Jean Renart and the Art of Romance

Jean Renart and the Art of Romance

Essays on *Guillaume de Dole*

EDITED BY

Nancy Vine Durling

University Press of Florida

GAINESVILLE TALLAHASSEE TAMPA BOCA RATON

PENSACOLA ORLANDO MIAMI JACKSONVILLE

Printed in the United States of America on acid-free paper

02 01 00 99 98 97 6 5 4 3 2 1

LIBRARY OF CONGRESS CATALOGING-IN-PUBLICATION DATA
Jean Renart and the art of romance: essays on Guillaume de Dole. / edited by
Nancy Vine Durling.
p. cm.
Includes bibliographical references and index.
ISBN 0-8130-1495-6 (alk. paper)
1. Jean Renart, 12th/13th cent. Guillaume de Dole. 2. Romances—History and criticism.
I. Durling, Nancy Vine, 1953– .
PQ1483.G453J43 1997
841'.1—dc21 96-53088

The University Press of Florida is the scholarly publishing agency for the State University System of Florida, comprised of Florida A & M University, Florida Atlantic University, Florida International University, Florida State University, University of Central Florida, University of Florida, University of North Florida, University of South Florida, and University of West Florida.

University Press of Florida
15 Northwest 15th Street
Gainesville, FL 32611

Contents

Acknowledgments vii

Introduction 1
NANCY VINE DURLING

Text and Context

1 The Uses of Embroidery in the Romances of Jean Renart: Gender, History, Textuality 3
NANCY A. JONES

2 "Once there was an emperor . . .": A Political Reading of the Romances of Jean Renart 45
JOHN W. BALDWIN

The Language of Lyric and the Language of Romance

3 Lyric Insertions and the Reversal of Romance Conventions in Jean Renart's *Roman de la rose* or *Guillaume de Dole* 85
MAUREEN BARRY MCCANN BOULTON

4 Suspension and Fall: The Fragmentation and Linkage of Lyric Insertions in *Le roman de la rose* (*Guillaume de Dole*) and *Le roman de la violette* 105
MICHEL ZINK

5 Jean Renart's Expanded Text: Lïenor and the Lyrics of *Guillaume de Dole* 122
REGINA PSAKI

6 On the Untranslatable Surface of *Guillaume de Dole* 142
PATRICIA TERRY

MUSIC AND PERFORMANCE

7 Jean Renart and Medieval Song 157
HENDRIK VAN DER WERF

Appendix 1: "Bele Aeliz": A Comparison of the Lecoy and Gennrich Editions 188

Appendix 2: Survey of Lyric Texts and Other Musical References 190

Appendix 3: Melodies 210

Selected Bibliography 223

Contributors 231

Index 233

Acknowledgments

Patricia Terry and I initially discussed the idea for this volume of essays as we completed our translation of *Guillaume de Dole*. Unfortunately, various logistical and temporal constraints made it difficult for us to collaborate on the project, and Professor Terry ultimately encouraged me to proceed on my own. Her contribution has nevertheless been invaluable, and I wish to express here my very deep appreciation for all she has done to help bring this collection of essays to its present state of completion.

It has been a privilege for me to work with all of the authors whose work is represented here; their patience and good will has made this collaborative project a real pleasure. I wish to thank Margaret Switten, who offered early encouragement of the project. I am also grateful to Matilda T. Bruckner and Harriet Spiegel, who made many helpful comments and suggestions. To Mildred Durling, who gave me the benefit of her expert proofreading skills, I extend my warmest appreciation. Robert M. Durling's support on all fronts is gratefully acknowledged.

It has been a pleasure to work with the editors at the University Press of Florida; the patience, interest, and expertise of Walda Metcalf, Alexandra Leader, Jenny Brown, and Deidre Bryan are greatly appreciated. For permission to reproduce the illustrations in this volume, I thank Oxford University Press and Photo Resources. I am particularly grateful to Leonard E. Boyle, director of the Biblioteca Apostolica Vaticana, who provided the photograph of a manuscript page of *Guillaume de Dole*.

Introduction

Nancy Vine Durling

The opening years of the thirteenth century witnessed a subtle shift in the orientation of courtly romance. While the Arthurian world of exotic adventures remained the setting of choice for contemporary writers, a new, somewhat more realistic, romance world also began to be explored. One of the most innovative voices in this transitional period belongs to a certain "Jean Renart." Unfortunately, we know nothing of this writer beyond his name, which is perhaps a nom de plume designed to evoke the wily figure of Renard the Fox.[1] A modest total of three works is now attributed to Jean Renart: *L'escoufle*, *Le lai de l'ombre*, and *Le roman de la rose ou de Guillaume de Dole*. Another romance, *Galeran de Bretagne*, refers to its author as "Renaus" (or "Renans" or "Renars"); it is not now attributed to Jean Renart.[2]

If we are to judge by the (admittedly unsatisfactory) criterion of quantity, *Le lai de l'ombre* would seem to have been the most successful of Jean Renart's works; it exists today in seven manuscripts. This 962-line poem relates the charming tale of a knight whose unrequited love at last finds fulfillment. The happy ending inspires the title: when the lady rejects the knight's gift of a ring, he drops it into a well in which he sees the reflection of her image, thus persuading her of his devotion. It is in this *lai* that Jean Renart first names himself; he also indicates in the prologue that he is the author of *L'escoufle*.[3]

In contrast to *Le lai de l'ombre*, Jean Renart's two romances exist today in single manuscripts. *L'escoufle* (Paris, Arsenal 6565) recounts the story of young lovers who elope in order to escape family opposition; accidentally separated, they undergo a variety of adventures before they are at last reunited. The earlier of Jean Renart's romances, it is perhaps not as skillfully written as *Guillaume de Dole,* but it is nevertheless a lively tale, told with considerable verve and wit.[4] Particularly successful are the vivid descriptions of a strong and self-reliant female protagonist, who makes her way in the world by dint of her skillful embroidery and ingenuity. The energetic sensuality of the young lovers is also described with refreshing clarity and candor.

Jean Renart's second romance, *Guillaume de Dole* (Vatican reg. 1725), is generally regarded as his chef d'oeuvre. A number of striking features distinguish it from prior romances, in particular those by Chrétien de Troyes. Marvelous adventures, fantastic creatures, tender exchanges between young lovers—all are markedly absent from *Guillaume de Dole.* In their stead we find zestful accounts of sexual dalliance in high places, handsome but self-serving knights, a beautiful woman whose decisive intelligence triumphs over daunting odds. Love may be the ostensible theme of *Guillaume de Dole,* but it is presented in a most unorthodox manner. The emperor Conrad decides to marry Lïenor (sight unseen) when his favorite jongleur artfully describes her physical charms. Even granting Conrad's noted weakness for beautiful women (he "knows all the tricks of love," we are told), his reliance on a court entertainer to determine his choice of empress seems (at best) remarkably eccentric. As for Lïenor, her determination to wed Conrad suggests her desire for a crown rather than desire for a man she has never met. These factors, among others, suggest that Jean Renart is poking fun at the established conventions of romance. In fact, *Guillaume de Dole* is filled with allusions to contemporary literature: there are close—and often mockingly ironic—borrowings from the *romans antiques,* a mysterious fragment of epic, and numerous references (both explicit and implicit) to the world of Arthurian romance. The author synthesizes these disparate elements with admirable élan; the result is a smooth and dazzling textual "surface" that often resists the interpreter's probe.

But the author's most widely recognized innovation is *Guillaume de Dole*'s hybrid form. Included in the narrative are partial texts of forty-six songs, some of them known to us from other sources and some of them famous. As the author himself observes, he combines the two genres, narrative and song, so successfully that they seem to have been written by the same person; it is for this reason that Jean Renart refers to his romance as "une novele chose"—something new, which will forever retain its freshness and originality [il . . . sera nouviaus toz jors] (v. 23). This statement reflects the author's confidence that his audience will receive

Guillaume de Dole with favor; it is therefore particularly disappointing that no concrete thirteenth-century evidence of Jean Renart's reputation has survived. Only two, somewhat indirect, indications of his status remain, more perplexing than informative.

Jean Renart's *Roman de la rose* does seem to have inspired his close contemporary Gerbert de Montreuil, who wrote the similarly named *Roman de la violette.* Like Jean Renart, Gerbert weaves fragments of song into the fabric of his narrative; the two romances also share important plot features. Gerbert does not, however, refer to his probable predecessor.

A second indication of *Guillaume de Dole*'s reputation in the thirteenth century is found in the one manuscript containing it. In addition to *Guillaume de Dole,* this late thirteenth-century codex contains three other romances: Chrétien de Troyes's *Chevalier de la charrete* and *Chevalier au lion* and Raoul de Houdenc's *Meraugis de Portlesguez.* The inclusion of Jean Renart's work with that of Chrétien is surely significant, although the precise meaning of the juxtaposition is hard to assess.[5] The scribe (or, more likely, the patron) may have based the selection purely on personal taste; or perhaps he (or she?) sought to highlight differences among the three authors. Raoul de Houdenc's romance (the earliest of the works attributed to this mid-thirteenth-century writer) draws heavily on Chrétien, evoking a world of *aventure* in a classic Arthurian setting. Yet although his tale is lively and entertaining, Raoul here lacks the sophistication of either Jean Renart or Chrétien. The reasons for anthologizing the four romances elude us.

Beyond the limited and inconclusive evidence of the manuscript and Gerbert's imitation, the record of the reception of *Guillaume de Dole* in the Middle Ages is silent. It is not until the late sixteenth century that *Guillaume de Dole* resurfaces, to become a topic of scholarly (if not popular) interest.

The Changing Fortunes of Guillaume de Dole

1580–1800

The first critical reference to *Guillaume de Dole* is found in the writings of Claude Fauchet, a pioneering literary historian and high court official under Henri III. Fauchet's efforts to collect and classify medieval literature may be viewed as part of a more general bibliographic trend.[6] Nevertheless, he appears to have amassed a library extraordinarily large for the time, claiming at one point to have owned some two thousand items. Had it not been for Fauchet's zeal as a collector, *Guillaume de Dole* could well have been lost forever.[7]

Fauchet mentions *Guillaume de Dole* in several of his works, calling attention in his *Recueil de l'origine de la langue et poésie françaises* to the insertion of the songs, whose poets he lists by name, and discussing in his *Origines des chevaliers, armoiries et héraux* the use of military vocabulary in the tournament scene.[8] In his posthumously published *Oeuvres,* Fauchet uses the subtitle *Guillaume de Dole* in order, as he explains, to distinguish the romance from the better known *Roman de la rose* of Guillaume de Lorris.[9]

Fauchet's political allegiance to the king ultimately brought disaster to his library. In the upheaval surrounding Protestant and Catholic claims to the throne, Henri was forced to flee Paris in 1589; he was accompanied by members of his entourage, including Fauchet. Fauchet remained in exile until 1594; during his absence from Paris, his collection was pillaged and dispersed by the soldiers of the duke of Mayenne.[10] We do not know the precise fate of the manuscript containing *Guillaume de Dole,* only that it appears in the catalog of the library of a certain Paul Pétau and was subsequently purchased, in 1650, by Queen Christina of Sweden.[11] The manuscript was acquired by the Vatican sometime after Christina's death in 1689. There it remained, undisturbed, for more than a century.

1800–1990

In the early part of the nineteenth century, short citations from *Guillaume de Dole* began to appear in studies by French and German scholars; a sample of the text was edited and published by Adelbert Keller in 1844.[12] Paulin Paris was especially interested in the use of songs in *Guillaume de Dole* and requested that a "mission scientifique et littéraire," sent to Italy by the French government in 1849, copy the lyric portions.[13] It was not until 1893, however, that *Guillaume de Dole* was published in its entirety; the edition, by Gustave Servois, at last provided scholars ready access to this "new" thirteenth-century romance. It was immediately recognized that *Guillaume de Dole* contained a fund of important lexicographical information; the precision with which certain aspects of daily life were portrayed was especially remarkable. Close analysis of both stylistic and lexical features soon led scholars to the conclusion that *Guillaume de Dole, L'escoufle,* and *Le lai de l'ombre* were all written by the same author.[14] A corpus of works was now attributable to the enigmatic figure known as Jean Renart.

The first major study of this corpus was Rita Lejeune-Dehousse's *L'oeuvre de Jean Renart,* published in 1935.[15] One of Lejeune's most remarkable contributions to our understanding of *Guillaume de Dole* was her discovery that Jean Renart had incorporated into it a number of historically identifiable secondary characters who interact with fictional ones. Her discovery led her to propose a hidden political agenda for *Guillaume de Dole,* which she viewed as a discreetly disguised pro-Welf (and thus anti-Philip Augustus) polemic; her analysis of the historical characters also served as the basis for a new dating of the romance, which she placed between 1208 and 1218. Lejeune's pioneering work, which includes close scrutiny of Jean Renart's language, also provides careful literary analyses of the romances. She argues that Jean Renart played an important role in the development of romance as a literary genre, thus implying that his romances must have been widely known.

Lejeune published her own edition of *Guillaume de Dole* in 1936.[16] Another edition, by Félix Lecoy, appeared in 1979, and a new (diplomatic) edition was published in 1995 by Regina Psaki. The romance was first translated into modern French by Jean Dufournet et al. in 1979, the beginning of a new era in Jean Renart studies.[17] It was also in 1979 that Michel Zink published his ground-breaking monograph, *Roman rose et rose rouge.*[18] Unlike Lejeune, Zink views *Guillaume de Dole* exclusively as a self-referential literary entity, arguing that elements of improbability in the plot are meant to draw attention to themselves and to the fictitiousness of the story. He views the presence of historical characters as a literary device by which the fictional nature of the story and its protagonists is made explicit. Similarly, he sees the plot as an extremely sophisticated commentary on the art of writing. Zink's study encouraged a trend in subsequent Jean Renart studies, many of which view the romance as "a form of literature about literature."[19]

Lejeune's and Zink's studies present widely differing approaches to a complex thirteenth-century romance that is only now beginning to receive the attention it deserves.[20] Happily, that attention is both scholarly and popular. New translations of *Guillaume de Dole* into modern French (1979), German (1982), and English (1993 and 1995) have made this entertaining tale available to a much wider audience; critical studies of the romance have increased dramatically in number since 1980. Nevertheless, despite steadily growing interest in Jean Renart, there has not yet been a volume of studies devoted exclusively to his work. This is all the more surprising since, as the essays in the present volume demonstrate, Jean

Renart's romances are now being studied from a variety of mutually enriching critical perspectives. Political and social history, women's studies, translation theory, musicology, as well as literary theory—all of these disciplines offer approaches to Jean Renart that add greatly to our understanding of his artistry.

A number of the essays published here offer new interpretations of old problems (such as the relation of the songs to the narrative and the interplay of fictional and historical characters); others address issues that have not previously been analyzed (the embroidery subplot and the difficult choices faced by the translator). Although the approaches vary widely, all seven of the essays share a common premise: Jean Renart's experiments with the genre of romance in *Guillaume de Dole* are even more innovative than has previously been realized. The essays have been organized into three interrelated sections.

Text and Context

In her essay Nancy A. Jones explores Jean Renart's romances "through the triple lenses of gender analysis, social history, and medieval conceptions of textuality." Her point of departure is the prologue to *Guillaume de Dole,* where Jean Renart evokes a striking textile metaphor to describe his authorial labors. Not only has the author "dyed his cloth red" with songs, he has also "embroidered [it] here and there with beautiful songs" (v. 14) [brodez, par lieus, de biaus vers]. Jones situates Jean Renart's claims to innovation within the broader social context of cloth production; the topic of embroidery, she argues, allows him to explore the interrelation of "cloth working, perjured femininity, and artistic virtuosity."

Another dimension of the cultural context in which Jean Renart wrote is explored by John W. Baldwin. Baldwin reexamines and refines Lejeune's thesis that Jean Renart's work is pro-Welf. In support of this thesis, he analyzes Jean's use of historically identifiable secondary characters and recognizable locales in both *Guillaume de Dole* and *L'escoufle;* he also examines the representation in the two romances of the imperial succession, a critical political problem in this period. The archival evidence that Baldwin brings to bear on these issues significantly advances our understanding of both the identity of certain characters and the reasons why they were included in Jean Renart's work of fiction. Baldwin's research recovers an aspect of the romance that would have been available to early thirteenth-century audiences but that has been lost to most subsequent readers.

The Language of Lyric and the Language of Romance

Maureen Barry McCann Boulton examines the contributions that lyric insertions make to the plot, especially their relation to the emperor's view of love, which evolves from the undemanding pleasures celebrated in *caroles* (dance songs) to the more complex emotions expressed in the *grand chant courtois.* She points out that the songs cannot always be understood as expressions of the characters' emotions; the emperor's, in particular, do not match those of the courtly lover singing his devotion to a beloved. In the return to the popular *carole* at the end of the story, she suggests, one may see an indication that Conrad's love for Lïenor will not be exclusive, a conclusion that is undercut by the narrative dénouement. Song and narrative, she argues, are often at odds.

Boulton speculates on whether the songs were really intended to be sung; in his essay, Michel Zink argues that the absence of musical notation in the manuscript is proof that they were not. In his view, *Guillaume de Dole* is to real life what its fragmentary lyrics are to real songs: presence and absence combined, just as the romance combines fictional characters and real people. He compares Jean Renart's use of lyric in *Guillaume de Dole* to that of Gerbert de Montreuil in *Le roman de la violette,* concluding that the use of lyrics in the latter work is a mere "system of abbreviations"; in *Guillaume de Dole,* by contrast, the fragmentation of the songs is an essential component of the author's "elliptical" style.

Another dimension of the lyric insertions is analyzed by Regina Psaki. Psaki argues that the heroine, Lïenor, serves as a figure for Jean Renart's overall poetic project in *Guillaume de Dole.* Just as the romance is composed of lyric fragments (and fragments of other genres as well), so Lïenor is presented to the audience in a fragmentary and elliptical way. The portrait of her is endlessly deferred, while our awareness of her presence is maintained by courtly songs celebrating love.

The multiple literary and topical references found in *Guillaume de Dole* present a special challenge for the translator. Can such references be made available to modern audiences, who are perhaps unfamiliar with the conventions of medieval romance or with thirteenth-century political history? The work poses other challenges as well. The shifting tone of the author's voice is especially difficult to pin down; to what extent can a translation reflect his mercurial style? This question becomes critical for the translator, who, by the very act of translating, offers an interpretation of the work. In her essay, Patricia Terry examines the linguistic phenomena that make such interpretation inevitable.

Music and Performance

Hendrik van der Werf's essay on music and performance explores the thirteenth-century musical context in which *Guillaume de Dole* was written. As van der Werf observes, the author's initial comment that the narrative is "both sung and read" does not provide a blueprint for performance. Unlike Zink, however, van der Werf believes that the original manuscript of *Guillaume de Dole* probably included music and that no conclusion can be drawn from the only extant version of the romance, which dates from the late thirteenth century. Although we do not know what actual performances of narratives were like, we do have musical notation for some of the lyrics. Drawing on contemporary references from both romance (in particular, the prose *Tristan*) and songbooks, van der Werf offers a compelling portrait of early thirteenth-century musical performance conditions. In three appendixes, he provides a survey of all references to music in *Guillaume de Dole,* a sample of extant melodies for twelve of the songs cited there, and a comparison of two edited versions of one song.

The essays in this volume bear witness to the complexities inherent in any modern interpretation of medieval romance. In the case of Jean Renart, those complexities are particularly profound. There is clearly much to be learned from this important writer; our new recognition of the richness of Jean Renart's work surely suggests that his claims to both novelty and durability were justified.

Notes

For full publishing information on short titles cited in the notes, see the selected bibliography. For titles not in the bibliography, full information is given in the notes.

1. The author specifically alludes to this famous figure of literary guile in v. 5421 of *Guillaume de Dole.*

2. It has been argued that Jean Renart is the author of the *fabliau Auberée* as well as two other works, *Le plait Renart de Dammartin contre Vairon son roncin* and *De Renart de Piaudoue.* Evidence in support of these attributions has not, however, been persuasive. On the debate about authorship of *Galeran de Bretagne,* see Franklin Sweetser's discussion in his introduction to *L'escoufle,* x.

3. The work is well known among medievalists for the role it has played in the development of modern text-editing practices. For a recent discussion and reassessment of this role, see Rupert T. Pickens, "The Future of Old French Studies in America: The 'Old' Philology and the Crisis of the 'New'," in *The Future of the Middle Ages: Medieval Literature in the 1990s,* ed. William D. Paden (Gainesville: University Press

of Florida, 1994), 53–86, especially 74–78. The most recent editions are by Félix Lecoy (*Jean Renart: "Le lai de l'ombre"*) and Margaret Winters (*Le lai de l'ombre* [Birmingham, Ala.: Summa, 1986]). For an English translation, see Patricia Terry, *The Honeysuckle and the Hazel Tree: Medieval Stories of Men and Women* (Berkeley: University of California Press, 1995), 149–78.

4. The first complete edition of *L'escoufle* was published by Paul Meyer in 1894; Sweetser's 1974 edition is the most recent. Two modern French translations have been published: André Mary, *"Le roman de l'escoufle" de Jean Renart, mis de rime ancienne en prose nouvelle* (Paris: Boivin, 1925), and Alexandre Micha, *Jean Renart. "L'escoufle": Roman d'aventures.* The work has not yet been translated into English.

5. A wide variety of narratives were anthologized with the romances of Chrétien; for a listing, see Keith Busby, Laurence Harf-Lancner, Terry Nixon, Alison Stones, and Lori Walters, "Appendix I: Other Contents of the Manuscripts of Chrétien de Troyes," in *The Manuscripts of Chrétien de Troyes,* ed. Keith Busby, Terry Nixon, Alison Stones, and Lori Walters (Amsterdam and Atlanta, Ga.: Rodopi, 1993), 249–62. It is possible that another of Chrétien's romances was originally included in the manuscript. As Terry Nixon has observed, the manuscript "is incomplete at the beginning . . . . According to an older foliation, forty-eight folios are missing before the present f. 1. Thus the manuscript may originally have contained another of Chrétien's romances before the *Lancelot*" ("Catalogue of Manuscripts," in *The Manuscripts of Chrétien de Troyes,* 1–85, here 62–63).

6. The first catalogs of vernacular French writers were compiled in the 1580s: *Le premier volume de la bibliothèque du Sieur de La Croix du Maine* (1584) and *La bibliothèque d'Antoine du Verdier, seigneur de Vauprivas* (1585). See Roger Chartier, *L'ordre des livres: Lecteurs, auteurs, bibliothèques en Europe entre XIVe et XVIIIe siècle* (Aix-en-Provence: Alinea, 1992), 50–52. As Roger Middleton has noted, however, Fauchet's *Recueil de l'origine de la langue et poésie françaises* (1581) "was the standard textbook on Old French literature for the next two hundred years, being quoted (with or without acknowledgement) by most subsequent writers (notably La Croix du Maine and Du Verdier) until it was superseded by work done in the eighteenth century" ("Index of Former Owners," in *The Manuscripts of Chrétien de Troyes,* 87–176, here 127).

7. For details of Fauchet's library, see Urban Holmes and Maurice Radoff, "Claude Fauchet and His Library," *PMLA* 44.1 (1929): 229–42. For an in-depth study of Fauchet, see Janet Girvan Espiner-Scott, *Claude Fauchet. Sa vie. Son oeuvre* (Paris: Droz, 1938).

8. Claude Fauchet, *Recueil* and *Origines.*

9. Claude Fauchet, *Oeuvres.*

10. See Holmes and Radoff (note 7) for further details.

11. The catalog was compiled by Pétau's son Alexandre some thirty-one years after his father's death. The Pétaus are discussed by Roger Middleton in his "Index of Former Owners," *The Manuscripts of Chrétien de Troyes,* 160–61.

12. Adelbert Keller, *Romvart: Beiträge zur Kunde mittelalterlicher Dichtung aus italiänischen Bibliotheken.* Small portions of the work had already been cited—for example, by Montfaucon and La Porte Du Theil in France and Joseph Görres in Germany (*Altdeutsche Volks- und Meisterlieder aus den Handschriften der Heidelberger Bibliothek*). The role of these early students of the work is discussed by Servois in the introduction to his edition.

13. Paulin Paris, "Archives des Missions Scientifiques," 5e cahier. Mission en Italie, 1er rapport. Paris, 10 May 1850, 241–92, here 249.

14. The attribution of the three works was also supported by Bédier's discovery of anagrams for the name "Jehan Renart" at the conclusion of both *L'escoufle* and *Guillaume de Dole.* Other significant early studies of Jean Renart's works include Henry Alfred Todd, "Guillaume de Dole"; C. A. Hinstorff, *Kulturgeschichtliches;* F. Loewe, *Sprache;* Ernst Färber, "Sprache"; Adolf Mussafia, *Kritik und Interpretation;* and Charles-Victor Langlois, *La vie en France au moyen âge,* 1:72–106. For a discussion, see Servois's introduction to his edition of *Guillaume de Dole.* A summary of the attribution question is provided by Rita Lejeune-Dehousse in *L'oeuvre de Jean Renart,* 19–24.

15. See note 12.

16. *Le roman de la rose,* ed. Rita Lejeune.

17. The first English translation was published in 1993 by Patricia Terry and Nancy Vine Durling. Professor Psaki's bilingual edition is a particularly useful tool for those who need assistance in reading the text in the original.

18. Michel Zink, *Roman rose.* For additional discussion of Zink's work and that of Lejeune, see the introduction to the Terry and Durling translation of *Guillaume de Dole.*

19. See, for example, Marc-René Jung, "L'empereur Conrad," 36.

20. See the selected bibliography at the end of the present volume.

Text and Context

CHAPTER 1

The Uses of Embroidery in the Romances of Jean Renart

Gender, History, Textuality

Nancy A. Jones

Much recent interest in Jean Renart's *Roman de la rose ou de Guillaume de Dole* has focused on the ingenious ways in which the romancer has incorporated lyrics into his narrative. Of prime interest to such studies are the prologue verses in which Jean Renart boasts of his formal innovation by comparing it to the improving of cloth:

car aussi com l'en met la graine
es dras por avoir los et pris,
einsi a il chans et sons mis
en cestui *Romans de la Rose,*
qui est une novele chose
et s'est des autres si divers
et brodez, par lieus, de biaus vers
que vilains nel porroit savoir. (vv. 8–15)[1]

[For just as one puts scarlet dye
into cloth in order to increase its praise
and worth/price,
just so has he put melodies and songs
into this *Romance of the Rose,*
which is a new thing.

And it is so different from other works,
being embroidered, here and there, with beautiful songs
that a coarse man could not understand it.]

The interpretive commentary devoted to this passage usually concerns the technical and hermeneutic implications of the textile imagery that Jean Renart uses to characterize his hybrid composition. Maureen Barry McCann Boulton examines the passage in terms of medieval poetic theory, while Roger Dragonetti argues that the embroidery and dye imagery works to dissolve the text's connection to history and culture.[2] I propose to examine the textile images from a broader perspective, through the triple lenses of gender analysis, social history, and medieval conceptions of textuality. The textile images have a broader interpretive significance, and they belong to a larger network of textile motifs at work in both *Guillaume de Dole* and *L'escoufle.* My readings of the textile motifs in these two romances will draw upon the diverse meanings of embroidery and textile crafts, especially those that in medieval culture are connected with femininity. We will see that Jean Renart's romance not only exploits the rich semiotic properties of embroidery and cloth but also draws on the cultural representation of embroidery as a traditional art and a commodity. Embroidery is a gendered activity, and gender is therefore a key component in the writer's handling of the ideological tensions produced by the conjunction of poetic and economic self-awareness.

Feminocentric Romance and the Embroidery Subplot

In the climactic court scene of *Guillaume de Dole,* the heroine Lïenor stages a masterful legal maneuver that confounds and exposes her treacherous calumniator. The scene has its analogue in other versions of the wager romance, where a virtuous woman (usually a wife but sometimes a betrothed maiden) is slandered as the result of a wager made about her chastity. Like the heroines of the other tales, Lïenor triumphs by virtue of her wit and daring. She outwits the would-be seducer who has slandered her and is publicly reclaimed by her royal suitor. Few would deny that Lïenor, and not her brother Guillaume or the emperor Conrad, is the pivotal figure in the plot of the romance. Similarly, in Jean Renart's earlier romance, *L'escoufle,* it is the heroine Aelis who shows the resourcefulness required to thwart parental opposition to her marriage with her lover Guillaume.

Jean Renart's proclivity for strong heroines is not a sign of his protofeminism; rather, it should be viewed within a larger context. As literary historians have long recognized, these early thirteenth-century works depart from the dominant twelfth-century model of French romance. Both *L'escoufle* and *Guillaume de Dole* can be assimilated into the large corpus of romance narratives in which tales of chivalric exploits, quests for the Holy Grail, and Celtic marvels are absent or subordinated to themes of persecuted heroines, separated lovers, abusive husbands, and marvelous reunions. These romances are built around a repertory of non-Arthurian motifs that are the stuff of folktale and fairy tale: twin siblings who are separated at birth and reunited only at maturity and whose resemblance sets off a series of mistaken-identity scenes; lovers separated by disapproving parents; foundlings whose noble births are revealed years later by means of birth tokens; imperiled virgins; wagers over a wife's or fiancée's chastity; evil stepmothers; and happy endings that coincide with the marriage of heroine and hero. They are familiar to readers of Greek romance, New Comedy, Old Testament stories, and hagiography. The emphasis in these romances on physical and economic suffering, chastity, and sentiment, especially on the part of women characters, provided a thematic alternative to the matter of Rome, France, and Brittany.

In texts such as *Galeran de Bretagne, Le roman de la violette, La Manekine, Berte as grans piés, Florence de Rome, Le roman du comte d'Anjou, Aucassin et Nicolette,* and *La fille du comte de Ponthieu,* variously categorized by literary historians as society romances, romances of adventure, Byzantine romances, wager romances, and idyllic romances, it is the damsel, not the knight, who "sets forth" into the forest of romance. Jean Renart's *L'escoufle* and *Guillaume de Dole* offer exceptionally sophisticated versions of this model, whose complexities have yet to be fully explored.

Given their early dates of composition, (1200–1202 for *L'escoufle* and circa 1210 for *Guillaume de Dole*),[3] Jean Renart's two romances may well have inaugurated the vogue for heroines whose resourcefulness and appeal far outdistance those of the hero to whom they are ultimately united in marriage. The heroine's narrative primacy (not reflected in the modern titles) may represent the changing tastes of the thirteenth-century public, encouraging writers to turn away from Arthurian themes and adapt elements from sentimental romance and folktale, albeit in a similar courtly spirit. Folktale morphologists classify these stories as "female fairy tales" with an "active" or "persecuted" heroine. The major typologist of romance, Northrop Frye, would characterize them as stories built around the perils of a virginal heroine.[4] While I do not attempt here to deal with the larger typological questions regarding women and thirteenth-century French romance, I do maintain that Jean Renart's romances present an exceptionally rich example of the feminocentric romance, particularly through amplification of what I will call the embroidery subplot.[5] While one can identify a number of generic and literary sources for these active heroines (notably, *Philomena* and Marie de France's *Lai de Fresne*), it is important to take into account some broader associations among cloth working, perjured femininity, and artistic virtuosity that were current during Jean Renart's time.

First, however, another feature of this corpus calls for discussion. A significant number of these feminocentric romances feature a peculiar episode involving the heroine. In several cases, the heroine, when expelled from her household or abandoned in the forest by father, husband, or other relative, shifts for herself by taking up embroidery. As an embroideress, she joins an all-female household in which she finds temporary refuge before returning to her original household and her role as the vessel for a noble lineage.

Not all versions of the embroidery subplot take the same form, nor do they all have equal prominence within the overall structure of the romance. Some versions are merely brief interludes, while others, such as that in *Galeran de Bretagne,* are developed across several episodes into a major segment of the narrative. We shall see how each of Jean Renart's two romances presents a distinct version of the embroidery subplot.

The embroidery subplot has yet to receive much critical attention, no doubt because it appears to be such a "natural" and even overdetermined feature in romance plots revolving around a heroine's fate. At first glance, the embroidery subplot appears to be an instance of the so-called thirteenth-century trend toward literary "realism." From this perspective, the texts simply portray a typical occupation of medieval women. The heroine's embroidery has also been viewed as a device used to enhance the audience's appreciation of her courtly femininity because embroidery was considered to be an aristocratic and virtuous accomplishment. The embroidery episodes may also respond to the tendency of many thirteenth-century romances to emphasize sartorial display, rather than chivalric prowess, as the sign of *noblesse.* The heroine's embroidery provides the opportunity for the writer to describe luxurious fabrics and serves a larger ideological function by evoking aristocratic power through descriptions of wealth and pageantry. One might observe, in addition, that the embroidery subplots facilitate the use of folktale motifs (for example, the embroidered birth token), which are often the key to narrative closure in the romances. Finally, the subplots provide the formal pretext through which courtly lyric can be inserted into the narrative in order to achieve a variety of literary and performative effects.

All of these observations contain some measure of truth. I would stress, however, that the thematics of embroidery represent an appealing, if ultimately unrealizable, ideological alternative to the genealogical narratives of medieval France. As an alternative to marriage or concubinage, life as an embroideress provides the characters with escape (however temporary) from male authority. All the heroines are described as naturally gifted embroideresses, and they quickly achieve economic success. These episodes show how closely linked are textile activity and female bonding. The refuge the heroines find in the textile workroom appears to provide an emotional, social, and perhaps sexual alternative to marriage. In this fictional space, women characters are freed from the coercions of the patrilineal system, in which female sexuality is tightly controlled and the female body is regarded as the coveted and feared vessel of the patrimony.[6]

In surveying these stories of exiled daughters and brides, Danielle Régnier-Bohler has remarked that embroidery or other cloth work enables the exiled heroine to reconstitute the lost gynaeceum (women's quarters). Her survey of thirteenth-century romance also notes that sewing, spinning, and weaving become the textual frame device for the onset of storytelling.[7] Furthermore, the embroidered objects that circulate in these stories have an intensified semiotic value. All of these factors indicate a broad tendency among Old French romancers to associate the gynaeceum and its textile arts with narrative art in general. This may be a fundamental pattern within Indo-European culture, to judge from the arguments advanced by Anne Bergren about women, weaving, and poetry in ancient Greece. Bergren writes that the "semiotic Greek woman was a weaver" and that the textile metaphors for poetic composition used by Greek writers represent a male appropriation of a female cultural discourse.[8]

Critics have also remarked that such episodes reflect male fascination with the gynaeceum within the feudal household. Georges Duby, among others, has described this female realm as the object of patriarchal anxiety about female sexuality.[9] Some romances, such as *Philomena,* depict the women's quarters as the place within which aggrieved women concoct revenge plots against their menfolk, while others, such as *Guillaume de Dole,* depict it voyeuristically as an alluring terrain vulnerable to male penetration. *Galeran de Bretagne,* the text most often compared to *L'escoufle,* does not portray a feudal gynaeceum but offers instead an idealized representation of an urban workroom whose function is to produce goods, not babies or gifts.

Embroidery and the Active Heroine: Medieval Models

By giving embroidery so central a place in his conception of heroinism, Jean Renart taps a set of age-old cultural connections between embroidery and femininity. These connections have been analyzed by feminist art historian Rozsika Parker, who notes that embroidery has always been considered to be a "natural" gift of women. She writes: "When women embroider, it is seen not as art, but entirely as the expression of femininity."[10] Similarly, Régnier-Bohler suggests that textile activity may accompany a kind of timeless female *communitas* (1988, 345–46). These discussions of cloth work, female space, and female sexuality help to illuminate several elements in Jean Renart's romances, yet they perhaps underestimate the historical foundations for the close interaction of embroidery, women, and romance in thirteenth-century texts. The connections are in fact multiple and contradictory, at once traditional and historically specific.[11]

Deeply rooted traditions in medieval culture virtually define women in terms of cloth work. The spindle, an ancient fertility symbol, was incorporated into Marial iconography from an early date. Moreover, considerable evidence linking textile work, including embroidery, with obedient and pious femininity survives from the era. The iconography of female domesticity, not surprisingly, is closely bound up with textile motifs throughout the Middle Ages. The virtuous wife of Proverbs 31, who spins wool and weaves cloth to dress her family, was a familiar didactic figure throughout the medieval period. Closer to Jean Renart's time, however, the image of Mary as a cloth worker becomes more frequent and explicit (see Figure 1). In fourteenth-century church windows, one finds Mary portrayed as a weaver at her loom, and in later courtly images, the Virgin appears as an embroideress.[12] This tradition was derived from the accounts of Mary's childhood in the apocryphal Infancy Gospels, the Book of James, and the Pseudo-Matthew Gospel, in which the girl Mary serves as a temple maiden and weaves a miraculously beautiful purple curtain to screen the tabernacle. These kinds of images reflect a growing interest in Mary's girlhood during the twelfth and thirteenth centuries. Much of this imagery is didactic in nature, but a writer such as Jean Renart may have been inspired by the dramatic elements in the Infancy Gospel narratives in creating his fictional heroines. In these texts, Mary becomes an unjustly accused maiden when her miraculous pregnancy leads to accusations of fornication. Finally, Jean Renart may have noticed how these texts, and the images inspired by them, link the Virgin's precocious virtue to her artistic skill with cloth.

FIGURE 1. Manuscript painting of the Virgin of the Annunciation holding a spindle. From the Gospels of Speyer Cathedral (Codex Bruschal), fol. 5. Landesbibliothek, Karlsruhe, Germany. Late twelfth century. By permission of Foto Marburg/Art Resource, New York.

One can cite other thirteenth-century visual examples where female handiwork illustrates the life of the Virgin in ways relevant to Jean Renart's heroines. On the portal of the North Porch at Chartres Cathedral (Mary's door), one finds a series of female figures representing the Active and the Contemplative Life: the former denoted by women processing wool for cloth and the latter shown by women reading and praying. Beneath the textile workers there was once a monumental figure of a woman sewing cloth, which was destroyed during the French Revolution (see Figures 2a and 2b).[13] The emphasis on textile imagery is not surprising, given the fact that the cathedral's holiest relic was the Virgin's tunic. The archivolt's imagery can also be related to several elements of Mary's legend, and the iconography of the Virgin's education alternately portrays the young girl Mary holding either a book or a cloth-working instrument. In addition to appearing as stone sculpture, embroidery itself was used as a medium for

FIGURE 2A. *(Left)* Woman winding wool, one of six figures representing the Active Life. Chartres Cathedral, North Porch, Left Bay archivolts, left side. Early thirteenth century. From E[tienne] Houvet, *La cathédral de Chartres: Portail nord (XIIIe siècle).* Chelles: Helio. A. Faucheux, 1919.

FIGURE 2B. *(Right)* Woman spinning wool or flax, one of six figures representing the Active Life. Chartres Cathedral, North Porch, Left Bay archivolts, left side. Early thirteenth century. From E[tienne] Houvet, *La cathédrale de Chartres: Portail nord (XIIIe siècle).* Chelles: Helio. A. Faucheux, 1919.

FIGURE 3. Cope of St. Maximin. (Detail: Mary working cloth in the temple with other virgins; a scene from the apocryphal *Life of Mary.*) Church of St. Maximin, Provence. Late thirteenth century. Reproduced from A. G. I. Christie, *Mediaeval English Embroidery* (Oxford: Clarendon, 1938).

such images. On the late thirteenth-century cope of St. Maximin, Mary is shown working cloth in the temple in the company of two virgins (see Figure 3).[14]

Such sources indicate that Mary was held as an exemplar of both the Active and the Contemplative life. The apocryphal narratives use textile work to express her gift for charitable works and the religious life in general but also as preparation for her role as divine consort and mother. It seems likely that the resourceful, virtuous heroines of thirteenth-century romance share some important characteristics with the Virgin of the Infancy Gospels, not least because of their proclivity for textile work but also because of their innate virtue and, in the case of Lïenor, her vulnerability to wrongful accusations of unchastity. Furthermore, the narrative sequence of the iconography inspired by the Infancy Gospels has a parallel in the structure of the feminocentric romances, in which the embroidery episodes figure as a kind of initiation ordeal and test of female prowess within a larger courtship narrative.

An old and related tradition associated embroidery with aristocratic feminine piety. Although Parker has argued that the traditional image of the virtuous queen who spends her time embroidering church vestments was largely a Victorian invention (23–39), medieval sources verify that such images have a basis in fact. Anglo-Saxon princesses, queens, and nuns are known to have produced fine ecclesiastical embroidery, establishing a tradition that would later become known as *opus anglicanum*. An anecdote about Pope Innocent III records his pleasure in receiving beautifully embroidered slippers crafted by the famous recluse and abbess Christina of Markyate. More often, however, royal women donors patronized professional embroiderers.[15] By the end of the twelfth century, aristocratic church needlework was largely superseded by professional embroidery workshops, and the literary representation of embroidery takes on a self-consciously archaic aura.[16]

Secular embroidery, on the other hand, is frequently mentioned in twelfth- and thirteenth-century romance, especially in descriptions of richly embroidered objects. These literary representations may more accurately reflect the productions of aristocratic women; however, some distortion is evident. The romances no doubt exaggerate the technical complexity of aristocratic embroidery and efface the role of professionals. Aristocratic women were likely to have been involved in more humble forms of sewing and cloth making, at least in a supervisory role.[17] This is far different from the picture drawn in the literary texts. The gynaeceum of romance does not produce the simple, pragmatic items necessary to a household; instead, it is the locus for the artistic production of luxury items.[18] Embroidered capes, girdles, and almspouches proliferate, and in a common topos, they are said to be the work of fairies.[19] Typically, embroidered objects figure as love or birth tokens, signifying the heroine's more or less conscious amatory desires.

Courtly heroines are praised for their accomplishments as well as their beauty, and talent at embroidery figures prominently in romance encomia. The most spectacular example is to be found in the twelfth-century romance *Philomena*, possibly an early work of Chrétien de Troyes. The narrator attributes every courtly and intellectual accomplishment to the maiden Philomena; she excels, we are told, at everything from falconry to dialectic! The detailed portrait concludes with the revelation that she is a virtuoso with her needle:

> . . . iert si bone ovriere
> D'ovrer une porpre vermoille
> Qu'an tot le mont n'ot sa paroille.
> Un diaspre ou un baudequin

Nes la mesniee Hellequin
Seüst ele an un drap portreire. (vv. 188–93)[20]

[she was so skilled
at working a piece of scarlet silk
that there was not her equal in all the world.
She would know how to embroider
fine silk with flowers or work heavy Baghdad silk
{and} even portray on cloth the Hellequin's demon horde.]

This same text presents another, darker side of women's textile crafts, which are here an expression of treacherous guile. Philomena's woven narrative of her rape by her brother-in-law Tereus incites her sister Progne to such fury that the latter murders and dismembers the couple's son. The reader is left to sort out the conflicting image of the heroine: while embroidery helps to establish Philomena as a courtly heroine and skilled narrative artist, her talent later serves to bring about a violent revenge against her rapist.[21]

The Embroideress and the Clerk: *Le roman de la rose ou de Guillaume de Dole*

There is no embroidery subplot in *Guillaume de Dole;* rather, Jean Renart presents a series of embroidery motifs within the framework of the wager tale. The embroidery motifs can be briefly summarized. First, Lïenor and her mother are initially introduced as industrious needleworkers who execute fine embroidered vestments for poor churches. Second, the two women perform and comment upon some *chansons de toile,* or cloth-working songs, whose scenario and themes, it has been pointed out, mirror and foreshadow Lïenor's own situation as a slandered woman who must win back her lover and reputation. Third, the pivotal scene in which Lïenor tricks the evil seneschal with a clever legal maneuver contains two embroidery-related details that often go unnoticed. Withholding her true identity, the heroine makes an appeal for justice to the emperor, claiming that she has been raped and robbed by the seneschal, on whom she has planted some incriminating evidence—notably, an embroidered girdle. Finally, after being acquitted of the slanderous charge of fornication, Lïenor is reclaimed by the emperor as his bride and is dressed in a magnificent robe embroidered with the story of the siege and fall of Troy.

Each instance of the embroidery motif merits analysis. The first scene I have mentioned takes place in the women's quarters of the manor house inhabited by Lïenor, her mother, and her brother. The occasion is the surprise visit of the emperor Conrad's envoy. As a mark of respect and gratitude for the honor of the visit, Guillaume leads the man into the presence of his mother and sister, with the remark that he is showing his "tresor" (v. 1115). Thus hailed by her brother and by the narrator's assertion that "ja mes n'entrera puis hui / en chambre a dame n'a pucele / ou il voie nule si bele" (vv. 1120–22) [after today he will never again / enter a lady's or a maiden's chambers / where he might see any so beautiful], Lïenor first appears in the romance as the object of a doubled masculine gaze that the reader is invited to share. Her beauty derives in part, it seems, from the charm of the gynaeceum, usually off limits to male visitors. Although Lïenor is presumably a skilled embroideress because she works alongside her mother, it is her mother's needlework that is singled out for praise by Guillaume: "Vez, fet il, biaus amis Nicole, / quel ovriere il a en ma dame. / C'est une mervellouse fame / et set assez de cest mestier" (vv. 1130–33) [Good friend, Nicole, he says, / see how skillful a needleworker my lady is. / She is a wonderful woman / and knows a great deal about this craft]. In the ensuing scene, the *chanson de toile* lyrics that the mother and daughter alternately sing serve as a kind of parody of their own activity. The chosen lyrics may mirror the two women's different relationship to their needlework and suggest that the maiden Lïenor, like the typical heroine of the *chanson de toile,* is a reluctant embroiderer. The mother performs verses from "Fille et la mere se sieent a l'orfrois," in which a mother chastises her daughter for neglecting her sewing and spinning because of love longing: "Aprenez, fille, a coudre et a filer, / et en l'orfrois orïex crois lever. / L'amor Doon vos covient a oublier" (vv. 1163–65) [Learn, daughter, to sew and weave / and raise gold crosses in the orphrey. / You'd best forget about the love of Doon]. Lïenor's response is to sing (reluctantly!) an excerpt from "Siet soi bele Aye," in which the refrain, "Hé! Hé! amors d'autre païs, / mon cuer avez et lïé et souspris" (vv. 1186–87) [Alas! Alas! love from another land, / you have captured and led off my heart], interrupts the song heroine's embroidery. In her second song, "La bele Doe siet au vent," there is no longer any mention of embroidery or needlework. Zink sees this progression as a sign of Lïenor's "légère indépendance," expressing her desire to escape from the confining realm of her mother's workroom and experience love in the open air.[22] The three songs foreshadow future events (Lïenor, for example, will indeed emerge from the gynaeceum to claim a noble suitor); it is, however, equally important to note that the sequence, while associating Lïenor with embroidery, at the same time deemphasizes her *literal* status as embroideress. By subtly appropriating the *chanson de toile* lyrics, Lïenor is in a sense "embroidering" upon the scene's archaic premise that women were actually wont to sing such songs over their needlework.

The courtroom scene takes this embroidery metaphor still further. Lïenor's ruse differs from the cruder tricks performed by other wager-tale heroines because it emphasizes the technical nature of her legal strategy. The scene is a vivid representation of the workings of medieval customary law, which sets it apart from the romances where virtue triumphs in a simpler fashion. Typically, the slandered heroine arrives before an assembly that includes her husband/suitor, her male kinsmen, and her calumniator. She then produces simple but infallible proof of her chastity or else tricks the slanderer into confessing his lie. Jean Renart, however, emphasizes the technicalities of feudal customary law, which oblige the heroine to pursue a complicated strategy in order to prove her innocence.

Under the accusatory system of customary law, a defamed person (here Lïenor) "cannot in her own person formally accuse the seneschal of deception or *tricherie* after what he has said of her, since a defamed person cannot legally accuse of *tricherie* another person in good repute."[23] Lïenor is thus obliged to appear disguised as another person and to accuse the seneschal of a crime for which she can produce the presumptive evidence to have him judged guilty. Jean Renart's portrait of her legal acumen is especially remarkable and ironic given the fact that French customary law did not automatically recognize a woman's right to speak for herself in court. As the scene opens, the narrator exclaims:

> Si vos di, s'ele fust as lois
> .v. anz toz plains sanz removoir,
> ce sachiez de fi et de voir,
> je ne sai por coi ne coment
> ele peüst plus belement
> son claim dire ne son afere. (vv. 4768–73)
>
> [I tell you, if she had been studying law
> for a full five years without stopping,
> this you can know for certain and true:
> I don't know how or in what way
> she could have stated her case
> or her claim more skillfully.]

Ultimately, it is customary law itself, as well as the seneschal, that Lïenor subverts and manipulates by inventing a plot to circumvent her legal handicap as an accused fornicator. She appears before the court armed with her beauty, her finery, and an ingenious fiction: she presents herself as an innocent maiden who was attacked by the seneschal *as she sat outdoors sewing:*

> Il fu uns jors, qui passez est,
> que cil la, vostres seneschaus
> (lors le mostre as emperiaus),
> vint en un lieu, par aventure,
> ou ge fesoie ma cousture.
> Si me fist mout let et outrage,
> qu'il me toli mon pucelage.
> Et aprés cele grant ledure,
> si m'a tolue ma ceinture
> et m'aumosniere et mon fermal. (vv. 4778–87)

> [One day, some time ago,
> that man over there, your seneschal
> (she pointed him out to the emperor),
> came by chance to a place
> where I was sewing.
> He did something ugly and shocking to me,
> for he robbed me of my virginity.
> And after committing that vile crime,
> he stole my belt
> and my almspurse and my brooch.]

Her testimony, of course, contains a trap for the seneschal, who carries the items on his person in the belief that they are secret love tokens bestowed upon him by a powerful countess.

The charge, however ingenious at the level of plot, is very selective in its presentation of narrative details. Notably, Lïenor specifies neither her own identity nor the precise site and time in which the purported offense took place. But she *does* specify what she herself was doing when the seneschal supposedly came upon her "by chance": she was sewing. The detail adds plausibility to her fictitious scenario because it implies a preoccupied state of mind that would have left her vulnerable to attack. But it also points to the broader ideological characterization of the embroideress as inherently tempting to male eyes because of her apparent passivity and self-preoccupation. Lïenor's credibility depends upon her listeners' unconscious acceptance of this stereotype. At the same time, Jean Renart is playing on the reverse image of the embroideress/cloth worker as a virtuous and resourceful figure who is capable of overturning all assaults upon her honor.

Lïenor substantiates her false charge by describing the objects she has had planted on the seneschal's person, particularly a girdle whose embroidered designs she describes. Of the three tokens found, the embroidered girdle is singled out as the proof of his guilt. The seneschal has been wearing it under his shirt, literally surrounding himself with his guilt. Her creative use of the embroidered belt (the sign of her virtue) thus removes the stigma of the rose on her thigh, which he claims to have seen.[24]

In his commentary on the court scene, Zink notes that the embroidery detail points back to the initial appearance of Lïenor and her mother in the romance. He sees the connection between the two scenes as proof that Lïenor knows how to present herself as a virtuous person (that is, as an industrious embroideress) in order to gain the emperor's sympathy without disclosing her actual identity. Assuming the guise of a genteel lady who does needlework on fashionable items such as girdles and almspouches, Lïenor is able to reveal herself to her lover in the chastity that constitutes her essential nature while she disguises herself by her verbal fiction of rape and robbery.

Lïenor's legal complaint of rape and robbery is a fictionalization of what actually happened to her. The seneschal's boastful lie almost had the same consequences as an actual seduction. Deemed guilty of fornication, Lïenor has narrowly escaped execution by a male kinsman enraged at her supposed loss of honor; and her brother has lost the material benefits of a family alliance with the emperor. Her version of their encounter exposes the sexual and economic aggression inherent in the gender relations of feudal society, here acted out against her by the seneschal. Metaphorically speaking, Lïenor's counterfiction of rape and robbery embroiders upon (in the sense of "works upon" and "improves upon") the seneschal's crude slander. Yet her victory over the seneschal produces no ideological rupture. She triumphs because she has adopted the image of the passive, sexually receptive, and male-identified *couseuse* of the *chanson de toile*.

Not only is Lïenor's courtroom fiction a kind of embroidery on the seneschal's story, it evokes those instances in classical myth when silenced women produce textile testimonies of male aggression. The embroidery detail links Lïenor's womanly guile with the romancer's literary *engin*. Her transformation of the slandered image of herself can be likened to Jean Renart's transformation of the old wager tale into a courtly romance. Her courtroom performance reminds one of the semantic overlap between *conteur* (legal advocate) and *conteur/narrateur* (teller of tales/narrator) then current in French.[25] The question arises: does Jean Renart, in privileging embroidery as a metaphor for his own artistry, wish to be seen as writing "from the woman's place"? Some clues to this issue may be found in the final embroidery scene.

While the prologue does not specify the gender of the cloth worker who improves a fabric with dye and embroidery, the subsequent references to embroidery portray it as a female activity. The last in the series of embroidery scenes takes place in another gynaeceum within the imperial palace. After being publicly reclaimed by the emperor as his bride, Lïenor is attended by a retinue of noble ladies who dress her for her wedding. They robe her in a splendid garment:

> D'un drap quë une fee ouvra
> fu vestue l'empereriz;
> il n'iert ne tiessuz ne tresliz,
> ainçois l'ot tot fet o agulle
> jadis une roïne en Puille,
> en ses chambres por son deduit.
> El i mist bien .VII. ans ou .VIII.,
> ainz que l'oevre fust afinee. (vv. 5324–31)
>
> [The empress was dressed
> in cloth embroidered by a fairy;
> it was neither woven nor coarsely trellised;
> long ago a queen of Apulia
> had done it all by needle
> for her own pleasure while in her chambers.
> And she had taken at least seven or eight years
> in order to complete the work.]

The masterful workmanship of the robe signifies, of course, Lïenor's worthiness to be empress and recalls the coronation robe donned by Erec at the end of Chrétien's romance.

Unlike Erec's robe and the magnificent embroidered ecclesiastical copes made for the medieval clergy, however, the iconography of Lïenor's imperial garment presents a set of contradictory messages. While the robe empowers Lïenor's image, the embroidered story it conveys—that of a mythical figure whose sex appeal caused the ruin of a great dynasty—also signals Lïenor's potentially destructive power as a woman. Embroidered on the robe is the story of the Trojan War, beginning with the abduction of Helen and ending with the departure of the victorious Greeks from the sacked city. One may object that this secular narrative may refer indirectly to Lïenor's own victimization by slander rather than by deed. Nevertheless, the visual magnificence of the robe seems to overwhelm the heroine with the force of its traditions, and she becomes a kind of icon.

Significantly, the robing of Lïenor in such a splendid artifact takes place in a gynaeceum in which the natural mother has been replaced by the well-wishing ladies of the court who adorn her with the work of an unseen yet benevolent mother figure, the unnamed "queen of Apulia." The robe, then, stands as a kind of visual counterpart to the earlier emblem of Lïenor's worth, the rose on her thigh, which was incautiously revealed by her mother to the seneschal with disastrous results. Might we not then view the rose as the mark of the carnal (and thus dangerous) beauty of the heroine, her veiled but receptive sexuality as imagined by men, and see the robe as the emblem of her spiritual, asexual beauty and grace, made miraculously manifest through the agency of the "good" (that is, nonbiological) mother?[26]

Encasing and effacing her body, the stiff embroidered fabric immobilizes the hitherto active heroine behind a set of imperial genealogical images. The scene suggests yet another dimension of embroidery—its institutional function in ceremonial display. The preciousness of the fabric represents the economic and political power of the imperial dynasty. Instead of generating wealth through her work, she now symbolically embodies her husband's wealth. It is at this moment that Lïenor ceases to be a (metaphoric) embroideress herself (a semiotic subject) and becomes instead an embroidered object or sign whose meanings are assigned by others. The scene exposes the gap between the embroideress heroine and the romancer, who, after all, will never cease to be a generator of signs. His implicit alliance with Lïenor turns out to have been opportunistic and appropriative. Thus, in retrospect, the gender-neutral status of embroidery in the prologue seems less innocent. It may signify the author's desire to keep the identification with his heroine submerged, for to feminize his art would risk contaminating it with the less transcendent qualities attributed to femininity and embroidery in medieval culture.

Embroidery, Economics, and Social Status: *L'escoufle*

L'escoufle, like other courtly romances, contains descriptions of fine clothing and fabrics. But the most spectacular development of the embroidery motif in this romance is the episode of Aelis's sojourn in the city of Montpellier. Here the heroine is thrust out of the courtly realm, and the meaning of her embroidery activity is altered. The episode has its analogue in the narratives mentioned earlier: *Berte as grans piés, Galeran de Bretagne, Florence de Rome,* and *Le roman du comte d'Anjou.* As a money-making enterprise, embroidery takes on an ambiguous social status in this romance, which is permeated with an aristocratic ideology.

The heroine is initially described in terms similar to those used to depict other embroideress heroines. She is not only skilled with her needle (she specializes in beautiful girdles) but is also a gifted *conteuse.* These dual traits foreshadow her resourcefulness and signal her bold, even uncourtly, daring. While her lover Guillaume falls back into despairing inertia over their forced separation (how like Guillaume de Dole!), it is Aelis who concocts the escape plan and decides to reclaim his rule in Rouen. Textiles play a part in subsequent events: she escapes from her room by means of a cord made from sheets; she arranges for Guillaume's mother to make them a "trousseau" of disguise outfits for their journey; and, of course, her scarlet almspouch becomes the pivotal device causing their separation. Apart from this one object, fabrics guarantee and restore bonds; hence, Aelis's embroidery indirectly leads her to reunion with Guillaume by bringing her into the household of the count and countess of Saint-Gilles.

Aelis's career as embroideress within the urban sphere suggests a historic shift in the European economy. The shift from a barter economy to a monetary economy that takes place between these two segments of the romance corresponds to a shift from a courtly, largely passive heroine to an active, entrepreneurial heroine and signals several ideological dimensions of the romance that have been largely overlooked.[27] They become more visible if read against a specific social intertext, namely the contemporaneous rise of a professional female labor force. Rather than reading the urban scenes as protorealist narratives, as some scholars have done, one could more profitably read the romance's contradictory representation of embroidery against certain developments taking place within the world of women's work during this period. By the mid-thirteenth century, embroidery was not only an art form but also a commodity produced within a fairly well-organized industry.

In an article on women and medieval guilds, Judith Bennett and Maryanne Kowaleski argue that the guilds "tended to treat women as second-class workers and second-class members" and that most skilled "women's work" (that is, embroidery and silk work) "never came under gild [*sic*] structure and supervision."[28] They note, however, that the situation was different in Paris, Rouen, and Cologne.

> At least five female-dominated gilds existed in medieval Rouen, but little is known of their histories. All focused on the textile trades, particularly in luxury items or linen (one of the city's major exports), and women had some measure of political power as gild officials in at least one of the gilds. In late thirteenth-century Paris, seven gilds (out of more than one hundred) were exclusively female or female dominated. These gilds specialized in detailed handwork and luxury textiles—spinning silk, weaving silk ribbons, and producing various types of fancy headgear and purses decorated with silk, gold thread and pearls. (1989, 18–19)

Bennett and Kowaleski add that the women of the Parisian guilds "operated independently of their husbands, sons or other male relatives and that they could become gild mistresses regardless of their marital status" (19). Furthermore, they suggest that ties between women might have been more important in such crafts than ties between women and men, noting that the embroiderers' guild included four sets of mothers and daughters and four sets of sisters (19). Indeed, the records reported by Bennett and Kowaleski offer an expanded version of the autonomous household that Aelis creates with Ysabeau in Montpellier. Given such information, one infers that Jean Renart was familiar with an urban world that included spheres of female economic and, perhaps, social autonomy.

Such a social intertext, despite its immediacy, remains occluded in the romance. In contrast to its symbolic, sentimental value, the economic value of embroidery is downplayed in the text. Whatever her technical skill and talents as a self-promoter/businesswoman, Aelis is not the enthusiastic entrepreneur that we find in the later romance, *Galeran de Bretagne.*[29] She is never depicted in the act of embroidering; and once she gains a place in an aristocratic household (albeit as a lady-in-waiting), no further mention of her embroidery work occurs. Nonetheless, she knows its value as a luxury product coveted by women, and she deliberately undertakes the conquest of the lady of Montpellier by embroidering a belt with the lady's husband's coat of arms. This mercenary spirit seems at odds with the antiministerial rhetoric of the romance. (The narrator inveighs against the *vilains* at court who were the undoing of both Guillaume's father and the emperor.) One should recall, however, that she was previously apt to express Guillaume's value in monetary terms.

This tension is, of course, resolved on one level by the plot, which reunites the lovers and restores them to their position in their noble lineages. At another level, however, we can read certain elements of the romance as attempts to deflect too close an identification of the heroine with the non-noble world of textile artisans who labored in cities such as Rouen and Montpellier.[30] The heroine's relationship with her doublet, Ysabeau, is a case in point. The romance stresses the hierarchy separating the two women through their relation to cloth: Ysabeau never becomes an embroideress (she makes a more humble product, *guimples*), and she is always depicted in terms of amiable servitude rather than sororal affection. Unlike the heroine's, her textile skills are not prestigious and do not give her economic security and autonomy (she is impoverished when they first meet), and she needs the noblewoman's supervision and direction.[31] Her subordination helps to ensure the impression that the heroine never completely leaves the feudal gynaeceum and her class prerogatives. The romance makes no serious attempt to represent an urban workshop whose goal would be to perpetuate itself. Instead, the heroine's textile labor is superseded by her popularity as a raconteuse among the courtly youth of Montpellier.

The central episode of the romance is a kite's theft of the heroine's silk pouch and ring after she has bestowed them upon her lover. The kite symbolizes the lovers' separation and their fall into a non-noble existence. The bird steals the love token because it mistakes the scarlet fabric for meat. From this detail, one might also infer a less obvious meaning. In a text that repeatedly contrasts aristocratic and courtly largesse with the grasping avarice of the *vilain,* the kite's carnal (and witless) appropriation of the textile love token represents the undiscriminating greed threatening the lovers' aristocratic world. The kite is, after all, the *vilain* of the bird world; and the *vilain,* if we recall line 15 of the prologue to *Guillaume de Dole,* is incapable of appreciating fine textiles. Whether or not we wish to see the episode in terms of explicit social allegory, we can once again perceive in the romance an encoding of social difference through the language of textiles. The lovers are reunited when Guillaume, in his wild devouring of a kite's heart, abandons the meek, servile behavior that has sustained him economically. Like Aelis, he is freed from the stigma of wage earning when he becomes a tale teller for a noble audience in the household at Saint-Gilles. Having "liberated" himself through an impulsive act of amorous revenge, he can be recognized by the heroine, who knows the value of fine fabrics, especially when they are bestowed as gifts. Given all these inflections of the plot by textile motifs, it is fitting that the romance concludes with an elaborate description of the garments worn at the lovers' imperial coronation. Aelis's coronation robe is not given a price value but is described as the work of a "sages et cortois mestre" (v. 8930) [skilled and courtly master], and the jongleurs are generously bestowed with ermine and silken clothes (vv. 8996–97). The opulent fabrics that adorn the characters and the hall do more than display imperial prestige; they also cover up the world of manufacturing and trade that the embroidery subplot had allowed us to glimpse. In this closing tableau, Jean Renart asserts the moral primacy of aristocratic exchange. In the epilogue tribute to his patron, the count of Hainaut, however, the romancer's punning on the words "conte" and "conter" (vv. 9058–80) hints at how illusory this socioeconomic vision might be. When received as a tribute of esteem by a noble spirit (such as that possessed by the count himself), a *conte* (tale) can transcend its lowly origins. But this is merely the assertion of a professional *conteur,* whose fictions are motivated by his material needs as much as by his desire to please.

The question of the writer's own relationship to embroidery and textiles brings us back to the prologue of *Guillaume de Dole.* Textile tropes are, of course, ubiquitous in statements about literary form, yet critics of this romance have perhaps not sufficiently appreciated the concreteness of the comparison for a medieval audience and its implications for our understanding of the hybrid textuality produced by the adornment of a romance with lyric insertions. In addition, the cultural connections between embroidered fabric and memory indicate that the lyric insertions have many implications for a dynamic interplay between medieval mnemonics and a developing sense of textuality. Finally, it will be necessary to consider the economic overtones of the prologue whereby an artistic innovation is directly linked to the processing, merchandizing, and pricing of cloth.

The opening lines of the prologue have a familiar quality, for they echo the artistic boast of Chrétien de Troyes in his prologue to *Erec et Enide* and feature the standard compliment to the noble patron, here Milon de Nanteuil. Like Chrétien, Jean Renart tells us that he has taken an oral tale and turned it into a romance:

> Cil qui mist cest conte en romans,
> ou il a fet noter biaus chans
> por ramenbrance des chançons,
> veut que ses pris et ses renons
> voist en Raincïen en Champaigne
> et que li biaus Miles l'apregne
> de Nantuel, uns des preus del regne. (vv. 1–7)

> [He who put this tale into {a} romance

where he has had beautiful melodies noted down
in memory of the songs,
wants for his worth and his renown
to be seen in Reims in Champagne
and that the handsome Milon de Nanteuil,
one of the worthy men of the realm, learn {of} it.][32]

Lines 2 and 3 echo Marie de France's prologue to her *Lais,* where she explains how she wanted to preserve in writing the Breton lays that she had heard, which had originally been part of an oral tradition.[33] Both claims—one of the writer's conversion of popular matter into courtly matter, the other of his or her preservation of a charming and perhaps fragile tradition (here courtly song)—are joined in Jean Renart's prologue. Indeed, the idea of comparing one's work to a fine fabric is a perfectly courtly one, given the delight that courtly romancers take in filling their texts with descriptions of richly embroidered objects and clothing.

In reviewing the history of medieval embroidery, Rebecca Martin describes how this textile art was used to convey political power:

> In one sense, art was a tool of the dominant institutions of society—the Catholic church and the aristocracy. They used architecture, sculpture, painting, tapestry, and objects of gold, enamel, and ivory as the back-drop and accoutrements for the pageantry and ceremony whereby they impressed others with their position and power. Sumptuous and costly textiles were an indispensable component of this display. Even the common laborer clad in rough woolens or linens had ample opportunity to admire the precious silks, cloths of gold, and tapestries that either adorned the churches on feast days or draped the streets for princely processions and entertainments.[34]

As a mark of position and privilege, therefore, precious fabrics offered an effective analogy for one's status as a courtly writer. Similarly, the writer's "gift" of a precious fabric to his noble patron enacts the value of largesse represented in many scenes of romance, where a ruler bestows a richly embroidered robe on a courtly hero. In such episodes, the gift of an embroidered robe or belt signifies a personal bond between lord and vassal that is implicitly superior to mercenary relations between individuals. The writer, from this perspective, relies on the generosity of his or her patron and may expect literal textile gifts instead of monetary payment in exchange for textual art. To pursue the textile analogy even further, one could say that the writer is contributing to a patron's cultural treasury, the court. By doing so, he or she ensures the distribution, or rather circulation, of his or her "fabric," since the lord's traditional function is to redistribute wealth among the members of his retinue.

As further evidence of the prologue's courtly quality, one might note that Jean Renart's metacritical use of cloth tropes is not without precedent in courtly romance. In his literary excursus near the beginning of his *Tristan,* Gottfried von Strassburg praises the poetic skill of certain of his contemporaries by comparing their art to that of dye masters and fairies:

> Hartman der Ouwaere
> âhî, wie der diu maere
> beid ûzen unde innen
> mit worten und mit sinnen
> durchverwet und durchzieret!
> wie er mit rede figieret
> der âventiure meine
> wie lûter und wie reine
> sîniu cristallînen wortelîn
> beidiu sint und iemer müezen sîn!
> . . . .
> Noch ist der verwaere mêr:
> von Steinahe Blikêr,
> diu sinen wort sint lussam
> si worhten vrouwen an der ram
> von golde und ouch von sîden,
> man möhte s'undersnîden
> mit criecheschen borten.
> er hât den wunsch von worten:
> sînen sin den reinen
> ich waene daz in feinen
> ze wundere haben gespunnen
> un haben in in ir brunnen
> geliutert unde gereinet:
> er ist binamen gefeinet. (vv. 4621–30, 4691–704)

[Ah, how Hartmann of Aue dyes and adorns his tales through and through with words and sense, both outside and within! How eloquently he establishes his story's meaning! How clear and transparent his crystal words both are and ever must remain! . . . But there are other "dyers." Bligger of Steinach's words are delightful. Ladies worked

> them with silk and gold on their embroidery frames—one could trim them with fringes from Byzantium! He has a magic gift of words. And I fancy his limpid invention was wondrously spun by the fairies and cleansed and refined in their well—for he is surely inspired by the fairies!][35]

Was Jean Renart familiar with this passage? It is impossible to know for certain, yet the fact that the two writers were chronologically and geographically close is intriguing. The connection becomes even closer when we recall that Jean Renart sets his romance in Flanders and the Rhineland and centers his romantic intrigue on a German emperor named Conrad. I cite this example merely to point out that both dyeing and embroidery appear to be part of a common code used to discuss romance aesthetics at the beginning of the thirteenth century.

The near coincidence of such similar imagery is striking, but the specific meanings of the images are very different. Gottfried uses the dye image to convey the memorable eloquence of Hartmann's diction and style with which he "permeates" his narrative matter. Hartmann's stylistic dye would seem to *enhance* and *clarify* his raw material—that is, his narrative matter—by bringing forth its hidden (or garbled) virtue. This is the classic courtly formula in which the *clerc* improves upon the jongleur. In a general way, dyeing does imply the enhancement of the aristocratic quality of the romance, in the sense that the lyric insertions ennoble what was originally a wager tale of popular origins.

In Jean Renart's text, however, the dyestuff image works quite differently. Lines 8 and 9 of the prologue do not give the common image of *immersing* the cloth in dye (contrary to the translation by Dufournet et al., which renders the phrase "com l'en met la graine / es dras" [vv. 8–9] as "comme on impregne de teinture rouge / les vêtements").[36] Rather, they refer to putting the grain (scarlet dye) *into* the cloth, as if marking it—an image that recalls the red rose on Lïenor's thigh. Indeed, the formal innovation in question, the lyric insertions, are more properly visualized as creating a kind of spotted effect on the narrative fabric. Dyeing thus more closely resembles embroidery that covers only part of the cloth's surface ("par lieus") and whose aesthetic effect derives from patterns created upon a ground.

Both are techniques of enhancement. While Gottfried's text plays upon this trope to praise a traditional form of artistic excellence, Jean Renart inflects it with a more technical quality in order to explain a new form of artistry. As he tells us, he has created "une novele chose" (v. 12). It is interesting to note that the special dyestuff used to create scarlet cloth was also a relatively new technique, for kermes or *graine* had first been introduced into Northern Europe within the previous fifty years.[37] The analogy between dyeing and embroidery that is established in the text works to undo the distinction between altering cloth (by dyeing it) and adorning cloth (by embroidering it). Jean Renart's is not simply an additive process but a transformative one.

The technical aspect of the prologue's dyestuff and embroidery imagery has other implications as well. It signals the romance's self-awareness of its transitional nature at a key moment in the development of vernacular literature, when courtly lyric was assuming textual form. It implies a rendering of the author's work as a text that can claim a power of memorization and monumentalization that had previously inhered in the memorized word of oral tradition. Along with textualization, so vividly evoked here by the physical activities of dyeing and embroidery, comes the attitude that the oral memory is fragile. By rendering invisible oral memory onto something concrete, the prologue implies that what was once handed down spontaneously in collective memory (without art) has become the basis for artistic elaboration on the part of an individual poet who now appears as the custodian of an anonymous tradition. The point is not that the oral memory is *inherently* fragile but that textualization inaugurates an ideology of its fragility. Physical metaphors for lyric poetry signal such a shift.

By dyeing and embroidering his romance with more than forty courtly songs or song fragments, "por ramenbrance," Jean Renart presents "a conspectus of the song-forms known in his day"—in other words, an anthology of the Occitan and northern French lyric traditions.[38] Sylvia Huot has written at length about the author's exploitation of compilational techniques and has established an analogy between the romance and the lyric *chansonniers*.[39] The mnemonic dimensions of this anthology format as it is figured by the image of dyed and embroidered cloth have, however, received less attention and deserve some comment.

Once again, a cultural perspective helps to illuminate a set of associations. In preindustrial societies, embroidery (and to some extent the dyeing process) represented the surplus labor stored up in the hoarding of precious materials (gold thread, costly dyestuffs). The embellished fabrics are thus themselves storehouses of value in both a literal sense (the inherent value of gold thread worked into a cloth) and a figurative sense (a record of the wealth required to support a highly skilled labor force producing nonutilitarian goods). Thus, from ancient times, embroidery signifies a type of cultural thesaurus or storehouse. It takes only a small conceptual leap to understand why embroidered fabric items figure so prominently in the inventories of royal and ecclesiastical treasuries. Such artifacts not only provided a means of storing wealth, as did gold plates and precious stones, but are also synecdoches for the treasury itself.

Turning back to Jean Renart's text, we can see that the anthology of song is in fact a treasury of song. Through his artful labor of "working" songs into his narrative, the author is not simply preserving the wealth of the courtly lyric tradition for future generations by binding them to the fabric of narrative but perhaps enhancing their value through a skillful disposition of the elements of that tradition. In other words, the combined acts of accumulating and arranging the songs on a new ground endow them with a new aesthetic dimension, just as gold thread becomes more beautiful as part of an embroidered design. The romance itself makes the connection between song, embroidery, and the concept of *trésor* (with the multiple meanings of treasury, storeroom, and treasure) in the scene where Guillaume introduces the emperor's messenger into the ladies' workroom or gynaeceum, where his mother and sister Lïenor are busy embroidering church vestments. Guillaume presents this female space as his *trésor*; then, in a carefully staged sequence, the female contents of this *trésor* sing some samples of the *chanson de toile*, forming a microtreasury of courtly lyric. The mise-en-abîme effect of this scene has been noted.[40] Rendering the textile image in a concrete form in no way undermines the dizzying tour-de-force quality of the work's textuality.

The mnemonic dimension of the prologue's textual image is still more complex, for *trésor* (treasury) regularly referred to the trained memory. Mary Carruthers, for example, notes that the Latin term *thesaurus*, meaning "storage-room" or "strong-box" (from which the word *trésor* is derived), is a major metaphor for this mnemonic power. The metaphor "refers both to the contents of such a memory and to its internal organization. . . . the structured memory [is seen] as a kind of inventoried set of bins . . . into which observations and knowledge, [and] all experience of the world however derived, are sorted and contained."[41] "The image of the memorial storehouse," she writes, "is a rich model of pre-modern mnemonic practice. It . . . gives rise to several allied metaphors for the activity of an educated mind, but all center upon the notion of a *designed* memory as the inventory of all experiential knowledge" (1990, 34). Thus, as a mnemonic thesaurus, or mental structure, the embroidered and dyed romance conjured up in the prologue offers access to the courtly lyric tradition not simply by *recording* and *storing* the songs but by artfully arranging them.

It cannot be said that the songs form a recognizable pattern in the "cloth" of the romance that could be memorized in the way that orators memorized elements of their argument by assigning them to imagined positions on a visual field. Rather, the technique of the lyric insertions involves a transformation of the ancient metonymically based mnemonic practice described by Carruthers. Jean Renart's hybrid text alters the image of the *trésor,* or treasury, moving beyond the somewhat arbitrary nature of its functioning. In *Guillaume de Dole* the tale is not just the frame for the disposition of songs but itself has independent value. Jean Renart has not simply "adorned" his narrative with beautiful lyrics in some pretty pattern but has *worked them into* his narrative, erasing the distinction between object and ground. This is partly another consequence of writing and textuality: the romance can break free of its mnemonic function as a *trésor* or storehouse of memory and develop its own form and meaning as an end in itself. As an example of this narrative integration, we can cite the *chanson de toile* episode. In fact, embroidery becomes a complex thematic element in the romance. Most notably, it plays a crucial role in the heroine's successful strategy to discredit the evil seneschal's lewd slander and also in the penultimate scene in which Lïenor is visually "worked into" the imperial lineage when she is dressed in a historiated wedding robe.

The semiotic complexity of the prologue's textile imagery extends still further. There remains one last connection to be made in the prologue among cloth, memory, and song as it appears in the author's allusion to his patron, Milon de Nantueil. Looking back at the text, we can see that the relationship among the various elements is syntactically mediated by textile imagery. Jean Renart has inserted two subordinate clauses expressing the wish that *his* worth and renown might travel to Champagne and that his patron learn of it. This is, of course, a typical courtly plea for material support; but the historical specificity of "met la graine / es dras" may lead us to a less courtly reading of the address to the patron. The phrase "met la graine es dras" describes an actual form of textile process used in Northern Europe to produce a luxury grade of wool. The term *graine* was used to denote the extremely costly scarlet dyestuff known as kermes, imported from the Mediterranean regions, because the desiccated insect matter (*coccus polonicus*) had a seedlike shape. The image evokes not only wealth but also a highly developed industry in the cities of northern France and Flanders. Thus, it is justifiable to reexamine the author's vocabulary of praise, specifically the terms *pris* and *preus.*

If Jean Renart is thinking of his hybrid romance as a *commodity,* then *pris* should be taken in its primary sense as "price" as well as the more courtly notion of "worth." If we translate *pris* as "price" in line 4, the possessive pronoun *ses* may not refer to Jean Renart himself, as Dufournet would have it, but to the cloth/text as the object that the author wishes to send to his patron, who, as a major diplomat and crusade leader, would have known how to value fine worked cloth both aesthetically and commercially. By calling Milon "uns des preus del regne," Jean Renart ingeniously flatters his patron by playing on the double sense of *preu,* which means both "valiant" and "expert." Milon de Nanteuil is not only a potential treasure store for this writer, who seeks to be monetarily "remembered" by his patron, but perhaps a connoisseur of fine textiles—and, one might speculate still further, of lyric poetry.

This reading of the textile elements in Jean Renart's fascinating prologue conflicts with the deconstructionist approach of critics such as Roger Dragonetti, who sees the textile tropes as the sign of the text's endless equivocations and artifice. In such an approach, embroidery represents the absence of the (historical) body; that is, it is a discourse of pure artifice. As the preceding reading of the prologue has shown, however, embroidery (and dyeing) *is* the body; and in the concrete image given to us by Jean Renart, they cannot truly be separated from the fabric of the romance. It is important not to overlook this concreteness of labor, ornament, and costly exchange implied in the embroidered fabric; for these, I would argue, are a source of interpretive wealth rather than poverty.

* * *

We have seen that Jean Renart's depiction of his heroines Aelis and Lïenor as embroideresses is not simply a hackneyed convention or an idle innovation. Likewise, the moral and aesthetic claims he makes for embroidery in his prologue to *Guillaume de Dole* have rich cultural and historical significance. At the outset of this chapter I asserted the centrality of gender and economic consciousness within his art, arguing that embroidery is the central organizing trope. As my readings of the romances have demonstrated, neither femininity nor economic exchange finds a utopian representation in these texts, for they are riddled by contradictions. Thus, while Jean Renart chooses to privilege a female character and celebrates the triumph of individual, aristocratic freedom over the forces of market exchange, his use of the language of embroidery and textiles ultimately undermines the ideological viability of such themes. It is the special property of embroidery to turn us simultaneously toward gender, history, and semiosis; and by aligning his art with it, Jean Renart has drawn us into the beautiful yet perplexing web of medieval textuality.

Notes

1. All quotations in the text are taken from the edition by Félix Lecoy (1979).

2. Maureen Barry McCann Boulton, *The Song in the Story*, 9–15; Roger Dragonetti, *Le mirage des sources*, 159–62, 183, 198–99.

3. See the remarks of Patricia Terry and Nancy Vine Durling about the dating of *Guillaume de Dole* in the introduction to their translation of the romance. See also Baldwin, chapter 2 in the present volume.

4. Northrop Frye, *The Secular Scripture: A Study of the Structure of Romance* (Cambridge: Harvard University Press, 1976), 65–93.

5. The term *feminocentric* was coined by Nancy K. Miller. See her *The Heroine's Text: Readings in the French and English Novel* (New York: Columbia University Press, 1980).

6. See Georges Duby's discussion of the social consequences of the rise of the patrilineal system in twelfth-century France in "The Aristocratic Households of Feudal France," in *A History of Private Life*, vol. 2, *Revelations of the Medieval World*, ed. Georges Duby, trans. Arthur Goldhammer (Cambridge: Harvard University Press, 1988), 35–85.

7. Danielle Régnier-Bohler, "Imagining the Self," 344–48.

8. Anne L. T. Bergren, "Language and the Female in Early Greek Thought," *Arethusa* 16.1–2 (1983): 71.

9. Georges Duby, *Mâle moyen âge* (Paris: Flammarion, 1988), 119.

10. Rozsika Parker, *The Subversive Stitch: Embroidery and the Making of the Feminine* (London: Women's Press, 1984), 5.

11. Emmanuèle Baumgartner has written an important article on the relation between women's cloth work and urban space in *L'escoufle* and *Galeran de Bretagne*. Her comments about the generic specificity of these texts overlap with some of my discussion. See "Les brodeuses et la ville," 89–95.

12. Jacqueline Lafontaine-Dosogne, *L'iconographie de l'enfance de la Vierge dans l'empire byzantin et en Occident*, vol. 2 (Brussels: Palais des Académies, 1965), 128–34; Robert Wyss, "Die Handarbeiten der Maria," in *Artes Minores: Dank am Werner Abegg*, ed. Michael Stettler and Mechtild Flury-Lemberg (Bern: Stampfli, 1973), 113–87. See also Odile Brel-Bordaz, *Broderies d'ornements liturgiques XIIIe–XIVe siècles* (Paris: Nouvelles Editions Latines, 1982), 54.

13. Emile Mâle, *The Gothic Image: Religious Art in France of the Thirteenth Century*, trans. Dora Nussey (New York: Harper, 1958), 129–30. Photographs of these figures appear in Mâle, *Notre-Dame de Chartres* (Paris: Flammarion, 1963), plates 87 and 88; see also Etienne Houvet, *La cathédrale de Chartres: Portail nord (XIIIe siècle)* (Chelles: Helio. A. Faucheux, 1919).

14. Parker, *The Subversive Stitch*, plate 31, top left.

15. Kay Staniland, *Medieval Embroiderers* (Toronto: University of Toronto Press, 1991), 7–12, 55.

16. See Michel Zink's commentary on the sewing scene in *Guillaume de Dole* in *Belle: Essai sur les chansons de toile*, 10–11.

17. David Herlihy, *Opera muliebria: Women and Work in Medieval Europe* (Philadelphia: Temple University Press, 1990), 57–59, 83–84.

18. A striking exception is the early scene in *Erec et Enide,* where the heroine first appears at work with her mother mending the household's clothing. The details of Enide's sewing and her shabby dress are meant to emphasize her poverty, which contrasts with her beauty.

19. Edmond Faral, *Recherches sur les sources latines des contes et romans courtois du moyen âge* (Paris: Champion, 1913), 345–46.

20. Text in C. de Boer, ed., *"Philomena": Conte raconté d'après Ovide par Chrétien de Troyes* (Paris: Geuthner, 1909).

21. I argue these points more fully in an unpublished essay, "The Daughter's Text and the Thread of Lineage in the Old French *Philomena.*" For a discussion of Philomena's textile work as a kind of subversive discourse, see E. Jane Burns, *Bodytalk: When Women Speak in Old French Literature* (Philadelphia: University of Pennsylvania Press, 1993), 128–32.

22. Zink, *Belle,* 8–9. See also the discussions in the present volume by Boulton (chapter 3), Zink (chapter 4), and Psaki (chapter 5).

23. Carl Frederick Riedel, *Crime and Punishment in the Old French Romance* (New York: AMS, 1966), 75.

24. Helen Solterer gives a very interesting commentary on this detail. Lïenor's "binding" of the seneschal's body with her girdle, causing his skin to redden and swell, suggests "a mock defloration, and of a man," exemplifying the romance's "deft play with the literal and the symbolic." See "At the Bottom of Mirage, a Woman's Body," 227.

25. M. T. Clanchy, *From Memory to Written Record: England 1066–1307* (London: Arnold, 1979), 221–22.

26. See Psaki (chapter 5 in the present volume) for a somewhat different interpretation of Lïenor's robe.

27. For an analysis of this shift as it applies to the hermeneutics of twelfth-century French romance, see Eugene Vance, "Chrétien's *Yvain* and the Ideologies of Change and Exchange," *Yale French Studies* 70 (1986): 42–62. My reading of the textile elements in *L'escoufle* owes much to Vance's model.

28. Judith Bennett and Maryanne Kowaleski, "Crafts, Gilds, and Women in the Middle Ages: Fifty Years after Marian K. Dale," in *Sisters and Workers in the Middle Ages,* ed. Judith M. Bennett, Elizabeth A. Clark, Jean F. O'Barr, B. Anne Vilen, and Sarah Westphal-Wihl (Chicago: University of Chicago Press, 1989), 12.

29. In a paper entitled "When Courtly Heroines Go to Work," delivered at the Conference on Medieval and Early Modern Studies: What Difference Does Gender Make? (University of North Carolina, Chapel Hill, 27–28 October 1995), I analyze the entrepreneurial spirit of this later romance.

30. See the remarks about the embroidery workshops of Rouen in the article by Bennett and Kowaleski cited in note 28. For information about the women textile workers of medieval Montpellier, see Kathryn L. Reyerson, "Women in Business in

Medieval Montpellier," in *Women and Work in Preindustrial Europe,* ed. Barbara Hanawalt (Bloomington: Indiana University Press, 1986), 117–44.

31. Ysabeau's destitution suggests the precarious existence of low-skill women textile workers profiled in Herlihy, *Opera muliebria,* 83–84. Such women were held in low esteem because they were sometimes obliged to work as prostitutes when their primary trade failed them.

32. The term *romanz* may refer to the genre of romance, to the (Romance) language in which Jean Renart is writing, or to both. The interpretation of these lines is the subject of an extended analysis by Michel Zink in his chapter in the present volume; see also Hendrik van der Werf's chapter.

33. Des lais pensai, k'oïz aveie.
Ne dutai pas, bien le saveie,
Ke pur remambrance les firent
Des aventures k'il oïrent
Cil ki primes les comencierent
E ki avant les enveierent.
Plusurs en ai oï conter,
Nes voil laissier ne oblier.
Rimé en ai e fait ditié,
Soventes fiez en ai veillié!

[Then I thought of the *lais* I'd heard.
I did not doubt, indeed I knew well,
that those who first began them
and sent them forth
composed them in order to preserve
adventures they had heard.
I have heard many told;
and I don't want to neglect or forget them.
To put them into word and rhyme
I've often stayed awake.]
(*Lais,* "Prologue," vv. 33–42)

Text from *Les lais de Marie de France,* ed. Jean Rychner (Paris: Champion, 1981); translation from *The Lais of Marie de France,* trans. Robert Hanning and Joan Ferrante (Durham, N.C.: Labyrinth, 1982), 29.

34. Rebecca Martin, *Textiles in Daily Life in the Middle Ages* (Bloomington: Cleveland Museum of Art and Indiana University Press, 1985), 9–10.

35. Gottfried von Strassburg, *Tristan,* ed. Friedrich Ranke (Stuttgart: Reclam, 1980); Gottfried von Strassburg, *Tristan,* trans. A. T. Hatto (Harmondsworth, England: Penguin, 1967), 105–6.

36. Jean Dufournet et al., trans., *Jean Renart: Guillaume de Dole,* 7.

37. John H. Munro, "The Medieval Scarlet and the Economics of Sartorial Splendour," in *Cloth and Clothing in Medieval Europe,* ed. N. B. Harte and K. G.

Ponting, Pasold Studies in Textile History (London, 1983), 15; Elizabeth Crowfoot, Frances Pritchard, and Kay Staniland, *Textiles and Clothing, c. 1150–1450* (London: HMSO, 1992), 20.

38. Christopher Page, *Voices and Instruments*, 34.

39. Sylvia Huot, *From Song to Book*.

40. Zink, *Belle*, 10–12; Dragonetti, *Le mirage des sources*, 159–62.

41. Mary Carruthers, *The Book of Memory: A Study of Memory in Medieval Culture* (Cambridge: Cambridge University Press, 1990), 33.

CHAPTER 2

"Once there was an emperor . . ."
A Political Reading of the Romances of Jean Renart

John W. Baldwin

Although they rarely comment on it, all readers of Jean Renart are aware that both his romances share a common political backdrop: the German Empire and its perennial problem, the imperial succession. *L'escoufle* achieves its climax with the coronation of an emperor at Rome, who obtains this position by marrying the daughter of a German emperor. The subsequent *Romance of the Rose* (often called *Guillaume de Dole*) opens with the lines: "In the empire, where the Germans have been lords for many days and years . . . once there was an emperor by the name of Conrad . . ." (vv. 31–34); it concludes with the emperor's finally submitting himself to the bonds of matrimony for the sake of producing an heir.[1] In this chapter I argue that Emperor Otto (IV) of Brunswick, the Welf candidate to the disputed imperial throne at the end of the twelfth and beginning of the thirteenth century, provides a historical context for reading these two romances. This Welf thesis was first proposed by Rita Lejeune in 1935 when she argued that Jean Renart fashioned an image of the emperor Conrad to be juxtaposed against Philip Augustus, Otto's Capetian antagonist. The role of Otto was merely implied; but in an important article in 1974, Lejeune further elaborated the "Welf tonality" of *Guillaume de Dole* by situating it in the geography of Liège, which was a bastion of Welf support. She offered the Welf thesis only as a hypothesis supported by scattered suggestions. In this chapter I propose to explore her insights by not only rereading the romance but also examining the wealth of historical evidence that can be culled from the political context—some of it as yet unedited—in an effort to show that Jean Renart can be intelligibly read against the historical events that took place in the empire during his time.[2]

In the 1970s literary critics began to abandon the historical-positivist perspective on medieval literature for an approach that concentrated on literary artistry and language. According to Michel Zink, the true *référant* in Jean Renart's romances was not external historical reality, which Jean saw only as an illusion, but the nature of the literary text itself. In an extreme statement, Roger Dragonetti argued that Jean Renart's goal was to employ rhetorical artifice and poetic language to play with, frustrate, and indeed subvert all reference to extratextual phenomena.[3] Without denying that Jean Renart's artistic and linguistic genius can fashion verse susceptible to readings on more than one level, I nonetheless return to Rita Lejeune's Welf thesis and resituate the two romances within the context of the crisis over succession that profoundly disturbed the German Empire from 1197 to 1218.

The Imperial Crisis over Succession: 1197–1218

Since the events of these two decades have long been familiar to historians of Germany, the relevant factors in the crisis over succession can be quickly recalled.[4] The sudden death of Emperor Henry VI on 28 September 1197 at the age of thirty-two, leaving an infant son Frederick as heir, jeopardized the impressive achievements of the Staufen dynasty. Not only had members consolidated and increased their territorial lands—Henry VI had acquired Sicily by marrying its heiress—but they had also attempted to establish a dynastic claim to the imperial crown. Two conflicting principles governed the succession of an emperor in Germany: election by princes and dynastic inheritance. For three generations the Staufens had persuaded the princes to elect members of the Staufen family. Now with an heir who was less than three years old the Staufens were acutely vulnerable both to their enemies within the empire and, more important, to those without.

The infant Frederick's claims were defended by his uncle Philip, duke of Swabia; but when the task appeared hopeless, he offered himself as candidate and was crowned king of the Romans (an intermediate step toward the emperorship) at Mainz on 8 September 1198. His adherents, who probably included the majority of the German princes, were concentrated in the south and southwest; but resistance arose among the princes in the north—particularly among those in the lower Rhine valley, all of whom received massive support from the kings of England. King Richard lavished subsidies on the archbishop of Cologne, the bishop of Liège, and the duke of Brabant and formed an alliance with Baudouin IX, count of Flanders, in 1197. The emperor Henry's death in the same year provided Richard with a splendid opportunity to promote a rival to the imperial throne. His candidate was furnished by the marriage of his sister Mathilda in 1168 to Henry the Lion, duke of Saxony and head of the Welf dynasty in northern Germany, who had often contested the Staufens. Among the children of this union were Heinrich, who succeeded to his father and married the heiress to the count of the Rhine Palatinate, and a younger brother, Otto of Brunswick, who was raised in the English court. Born in 1175/76, Otto was created count of La Marche, York, and Poitou by his uncle Richard. Because Heinrich was absent on a crusade, Otto became Richard's choice for the imperial throne. Proposed to the citizens of Cologne, who received financial inducements, Otto was elected king of the Romans and crowned at Aachen on 12 July 1198 by the archbishop of Cologne.

The rivalry between the two candidates prompted the intervention of a second outside power, the papacy. Newly elected in 1198, the young and energetic Innocent III inherited a policy of hostility toward the Staufens for their unfavorable treatment of the church and their aggressive designs on Italy—in particular, Sicily. Asserting authority to judge the claims of the candidates, he pronounced in favor of Otto in 1201.[5] The appearance of a Welf candidate bound by blood and silver to the English king also stirred the fears of a third outside power, Philip Augustus, the Capetian king of France. Alarmed by the potential cooperation between a German candidate and the English king, whose immense fiefs in France threatened the royal domain, King Philip was unfailing in his support of the Staufens and formed alliances with Philip of Swabia and later with the young Frederick.

During the two decades of disputed succession, the balance between the Staufen and Welf rivals oscillated widely. Philip of Swabia was assassinated in 1208 in an unrelated feud. On 4 October 1209 Pope Innocent finally crowned Otto in Rome, thus according him full recognition as emperor; but when the Welfs began to adopt the former Staufen policies in Italy, the pope excommunicated the emperor in 1210 and transferred his support to the Staufen Frederick, who was crowned king of the Romans at Mainz in 1212. In the meantime Otto's other external supporter, King John (who had succeeded his brother Richard in 1199), had suffered losses to Philip Augustus in France, relinquishing Normandy in 1204 and retreating south of the Loire by 1206. To recover his fiefs he offered large subventions and recruited allies from the Lowlands, including the counts of Boulogne and Flanders and his nephew Otto. While John attacked from the south, the allies converged on Paris from the north. Both prongs of the invasion were repulsed by the Capetians—most notably to the north at Bouvines, where Philip Augustus defeated the emperor and his English allies in a pitched battle in 1214. John retired to his island kingdom, and Otto's fortunes never recovered. The following year, the Lateran Council at Rome confirmed Frederick's election; and on 19 May 1218 Otto died with little to bequeath except the remaining imperial insignia, which he instructed his brother to transmit to the next duly elected emperor.

Within this rapid sketch of imperial history the importance of marriage and dynasty should now be evident. The marriages of the three Henrys—the Staufen Henry VI to Constance of Sicily, the Welf Henry the Lion to Mathilda of England, and the Welf Heinrich to the heiress of the Rhine Palatinate, among others—shaped the course of imperial politics for decades; but in the case of the imperial throne, the Staufen family eventually survived inopportune death, papal resistance, Welf ambition, and foreign intervention to transmit its political authority to another generation. It was not until Frederick II's death in 1250, without a legitimate heir, that the dynasty came to an end.

Framing the Context: The Addressees and the Chronology of the Romances

Requisite to a contextual reading of Jean Renart's romances are preliminary investigations into the historical identities of the author and his addressees, the date of composition, the time and space in which the narratives unfold, and other contextual indicators such as recognizable historical personages, which the author distributed throughout the text. Like his predecessors Béroul, Thomas of England, Marie de France, and Chrétien de Troyes, Jean Renart was reluctant to reveal his personal identity. He signed one of his works, *Le lai de l'ombre,* with *Jehan Renart* and concealed his name in the two romances by means of an anagram.[6] "Jean Renart" was undoubtedly a nom de plume, most probably adopted from the earlier *Roman de Renart,* to which the author pointedly alludes in *Guillaume de Dole* (vv. 5420–21). Like Chrétien de Troyes, Jean Renart not only intends his romances for the courts of kings and counts (*L'escoufle,*

v. 21; *Lai,* v. 49; *Guillaume de Dole,* v. 5646) but also identifies the recipients of each of his writings. *L'escoufle* was addressed to the noble count of Hainaut ("gentil conte en Hainaut," vv. 9060, 9079–80), the *Lai* to an unnamed bishop-elect ("l'Eslit," v. 41), and *Guillaume de Dole* to Milon de Nanteuil, who resided in the territory of Reims in Champagne ("en Raincïen en Champaigne / . . . li biaus Miles . . . / de Nantuel," vv. 5–7).[7] These three addressees help to situate and contextualize Jean Renart's writings at the outset.

The best candidate for the noble count of Hainaut is Baudouin (born in 1171/72), who became the ninth count of Flanders in 1194 and, in 1195, the sixth count of Hainaut by that name. He left his lands on 14 April 1202 to take part in the Fourth Crusade, was elected emperor of the Latin kingdom in Constantinople, was captured by the Bulgarians in 1205, and died in prison shortly thereafter.[8] Because this Baudouin inherited Hainaut from his father and Flanders from his mother, he could be appropriately designated as "conte en Hainaut" (*Chronique de Gislebert,* 229, tableaux 1, 4, 5).

Throughout *L'escoufle* Jean Renart dropped clues that would have been savored by Baudouin as the designatee. The heroine of the romance, for example, is called Aelis, a name that recalled Baudouin's grandmother, Alix de Namur (*Chronique de Gislebert,* 2, 60, 96). The fictional Aelis's fame extended from Montpellier, where she worked, to Mons[-en-]Hainaut (v. 5638), the chief seat of Baudouin's court. To search for Aelis, the hero Guillaume frequented popular pilgrimage sites. Weeks of waiting at the famous Santiago de Compostela produced only her donkey, but the shrine of Saint-Gilles was instrumental in reuniting the lovers. Saint-Gilles did not enjoy the same celebrity as Compostela, but it was a favorite of the family of Hainaut. Pilgrimages are recorded for Baudouin's mother and wife (*Chronique de Gislebert,* 150, 332).

The story of the ardent love and constant fidelity of the young Guillaume and Aelis, moreover, could have especially pleased Count Baudouin. Gislebert de Mons, whose history of Hainaut is dedicated to Baudouin, informs us of the count's own marriage to Marie de Champagne, contracted in 1186 when he was fourteen and his bride was twelve. The chronicler states explicitly that Baudouin loved his wife chastely and fervently, was content with her alone, and spurned all other women—qualities, as Gislebert adds, that were rarely found among other men. The bastards of Baudouin's own father and grandfather were openly recorded by the chronicler; and the bride's mother, Marie, countess of Champagne, was renowned for publicizing the axiom that marriage was incompatible with love, a sentiment that was shared in turn by her own mother, Eleanor of Aquitaine (*Chronique de Gislebert,* 191–92).[9]

Milon de Nanteuil, to whom Jean Renart sent *Guillaume de Dole,* came from the family of Nanteuil-la-Fosse (Marne, arr. Reims, can. Châtillon-sur-Marne). Milon first appeared at Reims as a candidate for the archbishopric of Reims in the contested election of 1202, following the death of Guillaume de Champagne, uncle of Philip Augustus. His youth and his modest origins from the lower nobility made him an unusual applicant for the foremost regalian see of France, a position that frequently went to men closely related to the royal family. Milon, however, was undoubtedly ambitious and perhaps even lacking in scruples. Robert of Courson, a theological master at Paris who was appointed as papal judge delegate in the affair, noted that the young man had offered three thousand marks from his inheritance to advance his case. Not only Milon, however, but also Philippe de Dreux, bishop of Beauvais, a royal cousin enjoying the king's support, and Baudouin, *prévôt* of the chapter, sought the post. All three, however, were obstinately opposed by the archdeacon, Thibaut du Perche. To settle the controversy, they finally appealed to Innocent III, who imposed his own choice in 1204.[10]

Appearing as canon of the cathedral chapter in 1206, Milon himself became *prévôt* of the chapter in 1207. For the next decade he held this position as leader of the chapter, second only to the archbishop.[11] In 1217 he was finally rewarded with election to the see of Beauvais, vacated by the death of Philippe, the royal cousin; he was not, however, consecrated until 1222. In the interval, Milon served as guardian of Reims during the archbishop's absence on a crusade in 1217; he himself left for the East in 1219.[12] Because Beauvais was a regalian see that usually went to men with connections to the king, Milon must have enjoyed initial royal favor; but before his death in 1234 he had antagonized the regency of Blanche de Castile and fallen into a dispute with Louis IX over the division of rights at Beauvais. In 1225, three years after his arrival at Beauvais, the cathedral was badly damaged by fire. Milon laid plans for rebuilding the edifice as the tallest cathedral in Christendom, and this construction undoubtedly consumed most of his time and energies during the time he was bishop.[13]

Jean Renart includes details in *Guillaume de Dole* that are meant to catch the attention of Milon de Nanteuil. For example, when he wishes to evoke the quantity of cloth consumed at the emperor Conrad's wedding, he affirms that it was sufficient to garb all the monks at Ourscamps and

Igny for three years (v. 5499). The latter was a Cistercian house that served as a necropolis for the lords of Nanteuil; along with the nuns at Longueau, Igny was a major beneficiary of the alms of Milon's family. (In 1222, for example, Milon's brother and wife gave Igny a rent from Nanteuil to buy fur cloaks for the nuns and tunics for lepers.)[14]

The careers of the addressees help us to establish approximate chronological limits for Jean Renart's writings. As a preliminary step, we notice that the relative chronology of the three works can be established more readily than the specific dates. Internal references suggest that the works were written in the following order: *L'escoufle, Le lai de l'ombre,* and *Guillaume de Dole.*[15] Sent to Baudouin VI, count of Hainaut, *L'escoufle* was composed between 1195, when Baudouin became count, and 1202, when he left on the Fourth Crusade. *Guillaume de Dole,* addressed to Milon de Nanteuil while he was at Reims, may be dated between 1202, when Milon first appeared as a candidate for election to archbishop, and 1218, when he was still guardian of Reims before leaving on the Fifth Crusade. The identity of the unnamed bishop-elect to whom *Le lai de l'ombre* was sent (and the resulting chronology) is less clear. It has usually been assumed that the designatee was also Milon de Nanteuil, while he was bishop-elect of Beauvais between 1217 and 1222. These dates, however, fit awkwardly between the two romances. As we shall see, another candidate for the Eslit might be Hugues de Pierrepont, bishop of Liège (1200–1229), whose diocese was of notable interest to Jean Renart and who was bishop-elect between 1200 and 1202. These dates would fit the chronological framework that I have outlined.[16]

In Search of Verisimilitude

Jean Renart's romances may be distinguished from those that preceded him by the vivid evocations in them of both geographical place and historical personage.[17] For the most part, his forerunners were interested in the geography of antiquity or of the Arthurian universe, which was composed of never-never lands filled with marvelous forests or the exotic settings of Brittany, both Greater and Minor. Rarely was geography mapped out with precision. In contrast, Jean Renart's spatial world was remarkably specific and localized, with a discernible concentration on Lotharingia, the middle territory between France and the empire. His predecessors also drew their cast of characters from antiquity or from Arthurian legend, with little effort to evoke identifiable contemporary personalities. Jean Renart, however, stresses his intention to portray actual events. In the preface to *L'escoufle,* he announces an agenda that privileges truth over fable: "Car ki verté trespasse et laisse / Et fait venir son conte a fable, / Ce ne doit estre chose estable / Ne recetee en nule court" (vv. 14–17) [For the one who goes beyond and abandons truth / and turns his story into a fable / this cannot be a stable thing / nor {should it be} recited in any court]. His successor and imitator, Gerbert de Montreuil, is even more explicit; in a programmatic epigram, he declares that his tale will not speak of the Round Table, Arthur, or his knights.[18] Although the chief protagonists of *Guillaume de Dole* are patently fictional, Jean Renart is the first author of romance to incorporate historically identifiable secondary characters. His use of actual places and persons was, it seems, a conscious attempt on his part to create an atmosphere of verisimilitude. But the specificity of the references, however delightful for his audience, creates a number of snares for modern readers, particularly those of the historical-positivist persuasion, who may understandably be tempted, for example, to identify the allusions in a manner not intended by the author. Such readers may assume that Jean Renart possessed the historical knowledge available to modern historians, allowing him to determine with precision the activities and dates of his characters. More perilously, readers may be tempted to plumb the author's intentions; why, for example, were certain personages included and others not? Modern readers should therefore be cautioned that Jean Renart could make mistakes about his historical characters and his full intentions may be impenetrable. We can at best take note of those places and personalities that *were* included and from them search for patterns that might help us to interpret the author and his work.

Geography and Personages

Since all of Jean Renart's works were written in Francien, the dialect of the Capetian lands, it might appear that they were composed for an audience at least neighboring the royal domain if not living there. Count Baudouin of Hainaut was ostensibly a Francophone; his father had been obliged to send him to the imperial court to learn courtesy and the German tongue (*Chronique de Gislebert*, 234). The county of Hainaut was a fief of the empire, but Jean Renart clearly hoped that his *Escoufle* would be known in France; he therefore defines Baudouin's renown as extending along the French borders from Tournai to Reims (v. 9066). Except for Normandy, however, he makes few geographical allusions to northern France. Only on rare occasions does he raise comparisons with the royal domain, citing Lendit (vv. 6528–38), Lorris (v. 7138), and Sens (v. 7160). By contrast, since Milon de Nanteuil was from Champagne (within the borders of the French kingdom), the references to France are naturally more abundant in *Guillaume de Dole.* Not only is more attention paid to the French participants at the tournament of Saint-Trond (despite their loss), but France is held up as the ultimate standard of chivalrous life. Clothes (vv. 1530–35), wine (v. 1838), and armor (vv. 1661–64) are all judged by French quality. Bishops covet promotion to the see of Reims (vv. 797–800) (as did Milon), and only the numerous daughters of the Capetian royal house are considered worthy of the emperor's hand (vv. 3040–41, 3514–15). In one telling slip of the pen, the poet has the emperor ask Guillaume whether he has ever been a familiar of the king of England, against whom "*our* king of France" [*noz* rois de France] (v. 1629) has long waged war.

Despite the fact that Baudouin and Milon were Francophones, both romances were clearly given geographical settings that lay beyond the French royal domain. In *L'escoufle,* Jean Renart takes particular pains to identify with precision numerous places in the duchy of Normandy (such as Montivilliers [v. 8593], Rouen [v. 8234], Caux [v. 60], Pont de l'Arche [v. 76], and Arques [v. 8089]). The story opens with Richard, count of Montivilliers, about to depart on a crusade. His itinerary follows the well-established crusaders' route through St. Bernard's pass, Lombardy, Brindisi, and then by boat to Acre (vv. 363–407). The travels of the young lovers, Guillaume and Aelis, constitute the major movement in the romance and extend from Italy to Normandy and back to Montpellier and Saint-Gilles. The chief dénouement, in which a kite causes the lovers to become separated, takes place in Lorraine, near Toul. In other words, the plot of *L'escoufle* unfolds in the middle space between the French royal domain and the empire.

Within this setting, the identity of the opening figure, the count of Montivilliers, would have been apparent to a contemporary audience. A Norman count called Richard, who confides his lands to an archbishop and departs on a crusade where he obtains a truce from the Saracens, would be scant disguise for Richard, king of England and duke of Normandy. Some features of the narrative are, of course, historically inaccurate because Richard actually embarked from Marseilles. Others are counterfactual because the German emperor Henry VI welcomed Richard with imprisonment rather than hospitality. Despite these variants, however, the audience would still have recognized the historical Richard. Indeed, as the count takes leave of the duchy, Jean explicitly designates him *cuers de lyon* (v. 298). The emblem of the lion was attached to many historical personages, but the epithet "lionheart" was closely associated with King Richard.[19] In a similar way, the count of Saint-Gilles (Toulouse), in whose household the lovers reunite and who knights the young Guillaume and leads him to

Rouen to be recognized as duke, could only have appeared to contemporaries as Count Raymond VI of Toulouse, who was King Richard's brother-in-law. (Jean Renart recognizes the family ties but mistakenly makes the count of Saint-Gilles Richard's first cousin [v. 7749].)

A romance that was addressed to Baudouin, count of Flanders and Hainaut, and that began by evoking Richard the Lionheart could well recall the origins of the Welf party by linking the two names. Not only had Richard offered subsidies to Baudouin in 1194, but he had also made a treaty of mutual assistance in 1197 to which his brother John, count of Mortain, and his nephew, Otto, count of Poitou, added their support.[20] Evocation of a successful crusader who had defeated the Saracens was likewise an important inspiration for Count Baudouin, who took the cross himself in 1200. But Jean Renart's account of the actions of Count Richard in the Holy Land also recalls another famous pilgrim. When Richard arrives in Jerusalem, his first act is to hasten to the Church of the Holy Sepulcher and pray for victory. Offering to the guardians a magnificent cup of ten marks of gold, which was profusely decorated with enamels, he places it upon the high altar and orders it to be suspended above the altar thereafter (vv. 549–639). No report survives of a comparable gesture by Richard the Lionheart; but when Henry the Lion, duke of Saxony and Otto's father, came to Jerusalem on a pilgrimage in 1172, he brought gifts of impressive treasure and endowed three lamps to be hung above the altar in the Church of the Holy Sepulcher and kept always burning. This deed was not only recorded in an extant charter but was also widely noted by contemporary chroniclers.[21] Once again Jean Renart added a detail to his romance that could be appreciated by a Welf audience.

Guillaume de Dole, even more than *L'escoufle*, furnished Jean Renart with an occasion to map geographical terrain with precision. Dole, where Guillaume and his sister Lïenor originate, was located in the empire but in the region of the Franche Comté, that middle space bordering the kingdom of France. Jean was well aware of the traditional imperial cities and castles in the valleys of the Rhine and Meuse—Mainz (vv. 4146, 5642), Cologne (vv. 2969–70), Kaiserwerth (v. 632), and Maastricht (vv. 1975, 2018)—but he took particular interest in alluding to numerous places situated in the diocese and principality of Liège: Dinant (v. 2521), Huy (v. 5528), Nivelle (v. 4677), Looz (v. 2386), and Namur (v. 2100). With careful attention to geography, he made the count of Boulogne break his journey at Mons-en-Hainaut on the medieval route to Saint-Trond (vv. 2110–11). At Saint-Trond itself, also not far from Liège, he located Guillaume de Dole's lodgings so precisely (at the crossing of two roads in front of the marketplace) that the site can still be identified from the city's present topography (vv. 2068–71).[22] As the French and German knights converge on the city for the tournament, the author distinguishes the Germanic/Flemish names of Boidin and Wautre (v. 2168) in the German retinues and notes that the Germanic greetings "wilecome" and "godehere" (v. 2595) are heard in the streets. A Francophone himself, he considers these dialects barbaric ("tïeschant come maufé" [v. 2169] [speaking Flemish like a devil]) and worthy of contempt. A Fleming (Tyois), for example, impolitely suggests that the evening's festivities be prolonged (vv. 2406–11). Jean Renart was well aware that Saint-Trond had for centuries lain at the linguistic frontier between the Germanic and French-speaking populations of the empire.[23]

Because of the attraction of the tournament at Saint-Trond, the diocese and principality of Liège provided the central geographical setting for the first half of the narrative of *Guillaume de Dole.* As Lejeune has suggested, this preoccupation with Liège may also reflect an interest in Welf politics (1974, 16–19). Baudouin, count of Hainaut, was a vassal of the emperor, but his immediate overlord was the imperial bishop of Liège who, in turn, was an early supporter of Otto of Brunswick's candidacy for the imperial crown (*Chronique de Gislebert,* 12, 100, 189, 331). When Otto was elected king in 1198, his candidacy was favored by the citizens of Liège; the bishop (Albert de Cuyck); and the chapter, of which Hugues de Pierrepont was the *prévôt.*[24] In 1200, when Hugues was elected bishop of Liège—the first French bishop after a long tradition of imperial incumbents—his candidacy was contested. Otto threw his support to Hugues by visiting the city and conferring on him the regalia.[25] Until Hugues's consecration in 1202, the king and the bishop offered each other close assistance. Thereafter, Hugues remained favorable to Otto until the latter's excommunication in 1210.[26] When the duke of Brabant, the longstanding enemy of the Liégeois, sided with Otto, the French king came to the defense of Liège, which in turn required loyalty from the bishop to the Capetians. Despite these reversals of allegiance, Hugues repaired the bridge at Maastricht in 1214, allowing Otto to cross the Meuse en route to the final campaign at Bouvines.[27]

After the tournament of Saint-Trond, set in the Liégeois, the plot shifts action, first to Cologne (for two weeks) and then finally to Mainz, the scene of the imperial assembly, Lïenor's vindication, and the wedding of Conrad and Lïenor. Liège, Cologne, and Mainz were the chief bastions of Otto's supporters in Lotharingia and the Rhine valley.

Welfs and Capetians: Historically Identifiable Characters

Jean Renart also populates *Guillaume de Dole* with scores of secondary characters who are readily identifiable as contemporary personages, most of whom had connections to the Welf party. A number of well-known Welfs are allotted prominent roles in the narrative; for example, among the first of the many named persons who sing lyrics are a "vallez" of the *prévôt* of Speyer ("prevost d'Espire," v. 520), and the son of the count of Dagsburg ("conte d'Aubours," v. 529). The *prévôt* of the cathedral of Speyer, whose name was also Conrad, was entrusted to carry an important letter for King John after October 1209. He belonged to the entourage of Conrad of Scharfenberg, bishop of Speyer and Metz and imperial chancellor from 1208 to 1212. As we shall see, the count of Dagsburg can be numbered among Otto's earliest supporters.[28] At the opening of the romance, when Jean Renart seeks to illustrate Conrad's imperial virtue as a peacemaker, he invents a war between the count of Gueldre ("li quens de Guerre") and the duke of Bavaria ("duc de Baiviere") in which the emperor intervenes on the side of the count and compels the duke to submit with a kiss of peace (vv. 621–30). At the time, the count of Gueldre was named Otto; he was present at Otto of Brunswick's coronation in 1198 and supported him through 1202.[29] On the other hand, Ludwig, the contemporary duke of Bavaria, was counted among the supporters of Philip of Swabia.[30] Most revealing, however, are the secondary figures who fought at the tournament of Saint-Trond. The French knights who represented the flower of chivalry at the turn of the century are the most numerous: Ansold or Eudes, lord of Ronquerolles ("li sires de Ronqeroles"); Guillaume des Barres ("li Barrois"); Enguerrand, lord of Couci ("cil de Couci"); Alain de Roucy ("Alains de Roussi"); Gaucher de Châtillon ("Gauchiers de Chastillon"); Guillaume, lord of Mauléon ("uns autres de Maulïon"); Gautier de Joigny ("Gautier de Joëgni"); and Count Renaud de Boulogne ("li quens Renaus de Boloigne," vv. 2094–110). On the tourney field their champion is Michel de Harnes ("Michiel de Harnes," v. 2719). All of these names can be found in the list of knights compiled in the contemporary royal registers of Philip Augustus, which help to furnish the first names omitted by Jean Renart.[31] They were accompanied by unnamed knights from Perche, Poitou, Maine, and Champagne (vv. 2087–88) and Artois, Alost, Wallincourt, and Balleul from the north (vv. 2674, 2699–703).[32]

Despite their numbers and the singular prowess of their champion, these celebrated French knights finally yield the field to the Germans, led by Guillaume de Dole. Less numerous than the French, the names of the German nobility provide a remarkable muster of Otto's avowed adherents: the duke of Saxony ("bon chevalier de Saissoigne / et . . . duc," vv. 2119–20) was none other than Otto's older brother Heinrich, who as duke and count-palatinate of the Rhine provided his brother with sustained help (with one notable lapse).[33] In the final scene of *Guillaume de Dole*, it is he who urges Conrad to marry Lïenor without delay (vv. 5290–92). The count of Dagsburg (Dabo) ("le conte d'Auborc," v. 2121) was Albert II, who was the first of the lay princes to write to the pope urging confirmation of Otto's election in 1198.[34] The duke of Limburg and his son Garan ("le mor Galran de Lanborc, / et le duc son pere," vv. 2122–23) were Heinrich III and Walram III, members of the Welf party from 1198. Heinrich remained true to Otto at Bouvines, but his son sided with Philip Augustus.[35] The count of Bar(-le-Duc) ("li quens de Bar," v. 2125) was Thibaut I, who allied himself with Baudouin of Hainaut against Philip of Swabia and Philip Augustus in 1199 and continued to shelter the king's enemies prior to Bouvines.[36]

These identified champions were followed by companies of knights from Lorraine, the Rhineland, Hainaut, and Burgundy, all imperial territories. During the festivities on the eve of the tournament, two further Welf partisans were mentioned: the duke of Louvain ("duc de Louvain," v. 2315) and the count of Looz ("le conte de Los," v. 2386). The former was Henri, duke of Louvain and Brabant, who was one of Otto's earliest—and most fickle—supporters but was nonetheless the consistent antagonist of the bishop of Liège. Although wedded to a daughter of Philip Augustus, he had arranged for his daughter to marry Otto in 1214 and appeared at Bouvines among the imperial allies.[37] The latter was Louis, count of Looz, close to Saint-Trond, who was caught in the feuds between the duke of Brabant and the bishop of Liège. By 1207 he had become a vassal of John and pledged support to the Welfs.[38] In the heat of the tournament, the count of Cleves ("li quens de Cleve," v. 2604) is introduced; this was Dietrich VI, another Welf partisan.[39] At the end of the tourney, the author identifies the victorious German knights as those from the Lowlands ("ceuls d'Avalterre," v. 2825), thus specifying the center of Otto's support. Because the German champions at Saint-Trond were, without exception, recognized partisans of Otto and were victorious against the French in the tournament, Jean Renart's Welf proclivities could scarcely pass unnoticed.

The final scene of *Guillaume de Dole* unfolds at the imperial city of Mainz, where Conrad has summoned all the princes of the empire to an assembly on 1 May to hear his matrimonial intentions. Jean Renart may have selected Mainz in order to recall Frederick Barbarossa's celebrated

Hoftage in the city in 1184 and 1188.[40] Nevertheless, the archbishopric was also eminently suited to the author's Welf politics. When Archbishop Conrad of Mainz died in 1200, at the beginning of the dispute over the imperial succession, one faction in the chapter elected the bishop of Worms, a partisan of the Staufens. Because this translation required papal approval, Innocent was able to block the move and secure the election of a Welf candidate, Siegfried of Eppstein, who remained archbishop throughout the controversy. Otto took possession of the city at the same time that the bishop was installed.[41] The archbishop of Mainz, however, is inexplicably absent from *Guillaume de Dole;* in his place we find the archbishop of Cologne. This archbishop, who apparently joins the imperial entourage after Conrad makes a stop at Cologne, administers the ordeal in the church of St. Peter, officiates at Conrad's and Lïenor's wedding, and finally commissions the story to be written down; all of these activities occur in Mainz. It is significant that, throughout the controversy over the imperial succession, the archbishops of Cologne were the earliest and most influential of Otto of Brunswick's supporters. Claiming the right to consecrate the king of the Romans, Archbishop Adolf of Altena (1193–1205) promoted Otto's election at Cologne in June 1198 and crowned him at Aachen in June.[42] When Adolf defected from the Welf party in November 1204, Innocent deposed him and had Bruno of Sayn elected; as provost of Bonn, Bruno had long been a partisan of Otto.[43] Bruno's death in 1208 led to the election of Dietrich of Hengebach, who remained in the Welf camp.[44]

Otto of Brunswick

With the fictional emperor Conrad consistently portrayed in Welf territories and surrounded by characters drawn from contemporary Welf politics, Jean Renart's audience may well have been tempted to see a reference to Conrad's historical counterpart, the youthful Otto of Brunswick. The names of the principal characters also convey significant family associations. Guillaume, the brother of Lïenor, recalls Otto's younger brother born in England; Lïenor herself is perhaps named in memory of Otto's mother, Mathilda of England. The troubadour Bertran de Born, who knew Mathilda at Argentan in Normandy while Henry the Lion was absent on his pilgrimage, addressed her as Lana/Laina/Leina/Eleina in his lyrics. Lïenor had therefore become the literary name of Otto's mother.[45] When Jean Renart's audience heard Conrad exclaim to the seneschal that he does not despise Lïenor because she is not the sister of the king of England (he has, after all, sufficient goods and lands for two [vv. 3574–77]), they may well have recalled that Otto's mother was in fact the sister of an English king.

In romance and in life, however, the chief means for revealing the identity of all knights encased in anonymous armor was heraldry. In the opening scene of *Guillaume de Dole,* Jean Renart describes the blazon on Conrad's shield: "He carried a shield divided in half between the arms of the noble count of Clermont and a rampant lion of gold on a field of azure" (vv. 68–71). Because Clermont was a common name, scores of such toponyms exist; but there was a *seigneurie* of Clermont-en-Hesbaye near Liège and Huy, the region to which Jean devoted so much attention. This family had adopted the heraldry of the eagle, or the famous imperial *Reichsadler,* in use since Henry VI. In other words, Conrad carried a shield divided between the imperial eagle and the lion of either the kings of England or the house of Welf. (The name Welf means lion whelp.) In the middle of the thirteenth century, the English historian Matthew Paris furnished a colored sketch of Otto's heraldry in the margin of his chronicle with a half eagle and three half lions and described it verbally as half imperial and half the shield of the king of England. Matthew's representation of Otto's shield was confirmed on the reverse of the seal of Otto's second wife, Marie de Brabant, which is divided between three lions and an eagle, as well as on the handle of Otto's ceremonial sword (the "Mauritius sword") and the Quedlinburger casket. Conrad's shield, however, is divided between the eagle and a single lion. Most of the coins that Otto minted while king of the Romans and emperor contained either the imperial eagle or, more commonly, the crowned lion of the Welf tradition. On occasion, however, coins with both a rampant lion and an eagle were minted, in one case a *Reichsadler.* Despite the discrepancy between one and three lions, those familiar with these coins might well have recognized Conrad's shield as adopting Otto's symbols. This identification was, in fact, made by another poet who was a contemporary of Jean Renart. The celebrated minnesinger Walther von der Vogelweide addressed a Middle High German *Otteton* to the Welf emperor and declared: "ir tragt zwei keisers ellen, / des aren tugent, des lewen kraft: / die sint des hêrren zeichen an dem schilte / die zwêne hergesellen" [You bear the prowess of two emperors: / the eagle's virtue and the lion's strength. / These two comrades-in-arms / are the lordly emblems on your shield].[46] In effect, therefore, two contemporary writers, French and German, described the same shield, which Walther attributed explicitly to Otto. Whatever the discrepancies between the literary descriptions and Otto's actual shield, Jean Renart's audience could scarcely have missed a reference to Otto.[47]

Milon de Nanteuil

If Baudouin, count of Hainaut, and Hugues de Pierrepont, bishop of Liège, fit easily into the Welf constituency, Milon, *prévôt* of the chapter of Reims, does not. At first glance, his family of Nanteuil-la-Fosse seems clearly allied with the Capetians against the Welfs. His father, Gaucher I de Nanteuil, adopted the name when he married the heiress of Nanteuil, Helvide; but he was the younger son of Gaucher II de Châtillon-sur-Marne, whose older brother Guy II de Châtillon married Alix de Dreux, a royal cousin. Their oldest son, Gaucher III de Châtillon, accompanied Philip Augustus on the crusade and the Norman campaign and was rewarded with marriage to Elizabeth, countess and heiress of the county of Saint-Pol; he finally sided with the French king at Bouvines.[48] Jean Renart recognized Gaucher de Châtillon's adherence to the Capetians by placing him among the French knights at the tournament of Saint-Trond (v. 2097). Milon de Nanteuil was therefore the first cousin of Gaucher III de Châtillon, count of Saint-Pol, and an acknowledged supporter of the Capetian cause. In addition to Milon, Gaucher and Helvide de Nanteuil produced four other sons: Gaucher II, Guy, Guillaume, and André. Gaucher, Guillaume, and André were listed among the French knights in Philip Augustus's registers; more important, Gaucher II de Nanteuil and his cousin Gaucher III de Châtillon were recipients of *fief-rentes* from the king, unmistakable evidence of their attachment to the Capetians.[49]

Although a family such as the Nanteuil was securely allied with the Capetians, in times of crisis it might be tempted to hedge its allegiances through marriage alliances with the opposing side. An extreme form of this behavior was exhibited by the duke of Brabant: as we have seen, although he was married to the daughter of the king of France, he offered his own daughter to the emperor Otto in 1214. Perhaps the tensions leading up to the battle of Bouvines induced the lords of Nanteuil-la-Fosse to wager such a marriage between 1209 and 1214. In July 1209, while Gaucher II, lord of Nanteuil, was absent on a crusade against the Albigensian heretics in the south, his wife, a certain Sophie, perhaps de Chevigny, fell gravely ill and confirmed to the nuns of Longueau donations made by her husband.[50] Apparently Sophie died soon after, because in May 1214 Gaucher, now ill himself, drew up his own testament in favor of the Cistercians of Igny in which he referred not only to a deceased (first) spouse but also to a second wife, Aleyde de Béthune.[51] (Gaucher did not, however, die from this illness, for he continued to issue charters with Aleyde through 1224.)[52]

Aleyde was the daughter of Guillaume II, lord of Béthune, and Mathilde de Dendermonde. She was named in a charter of 1194 along with her brothers Daniel, Robert, and Baudouin and a sister Mathilde.[53] The family of Béthune was pivotal in the conflict between the Capetians and the Welfs at the end of the twelfth and the beginning of the thirteenth century. Aleyde's uncle, Robert VI de Béthune, was head of the family until he died in 1193/94; he had been generally loyal to the French monarchy. Her father, Guillaume II, supported Philip Augustus in the crisis of 1197 with the count of Flanders and accompanied Baudouin to the East in 1202. Her brother Daniel was out of the country on a crusade during the tumultuous years of 1213–14. If these members of the family generally acquiesced to Capetian authority, others were more prominent on the opposing side. Aleyde's uncle Baudouin accompanied King Richard on his crusade, shared his captivity, and was rewarded with marriage to the countess and heiress of Aumale in Normandy. He was in Richard's original embassy to secure the election of Otto. Aleyde's brother, Robert VII de Béthune, served on two missions between the Welf allies and England, participated in the attack on the French fleet at Dam, and entered the battle of Bouvines on the side of Otto and his allies. It was her uncle Jean, however, who was most visible in behalf of the Welfs. He entered his ecclesiastical career as *prévôt* of Douai and Seclin, where he was a flagrant pluralist and was even suspected of forging papal letters. Despite his unsavory reputation, he was elected bishop of Cambrai in 1200 and became Otto's most trusted and active agent in France. As early as 1198, for example, Jean served in Richard's embassy, which promoted Otto's election; and in 1209/10 he was one of the messengers on an imperial mission to seek peace with Philip Augustus.[54] By marrying into a prominent Welf family such as the Béthunes between 1209 and 1214, Gaucher de Nanteuil was perhaps protecting himself in case the Capetians were the losers.

But if Jean Renart was looking for a Welf patron in the form of a recent convert, why did he send his romance to Milon, the *prévôt* of Reims—a younger brother and a cleric—and not to Gaucher himself? The answer may lie in the strategic position of Reims on the eastern borders of France. In the autumn of 1203, when King John's fortunes were at their lowest as Philip Augustus's invasion of Normandy proceeded unhindered, success was favoring Otto of Brunswick's campaign in the empire. At that moment, with a burst of generosity, Otto sent his uncle a letter in which he proposed to negotiate a truce with Philip of Swabia for a year or two so that he could come to the aid of John by attacking France either through Reims or Cambrai.[55] The strategic importance of Reims as a bulwark against the east had long been recognized by the Capetians. In 1124 Louis VI had rallied the French barons there to meet the threatened invasion of Emperor Henry V. Philip Augustus had summoned the armed men of the chapter of Reims in 1197, and again in 1200, to meet Richard and Baudouin of Flanders. These obligations were renewed in 1207 as the menace from Flanders and the empire increased. By 1209 the king had loaned money to the archbishop to help strengthen the city's fortifications.[56]

From Otto's standpoint in 1203, however, Cambrai was in friendly hands; Jean de Béthune had been bishop there from 1200, but the archbishop of Reims was unknown because the election was still under dispute. We remember that the family of Nanteuil had attempted to win the position by promoting the candidacy of Milon with a large financial subsidy. In this attempt to acquire an episcopal see for their family, they were acting no differently from the Béthunes at Cambrai or the Rethel-Pierreponts at Liège. (In fact, the Nanteuils were distantly related to the Pierreponts.)[57] They were, however, unsuccessful and had not yet formed ties with the Welf family of Béthune.

Another family with Welf connections also had designs on the position. The archdeacon Thibaut du Perche had not only opposed the leading contenders in the election but also put forward his own candidacy. He was the son of Rotrou IV, count of Le Perche on the Norman frontier, and Mathilde, daughter of Thibaut IV, count of Blois. In 1189 his older brother Geoffroi IV, count of Perche, had married Mathilda of Saxony, the sister of Otto of Brunswick. Between 1202 and 1204, therefore, the see of Reims was sought by a candidate who was a brother-in-law of Otto, but he, too, failed in this attempt.[58] Because the election was contested, it was eventually resolved by Innocent III, Otto's leading backer after King Richard. The pope conferred the see on Guy de Paray (-le-Monial?), cardinal, papal legate, and Innocent's agent in Germany promoting Otto's cause there. Guy was formerly abbot of Cîteaux, whom Richard had sent to Rome to plead Otto's cause. Innocent elevated him to cardinal-bishop of Preneste and made him papal legate to Germany in 1201 to resolve the dispute over the succession to the empire. For the next three years he tirelessly attempted to persuade the German prelates and princes to accept Otto.[59] At the same time he also supported the candidacy of Hugues de Pierrepont to Liège, finally consecrating Hugues in 1202.[60] So energetic were Guy's efforts that the adherents of Philip of Swabia wrote to the pope in 1201 protesting the legate's partisanship (*RNI*, no. 61).

If, in the end, Guy failed to recruit sufficient German princes to secure Otto's cause, his accession to Reims nonetheless fitted well with Welf interests in France. He was hardly a candidate to please Philip Augustus; the king undoubtedly remembered that the prelate had been part of the papal delegation that had investigated the charges of Philip's estranged wife Ingeborg in 1196. Like Jean de Béthune at Cambrai, Guy might be counted on for continued support, or at least neutrality, if Otto chose to approach France from the northeast. Guy de Paray, however, was most likely an old man; he died two years later. His successor in 1206 was Master Albéric, archdeacon of Paris, who was recommended for the position by Eudes de Sully, bishop of Paris and the chief ecclesiastical advisor to Philip Augustus. Although Albéric's career permits little suspicion of disloyalty to the French monarchy, he was nonetheless absent from the climactic battle at Bouvines, although he and his chapter had been long prepared for the event.[61] Otto's ultimate interests in Reims, therefore, had at least been preserved. A partisan archbishop was succeeded by one who was neutral in the conflict. The role played by Milon de Nanteuil as *prévôt* of the chapter remains, however, wholly in the realm of conjecture. During the decade preceding Bouvines, the chapter had apparently contested the king's assessment of its military duties. In October 1207, Milon, as head of the chapter, finally conceded that Reims, like all the other chapters of France, was obligated to answer a royal summons for the defense of the crown and kingdom; but in fact Reims did not appear at Bouvines in 1214.[62]

Jean Renart, whose interests and sympathies for Welf politics we have been exploring, wrote two romances for Francophone audiences. *L'escoufle,* which opens with a crusade reminiscent of King Richard the Lionheart's, was appropriately addressed to Baudouin, count of Hainaut and Flanders. Why *Guillaume de Dole,* which is even more oriented to Welf politics, was sent to Milon, a member of the Nantueil family and *prévôt* of Reims, remains open to speculation. If, as I have suggested, the dedication was occasioned by the marriage of Milon's brother to Aleyde de Béthune, whose family had important ties to the Welfs, its purpose may have been to encourage Milon's receptivity to the cause of Otto of Brunswick. After the death of Archbishop Guy de Paray in 1206, Milon was the head of the chapter of Reims, while the new archbishop Albéric was staunchly loyal to the Capetians. During the brief interval between the death of Philip of Swabia in June 1208 and Otto's imperial coronation at Rome in October 1209, the emperor's political fortunes were at their height. Thus encouraged, the emperor explored contradictory policies. He wrote letters to his uncle John, urging him to become reconciled with the English church and promising him aid against the French. At the same time, he also commissioned the bishop of Cambrai to explore the possibilities of peace with

Philip Augustus. Philip Augustus was keenly aware of the dual danger. The chronicler Pierre des Vaux de Cernay reports that the king excused himself from the expedition against the Albigensians in May 1209 because he had two great and threatening lions at either side: the so-called emperor Otto and King John of England, both of whom worked to destabilize the French kingdom.[63] In this period of Welf ascendancy, therefore, Jean Renart may likewise have written a romance for an influential dignitary of the strategic church at Reims, whose family was recently allied by marriage with the bishop of Cambrai. His purpose was to bring about a rapprochement with the Welf emperor.

Chronology Revisited

This political context may also help to refine the chronology of Jean Renart's two romances. The dates for *L'escoufle* (1195–1202, as defined by the career of Baudouin, count of Hainaut) may be limited to 1200–1202. If, in order to draw the favor of a prospective crusader, he prefaced his romance with a crusade, the work would likely have been written between 1200, when Baudouin took the cross, and 1202, when he finally departed. Milon's career at Reims provides the outside dates of 1202–18 for *Guillaume de Dole*. The work was probably composed before 1215, however, because the cold water ordeal performed by the archbishop of Cologne in the church of St. Peter at Mainz was formally prohibited by the Fourth Lateran Council at that time.[64] It was also most likely composed before the battle of Bouvines on 27 July 1214. To represent a fictional tournament at Saint-Trond between Capetian and Welf parties (but composed of authentic contemporary figures) and to accord victory to the Welfs after Bouvines would undercut the authenticating realism of the tournament. It would also be extremely provocative, since at least seven of the participants were actually present on both sides at Bouvines, including Gaucher de Châtillon, Milon de Nanteuil's first cousin. Jean Renart places Renaud, count of Boulogne, among the French, which also helps to clarify the dating. An author of a romance cannot be expected to follow specific political allegiances with accuracy, especially when many individuals vacillated; the tergiversations of Renaud, however, were well publicized in France. From 1201 to 1211, he was officially on friendly terms with Philip Augustus. After November 1211, however, he was judged forfeit of his fief of Mortain, openly cooperated with the Welf allies by 1212, fought valiantly against the French at Bouvines, was captured, and imprisoned at Péronne until his death in 1227.[65] To place him among the French after 1214, or even 1211, would have violated all appearance of political verisimilitude. The most appropriate time for the composition of *Guillaume de Dole* may be suggested by the convergence of two factors: the marriage alliance between the families of Nanteuil and Béthune (1209–14) and the political apogee of Otto at his coronation in 1209. Without imposing further precision, we may conjecture that the years immediately following 1209 appear to be the most appropriate time of composition.[66]

Imperial Succession: Consecration, Election, and Heredity

At a time when the German Empire was convulsed with struggles over the imperial succession, Jean Renart also placed this constitutional problem at the center of his two romances.[67] In *L'escoufle,* the emperor has no son to succeed him; in *Guillaume de Dole,* Conrad remains a carefree bachelor with no thought of an heir. Not only was royal succession pertinent to contemporary politics, but it also had become a topos in the romances that formed the literary horizon of both Jean Renart and his audiences. It is true that royal succession hardly surfaced in the Arthurian tradition. The legendary monarch never grows old (or older), has no children, makes no effort to designate his nephew Gauvain in his place, and takes no thought for the future of his kingdom. In contrast, the Tristan legend, which thoroughly informs Jean's two romances, reasserted the dynastic principle of succession. King Marc of Cornwall and England adopts his nephew Tristan as successor; but his close barons, fearing that this choice will incite civil war, urge him to take a wife to produce an heir of his body. Accordingly, Marc marries Iseut, but the marriage is compromised by the treasonous love between the queen and the nephew. Chrétien similarly raises the problem of succession in the Greek Empire in his *Cligès,* where the uncle Alis contests the nephew Cligès, each desiring the same woman, as in the Tristan legend. The objects of their desires, however, are always of royal blood. Iseut la Blonde is a royal princess from Ireland; Fénice is the daughter of the German emperor.

The contemporary crisis over succession in the empire gave the papacy the opportunity to intervene for its own advantage. Asserting the doctrine of *translatio imperii* and possessing the imperial insignia, Pope Innocent III claimed the sole right of judging contested elections. In a long speech before the papal consistory in 1200/1201, he reviewed the qualifications of the three candidates: the infant Staufen Frederick, whom he called a child ("puer"); Philip, duke of Swabia; and Otto of Brunswick. Judging each by the criteria of what was licit, fitting, and expedient and citing arguments pro and contra in scholastic fashion, Innocent analyzed from the papal standpoint the three fundamental elements governing imperial succession: consecration, election, and heredity. Dynastic succession was the least determinative because it had produced, in the case of Frederick, a child who was unfit to rule and, in the case of Philip, a Staufen who was under excommunication for family policies prejudicial to the church. Although Otto had been elected by the minority of the princes, they were nonetheless the most qualified to choose. Privileging election over heredity, therefore, Innocent decided in favor of Otto, whose election he proposed to confirm by papal right of consecration (*RNI,* no. 29).

Like Innocent III, Jean Renart addresses the three fundamental elements of imperial succession. His two romances show, however, that he differed with the pope on one important issue: he attaches little significance to papal consecration. Because Conrad has already been made emperor when the romance begins, the question does not arise in *Guillaume de Dole;* in *L'escoufle,* however, the romance culminates with the coronation of Guillaume at Rome, "the master seat of the empire" (v. 8768). In romance fashion, Jean Renart is preoccupied throughout his narrative with the mundane aspects of the festivities. Guillaume and Aelis are greeted at the gates by one hundred dukes and counts who offer homage. Aelis enters Rome on the right hand of the king of Sicily. The poet lavishly describes the festooning of the city and the clothing of the principals, especially the dress of the future empress. Amid these celebrations, the participation of ecclesiastics can also be detected. Church bells peal on the first day of the couple's entrance. Two weeks later, on the feast of Pentecost, they are led in a great procession of countless archbishops, bishops, and abbots to an unspecified destination. Although the pope ("apostoiles") bestows the scepter, miter ("cor"), and crown on Guillaume, Jean Renart treats the constitutive ceremony with remarkable economy.[68] Only by comparing gold embroidered garments with ruddy visages does he allude to the consecration—from the papal standpoint, the essential element in creating an emperor and empress.[69] The author excuses himself, however, from lingering over details and hastens on with uninhibited pleasure to the postcoronation banquet and its attendant entertainments (vv. 8974–76).

Although Jean Renart neglects papal rights, the princes' role in electing an emperor figures prominently in both romances, just as it did in the German Empire. When the emperor of *L'escoufle* determines to marry his daughter to the young Norman Guillaume and make him his successor, he calls an assembly of high barons of the empire to secure their consent (vv. 2150–96). Composed of dukes, princes, counts, bishops, abbots, and archbishops, this *parlement* is initially reluctant but eventually swears to support Guillaume's succession to the crown (vv. 2218–340). After the emperor's death at the end of the romance, these native princes ("li naturel prince") call Guillaume from Rouen to take his elected place (vv. 8528–91). In *Guillaume de Dole,* after the emperor Conrad has decided to marry Lïenor, he summons princes, masters, and dignitaries of the empire to an assembly at Mainz to obtain their agreement (vv. 3036–95).[70]

Despite the prominent role Jean Renart assigns to the princes, he nonetheless follows the literary conventions of the Tristan story and *Cligès:* the princes accept a dynastic solution to the imperial succession. In order to retain the imperial succession within his family, the emperor in *L'escoufle* proposes Guillaume, son of the count of Montivilliers, as the husband of his only daughter (vv. 2150–53). In *Guillaume de Dole* the imperial succession is threatened because Conrad, indulging in the delights of bachelorhood, shows little inclination toward matrimony. He has received his name, and therefore presumably his title, from his father, "who was emperor before him" (vv. 35–36). On numerous occasions the high barons had tried to persuade him to marry and thus produce an heir (vv. 121–37). They argue that, if he died or went overseas on a pilgrimage, they would have no king from his lineage; another ruler, one without Conrad's training ("norreture"), would treat them more cruelly (vv. 3058–71). Indeed, as Conrad himself relates, they are afraid that the kingdom will escheat to another who does not know how to honor and serve them as he does (vv. 5121–27). Both of Jean Renart's emperors, therefore, are in search of heirs—one through a husband for an only daughter, the other through a duly married wife.

Dynastic right was precisely the solution to royal succession exploited by the Capetians and the Staufens. The Capetians had regulated the problem of royal succession in France by establishing the hereditary right of their dynasty to the throne through association of son with father before the latter's death. At the birth of Philip Augustus in 1179, the seventh generation of his dynasty, a monk at Saint-Germain-des-Près celebrated the Capetian dynastic achievement while rewriting Suger's notes on a biography of Louis VII. To enhance French success, he noted the difficulties that contemporary English and German kings had in producing heirs. Henry I's lack of a son in 1135 brought civil war and devastation to his English kingdom; and the problem was more acute in the empire in 1125, when the Salian emperor Henry V died without a direct heir. The candidacy of Frederick, Henry's nephew and duke of Swabia, was rejected by the archbishops of Cologne and Mainz, who championed Lothar, duke of Saxony, whom they crowned at Aachen. Even with the support of Pope Innocent II, however, Lothar was unable to prevent strife and chaos for the empire because, in the French view, the kingdom of the Germans had failed to benefit from a hereditary right to succession.[71]

After the Salians, the Staufens also sought to establish their dynastic right to the imperial throne with the advent of Conrad III. Although Conrad had passed over his six-year-old son in favor of his nephew Frederick of Swabia, this Frederick, who became the renowned Barbarossa, chose his own son Henry as direct successor. When this Henry VI died in 1197, leaving his infant son Frederick, the fate of the former Salians once again threatened imperial succession. By baptizing the emperor in *Guillaume de Dole* with the Staufen name Conrad and having him seek an heir by his body (thereby recalling the origins of the Staufen dynasty), Jean Renart may well have been suggesting to Otto of Brunswick that he adopt the Staufen policy of dynastic succession for the Welf family. (Milon de Nanteuil, we may note, was also distantly related to the first Staufen. Conrad was therefore an imperial name that would resonate in the memory of the Châtillon-Nanteuil family.)[72]

Like the fictional Conrad, the historical Anglo-Welfs were singularly unconcerned with matrimony, preferring protracted *fiançailles* to marriage. Richard the Lionheart was affianced to Alix de France (daughter of Louis VII and Constance of Castile) in 1168, when he was eleven and she eight. After more than twenty years, however, he resolutely refused to marry her, claiming, it was said, that she had been abused by his father. When in 1191 he did marry Berengaria, daughter of King Sancho of Navarre, as a measure to protect his fiefs in southern France, their union was without issue, perhaps because of her barrenness or, more likely, because he saw little of her. His unexpected death in 1199 precipitated a disputed succession between his brother John and his nephew Arthur. Whether or not he was homosexually inclined, his preoccupations were—to say the least—not matrimonial, for which he was severely blamed by contemporaries.[73] Like his uncle, Otto of Brunswick also spent more time as a fiancé than as a husband, and his engagements were likewise politically motivated. Affiancing Marie, daughter of his early supporter Henri, duke of Brabant, in 1198, he broke the engagement in 1206 to become affianced in 1207 to Beatrix, daughter of his rival Philip, duke of Swabia. He married Beatrix in July 1212; her death the next month enabled him to return to Marie, whom he wed in 1214, in time to secure the loyalty of her father before the showdown at Bouvines. Without children when he died in 1218, his testament directed his brother Heinrich to transmit the imperial insignia within twenty weeks to the one whom the princes had elected unanimously.[74]

In contrast to this matrimonial reluctance, Jean Renart arranged for his two fictional representatives of the Anglo-Welfs to fulfill their dynastic duties. In *L'escoufle,* when Richard, count of Montivilliers, decides to go overseas to save his soul, the author immediately notes that the count has no children or wife to whom he will leave his lands (vv. 126–27). His position was effectively that of the historical Richard I of England (also duke of Normandy), who was without heirs at the time of his departure on crusade, although he had technically married Berengaria before he reached the Holy Land. When the fictional Richard does marry and produce a son at Rome, this Guillaume is always considered the legitimate heir to Normandy, even though he has never seen the duchy. Shortly before his father's death, ten Norman knights appear in Rome to ask that the son return to take possession of the land (vv. 3488–93); and in the end Guillaume returns to claim the duchy as his heritage ("l'iretage," v. 8097). The celebrations at Rouen demonstrate that hereditary succession is in full vigor in the Normandy of Jean Renart's imagination.

At the opening of *Guillaume de Dole,* Conrad is clearly a *iuvenis,* as yet unmarried, like Otto at his accession in 1198, when he was no more than twenty-three. Conrad steadfastly resists marriage because his youth ("genvrece," v. 136), which governs him, will never let him accede. "If I had a wandering heart [cuer volage], it came from my childhood and youth" [enfance et jonece] (v. 3496–97), he later explains. By concluding the romance with Conrad's marriage to Lïenor, which the duke of Saxony urges without delay, Jean Renart might be suggesting to Otto of Brunswick that he start a new Welf imperial dynasty, just as Conrad III had inaugurated the Staufens. In history, however, it was the continuing dynasty that prevailed in the dispute over imperial succession at the turn of the century. Despite the subsidies of the English and the pope's deployment of election and consecration, the Staufens transmitted the crown finally to Frederick II, thus postponing the dynastic crisis for another generation.

In both romances, the contention was not so much about dynastic right as about the choice of the emperor's spouse. The princes propose candidates of royal blood, as princes generally do in the romance tradition (one thinks of Iseut and Fénice). In *L'escoufle* they suggest the French king (v. 2166), in *Guillaume de Dole* one of his daughters (vv. 3040, 3515). (Since the time of Louis VII, royal daughters had been in abundant supply.)[75] Both emperors counter with marriages far below their station. It is true that Guillaume is a count's son in *L'escoufle,* but the values ascribed to him and his father are those of knights ("chevaliers hardis et adrois," v. 2799). As Aelis crouches at the windowsill to leap into elopement, her thoughts are torn between *sens* and *amors,* which in romance fashion compete for her decision (vv. 3891–963). Although Guillaume is a count, "sens" upbraids her for disgracing her "lignage" by consenting to this concubinage ("soignentage"); but love finally wins her for her "ami." In *Guillaume de Dole,* however, because Lïenor is clearly the sister of a lowly knight, the emperor Conrad must reassure her brother Guillaume that, as a "prodom," his "lignage" is worthy of a kingdom (vv. 2973–77). The princes and high barons oppose both marriages on the grounds of lineage. Guillaume is condemned as a parvenu ("avolés") of the Germans and Romans (*L'escoufle,* vv. 2792–93), and Lïenor observes that the seneschal has always despised her lineage (*Guillaume de Dole,* v. 5063). Jean Renart's emperors, therefore, sought to resolve the dynastic crisis by plotting a pair of mésalliances with the countal/knightly ranks. To gain the princes' agreement with their desires, the two emperors ask for a boon: that the princes will swear to follow their will without knowing the contents of the oath (*L'escoufle,* vv. 2186–89, 2280–81; *Guillaume de Dole,* vv. 3082–90). These oaths would have been recognized by the audiences of romance as the conventional *don contraignant* or *don en blanc,* frequently deployed to obtain outrageous goals.[76] With few parallels in contemporary history, this solution must have been a romance fantasy calculated to please the audiences of knights and ladies who swelled the entourages of Baudouin de Hainaut and Milon de Nantueil. In the romances of Jean Renart, knightly lineage is conveniently allied with the emperors to provide resolution to the political issue of the imperial succession; in like manner the celebration of the matrimonial successes of Guillaume de Montivilliers and Lïenor de Dole nourishes the wildest dreams of countless knights and ladies of the lower levels of the French aristocracy.

Notes

1. I consult the following editions of Jean Renart: *L'escoufle,* ed. Franklin Sweetser; *Le roman de la rose,* ed. Félix Lecoy; and *Le lai de l'ombre,* ed. Félix Lecoy.

2. Rita Lejeune-Dehousse, *Oeuvre,* 64–67, 355, and "Le *Roman de Guillaume de Dole,*" 1–24, especially 17–18. From her impressive historical scholarship Lejeune has assembled suggestive data that constitute the point of departure for my chapter.

3. Michel Zink, *Roman rose et rose rouge,* 120–22, and *La subjectivité littéraire: Autour du siècle de Saint Louis* (Paris: Presses Universitaires Françaises, 1985), 42; Roger Dragonetti, *Le mirage des sources.*

4. The most recent, comprehensive, and authoritative study of the period is now Bernd Ulrich Hucker, *Kaiser Otto IV., Monumenta Germaniae Historica* (hereafter, *MGH*), Schriften 34 (Hannover, 1990). Previously, the fundamental studies were

Eduard Winkelmann, *König Philipp von Schwaben, 1197–1208* and *Kaiser Otto IV. von Braunschweig, 1208–18,* Jahrbücher der deutschen Geschichte (Leipzig, 1873, 1878), 2 vols. The documentation has been calendared in *Regesta imperii* 5 (1,2), *Die Regesten des Kaiserreichs unter Philipp, Otto IV, Friedrich II . . . 1198–1272,* ed. J. F. Böhmer, J. Ficker, and E. Winkelmann (Innsbruck, 1881–94), and *Nachträge und Ergänzungen,* ed. Paul Zinsmaier, in *Regesta imperii,* ed. Böhmer (Cologne, 1983), 5:(4). For another recent interpretation, see Theo Holzapfel, *Papst Innozenz III., Philipp II. August, König von Frankreich und die englisch-welfische Verbindung, 1198–1216,* Europäische Hochschulschriften 3 (Frankfurt-am-Main, 1991), 460. A recent overview of the cultural activities of Otto IV's court appears in Hans Martin Schaller, "Das geistige Leben am Hofe Kaiser Otto IV. von Braunschweig," *Deutsches Archiv für Erforschung des Mittelalters* 45 (1989): 54–82.

5. The pope was so preoccupied with the imperial election that he devoted to it a separate volume of chancery registers entitled *Regestum Innocentii III papae super negotia Romani imperii* (cited hereafter as *RNI*), ed. Friedrich Kempf, Miscellanea historiae pontificiae 12 (Rome, 1947), which contains the principal documentation of interest to the papacy.

6. His name appears in *Le lai de l'ombre* (v. 953). The anagrams occur in the two romances in passages where the surname of the author is evoked. They may be deciphered by reading backwards. *L'escoufle:* "fait par bien povre" = povRE bieN pAR faiT (v. 9100) and povRE seurnoN A coRT (vv. 9100–9101); *Guillaume de Dole:* "qu'il enTRA eN REligion" (v. 5655). Joseph Bédier made the discovery in his edition of *Le lai de l'ombre* (Paris: Champion [SATF], 1913), vii-xx.

7. Chrétien de Troyes, *Erec et Enide,* v. 20. His *Chevalier de la charrete* was addressed to "ma dame de Champaigne" (v. 1) [Marie, countess of Champagne] and his *Conte du Graal* to "li cuens Phelipes de Flandres" (v. 13) [Philippe d'Alsace, count of Flanders]. Marie de France's *Lais* were written for a "nobles reis" (probably King Henry II of England) and her *Fables* for a certain "cunte Willame" (perhaps William Longsword, who died in 1226).

8. The most convenient summary of his career appears in Robert Lee Wolff, "Baldwin of Flanders and Hainaut, First Latin Emperor of Constantinople: His Life, Death and Resurrection," *Speculum* 27 (1952): 281–322. *De Oorkonden der Graven van Vlaanderen (1191–aanvang 1206),* ed. W. Prevenier, Commission royale d'histoire, Recueil des princes 5 (Brussels, 1964–71), is the edition of his charters. *La chronique de Gislebert de Mons* (ed. Léon Vanderkindere, Recueil de textes pour servir à l'étude de l'histoire de Belgique [Brussels, 1904]) was written on his behalf. Less likely candidates are Baudouin VI's father, Baudouin V (1171–95) of Hainaut (VIII of Flanders) and Ferrand (1212–33), who married Baudouin VI's daughter Jeanne but was imprisoned by Philip Augustus after Bouvines from 1214 to 1226. Baudouin V, father-in-law of Philip Augustus, remained generally favorable to the Capetians and made no alliances with Richard. Originating from Portugal, Ferrand was count for only a brief, tumultuous two years before his lengthy imprisonment.

9. *Chronique de Gislebert,* 191–92. For Baudouin IV's and V's bastards, see tableaux

IV and V. The mother Marie's theories about love and marriage were publicized by Andreas Capellanus, *De amore* (ed. P. G. Walsh [London, 1982], 154–57), and the adulterous leitmotif of Chrétien de Troyes's *Chevalier de la charrete* was dedicated to Marie.

10. The disputed election of 1202–4 is recorded in Innocent III, *Regesta, PL* 215:16, 224, 398; *Regesta pontificum Romanorum*, ed. August Potthast (Berlin, 1874), nos. 1841, 2085, 2269; *Chronicon Laudunensis canonici, Recueil des historiens de la France* (cited hereafter as *RHF*), 18:712, 713; and Aubry de Trois-Fontaines, *Chronica Alberici*, ed. P. Scheffer-Boichorst, *MGH SS*, 23:884. Robert of Courson's text comes from his *Summa* (Paris, B.N. lat. 14524, fol. 38v.): "Unde ecclesia Remensis repulit adolescentem nobilem et offerentem illi redditus trium milium marcuarum quos habebat iure hereditatis ut promoveretur in archiepiscopum" [Hence the church of Reims rejected the noble adolescent and his gift of a revenue of three thousand marks, which he had by hereditary right so that he might be elevated to the position of archbishop]. See John W. Baldwin, *Masters, Princes, and Merchants: The Social Views of Peter the Chanter and his Circle* (Princeton: Princeton University Press, 1970), 1:19, and *The Government of Philip Augustus: Foundations of French Royal Power in the Middle Ages* (Berkeley: University of California Press, 1986), 181.

11. Milo was listed as canon of Reims in 1206 in the Cartulary of Saint Martin de Laon, Laon Bibl. mun. 532, fol. 61; his two brothers are also listed. His first appearance as *prévôt* was in October 1207 (*Layettes du Trésor des chartes*, ed. Alexandre Teulet, Joseph de Laborde, Elie Berger, H. F. Delaborde [Paris, 1863–1909], vol. 1, no. 827 bis). Thereafter he is cited in numerous charters. In 1208 he was also designated as *prévôt* of Rozoy and Saint-Quiriace at Provins (Michel Veissière, *Une communauté canoniale au moyen âge: Saint-Quiriace de Provins (XIe-XIIIe siècles)* [Provins, 1961], 141, 296, 297). On his career at Reims, see *Gallia christiana in provincias ecclesiasticas distributa* (Paris, 1739–1877), 9:167–68; Guillaume Marlot, *Histoire de la ville, cité, et université de Reims* (Reims, 1843–46), 1:651; and Pierre Desportes, *Reims et les Rémois aux XIIIe et XIVe siècles* (Paris, 1979), 91n.185, 155. See also Lejeune, *Oeuvre*, 77–80. I am grateful to Pierre Desportes for confirmation on Milon's career at Reims.

12. *M[ilo] Belvacensis electus vices domini Remensis gerentes* (June 1218), Cartulary of the chapter of Laon, Arch. dép. Aisne G 1850, fol. 64r.; *M[ilo] Belvacensis electus vices gerens domini Rem[ensis]* ([July 1218] the charter also includes his two brothers); Cartulary B of the chapter of Reims, Arch. mun. fol. 345v-346; Cartulary G of the chapter of Reims, Arch. mun. fol. 69v., 101v.; *M[ilo] Belvacensis electus . . . Actum Remis, vacente sede Remensi* (March [1219]), Cartulary G of the chapter of Reims, Arch. mun., fol. 82r.; Desportes, *Reims*, 126n.216. For his departure on the crusade with his brother in 1219, see *Chronica Alberici*, 908.

13. On his reputation, see *Récits d'un ménestrel de Reims au treizième siècle*, ed. Natalis de Wailly, Société de l'histoire de France (Paris, 1876), 96–99. On his dispute with Louis IX, see Odette Pontal, "Le différend entre Louis IX et les évêques de Beauvais et ses incidences sur les conciles (1232–1248)," *Bibliothèque de l'Ecole des Chartes* 123 (1965): 5–34. On his career at Beauvais and his contributions to the

rebuilding of the cathedral, see Stephen Murray, *Beauvais Cathedral: Architecture of Transcendence* (Princeton: Princeton University Press, 1989), 29, 35–38, 61–62, 83. For an account of his career after 1217, see Louis-André Vigneras, "Sur la date de 'Guillaume de Dole'," 113–15.

14. André DuChesne, *Histoire de la maison de Chastillon-sur-Marne* (Paris, 1621), 613–18. Numerous gifts are found in the documents of Igny in Arch. dép. Marne 19 H 1–67 and the Cartulary of Igny, Paris, B.N. lat. 9904, as well as the Cartulary of Longueau, Arch. dép. Marne 72 H 2. For the latter, see the inventory in Paul Pellot, "Le cartulaire du prieuré de Langueau," *Revue de Champagne et de Brie,* 2ème série, 7 (1899): 19–39, 161–80, 279–88, 337–50, and, separately, *Cartulaire du prieuré de Longueau* (Arcis-sur-Aube, 1895). The gifts of clothing are recorded in Arch. dép. Marne 19 H 49 (2), Cartulary of Igny (fol. 241v.-242r.). A similar gift was made to Longueau in May 1224, Cartulary of Longueau, fol. 14r.-v.

15. The *Lai* (vv. 22–23) and *Guillaume de Dole* (v. 5417) contain direct references to *L'escoufle. Guillaume de Dole* (vv. 656–69) alludes to a brave knight from Champagne who loved a woman on the march of Perthois; this description corresponds to the story of *Le lai de l'ombre* (compare vv. 53–59). This order has been accepted by Harry F. Williams, "The Chronology of Jehan Renart's Work," *Romance Philology* 9 (1955–56): 223, 224; Félix Lecoy, "Sur la date du *Guillaume de Dole,*" 396; and Lejeune, "*Guillaume de Dole,*" 19. On the reference in *Guillaume de Dole* to *L'escoufle,* see V. Frederick Koenig, "New Studies on Jean Renart: The Date of the *Escoufle,*" *Modern Philology* 32 (1934–35): 344. On the reference to the *Lai* in *Guillaume de Dole,* see Williams, "The Chronology," 225. For the technique of intertextual dating, see Philippe Walter, "Tout commence par des chansons," 189–91.

16. For a summary of the arguments for Milon de Nanteuil, see the *Lai,* ed. Lecoy, xii-xiv. On Hugues de Pierrepont, see the discussion later in this chapter.

17. For the group of romances that shared Jean Renart's conceptions of space and personage, see Walter's suggestions in "Tout commence par les chansons."

18. Gerbert de Montreuil, *Le roman de la violette,* ed. Douglas Labaree Buffum (Paris: Champion [SATF], 1928), vv. 34–35: "N'est pas de la Reonde Table, / Dou roi Artu ne de ses gens" [It is not about the Round Table, / about Arthur or his folk].

19. In *The Legends of King Richard I, Coeur de Lion* (The Hague: Mouton, 1966), 116–17, Bradford B. Broughton has discussed the evidence.

20. *Chronica magistri Rogeri de Houdene,* ed. William Stubbs (London, 1870), 3:234; *De Oorkonden der Graven van Vlaanderen,* no. 66; *Foedera, conventiones, litterae,* ed. Thomas Rymer (London, 1816), 1(1):67. Gervase of Tilbury, an apologist for Otto of Brunswick, also recognized the matrimonial ties between the Welf emperor and the house of Toulouse. See *Otia imperialia,* ed. G. W. Leibniz, *Scriptores rerum Brunsvicensium* (Hannover, 1707–10), 1:947; ed. R. Pauli, *MGH SS,* 27:383. Raymond VI also called upon Otto for help against Simon de Montfort in 1210 and 1213 (Winkelmann, *Otto IV. von Braunschweig,* 293–94; Hucker, *Otto IV.,* 209).

21. *Die Urkunden Heinrichs des Löwen, Herzogs von Sachsen und Bayerne,* ed. K. Jordan *MGH,* C.3, Laienfürsten- und Dynastenurkunden der Kaiserzeit 1 (1941–

49): 49. The chief source was Arnold of Lübeck's *Chronica Slavorum*, ed. G. H. Pertz, Scriptores rerum Germanicarum in usum scholarum (Hannover, 1868), 22 (hereafter cited as *Arnoldi chronica*), completed about 1195 and probably an eyewitness account, but it was also found in the works of ten other chroniclers, including those from Normandy and Cologne. For a full study, see Einar Joranson, "The Palestine Pilgrimage of Henry the Lion," *Medieval and Historiographical Essays in Honor of James Westfall Thompson*, ed. James L. Cate and Eugene N. Anderson (Chicago: University of Chicago Press, 1938), 146–92. Most of the attention devoted to Count Richard's gift has concerned the anomaly of the cup's decorations, which consisted of the Tristan and Iseut legend. See Linda Cooper, "L'ironie iconographique."

22. Lejeune (*Oeuvre*, 130–38, and "*Guillaume de Dole*," 1–16) has studied the geography of the romance with great care. For another interpretation of Jean Renart's geography, see Marie-Claude Struyf, "Symbolique des villes."

23. For a discussion of this linguistic frontier, see Albert Henry, *Esquisse d'une histoire des mots wallon et wallonie*, 3d ed. (Mont-sur-Marchienne: Institut Jules Destrée, 1990), 18–21. I am grateful to Paul Maevert for this reference. In the *Philippidos*, Guillaume le Breton calls Lotharingia bilingual and records French disdain for "barbaric" Flemish ("Lotharingi bilingue," *Oeuvres de Rigord et de Guillaume le Breton*, ed. H. F. Delaborde [Paris, 1885], 2:272–73, 296).

24. On the career of Hugues de Pierrepont, see *Actes des princes-évêques de Liège, Hugues de Pierrepont, 1200–29*, ed. Edouard Poncelet, Commission royale d'histoire, Recueil des actes des princes belges 3 (Brussels, 1941), vii-xiv. The Pierreponts were associated with the counts of Hainaut as early as 1184. In that year Guillaume de Pierrepont, Hugues's brother, received a *fief-rente* from Baudouin V (*Chronique de Gislebert*, 175). Hugues was related through his mother to the family of Albert de Rethel, who as *prévôt* of the chapter had long been influential in the affairs of Liège. See Jean-Louis Kupper, *Liège et l'église impériale. XIe-XIIe siècles*, Bibliothèque de la Faculté de Philosophie et Lettres de l'Université de Liège 228 (Paris: Les Belles Lettres, 1981), 182, 301, 343–44.

25. *Reineri annales*, ed. G. H. Pertz, *MGH SS*, 16:655. In 1203 Hugues dated a charter by referring to the reign of Otto (*Actes des princes-évêques de Liège*, no. 13). This was a rare practice among Otto's partisans. See Georg Scheibelreiter, "Der deutsche Thronstreit 1198–1208 im Spiegel der Datierung von Privaturkunden," *Mitteilungen des Instituts für Oesterreichische Geschichtsforschung* 85 (1977): 40, 72, 73.

26. It is also noteworthy that the bishop and the chapter of Liège formed a confraternity (*societas*) with Hildesheim in 1204, when the bishopric of Hildesheim was occupied by Hartbert (1199–1216), a partisan of Otto (Hucker, *Otto IV.*, 439). Liège had similar ties with Reims and St. Gereon in Cologne, also churches favorable to Otto (*Actes de princes-évêques de Liège*, no. 29; Scheibelreiter, "Der deutsche Thronstreit," 62).

27. *Reineri annales*, 671. For the complications of the situation see Holzapfel, *Papst Innozenz III.*, 239–41.

28. On the *prévôt* of Speyer, see Hans-Eberhard Hilpert, "Zwei Briefe Kaiser Ottos IV. an Johann Ohneland," *Deutsches Archiv für Erforschung des Mittelalters* 38 (1982): 134–37, 140, and Hucker, *Otto IV.*, 214. On Conrad of Scharfenberg, see Paul Zinsmaier, *Die Urkunden Philipps von Schwaben und Ottos IV. (1198–1212)*, Veröffentlichungen der Komission für geschichtliche Landeskunde in Baden-Württemberg, Reihe B. Forschungen 53 (Stuttgart: Kohlhammer, 1969), 59, and Hucker, *Otto IV.*, 415–16. On the count of Dagsburg, see p. 57.

29. He was a vassal of the bishop of Liège (*Actes des princes-évêques de Liège*, xxix-xxxii; *Regesta imperii*, 5[1]:57, 67). His successor, Gerhardt, also participated with the Welfs in 1212 (*ibid.*, 146).

30. Ludwig I, duke of Bavaria, was an elector of Philip of Swabia. See Scheibelreiter, "Der deutsche Thronstreit," 347, 348. By 1212, however, he had made peace with Otto (*MGH Constitutiones*, 2:49–50,n.40; Hucker, *Otto IV.*, 99, 644, 657).

31. Lejeune (*Oeuvre*, 88–107, modified in "*Guillaume de Dole*," passim) was the first to identify the names. All were included in Register A (1204–8) of Philip Augustus and, except for Guillaume des Barres, at least twice. For the references, see *Les registres de Philippe Auguste*, ed. J. W. Baldwin, F. Gasparri, M. Nortier, and E. Lalou, *RHF*, Documents financiers et administratifs 7 (Paris, 1992): Ronquerolles, 318, 334; Barres, 319; Couci, 317, 329; Roucy, 318, 334; Châtillon (as "comes Sancti Pauli"), 316, 328; Mauléon, 313, 314, 329; Joigny, 320, 332; Boulogne, 315, 328; and Harnes, 315, 316, 333. Mauléon may be identified with the Guillaume of the Registers rather than the more noted Savari de Mauléon, who fits with difficulty into the present context.

32. Jean Renart states that a contingent of knights was led by the count of Champagne ("li quens de Champaigne i amaine," v. 2088). Count Thibaut III took the cross in 1199 and died prematurely in 1201. His successor, Thibaut IV, did not come of age until 1222. The Champenois may have been led by someone other than the count; for example, on the field of Bouvines they were led by the count of Grandpré. See Guillaume le Breton, *Gesta*, in *Oeuvres*, 1:276, and Baldwin, *Government of Philip Augustus*, 285.

33. *RNI*, nos. 11, 40, 41, 121; *Regesta imperii*, 5(1):60, 136, 137; Scheibelreiter, "Der deutsche Thronstreit," 58, 59; Lejeune, "*Guillaume de Dole*," 9. Along with Adolf of Cologne, Heinrich briefly defected from Otto in 1205/6. He owed his title as duke of Saxony to Otto (Hucker, *Otto IV.*, 40–46, 359–67).

34. *RNI*, nos. 8, 11, 35, 45; Winkelmann, *Philipp von Schwaben*, 78, 79, 85, 86; Lejeune, "*Guillaume de Dole*," 8; Hucker, *Otto IV.*, 24, 36.

35. *RNI*, nos. 40, 59; *Regesta imperii*, 5(1):57, 59, 60, 67, 71, 72, 80, 136, 148; Guillaume le Breton, *Gesta*, 266, 287; *Philippidos*, in *Oeuvres*, 2:297; Lejeune, "*Guillaume de Dole*," 7; Hucker, *Otto IV.*, 307, 318, 688.

36. *Oorkonden der Graven van Vlaanderen*, no. 114; Guillaume le Breton, *Gesta*, 243; Lejeune, *Oeuvre*, 110–12; Marcel Grosdidier de Matons, "Le comté de Bar des origines au traité de Bruges (950–1301)," *Mémoires de la Société des lettres, sciences et arts de Bar-le-Duc* 43 (1918–21): 203–39; Georges Poull, *La maison*

souveraine et ducale de Bar (Nancy, 1994), 133–34. Thibaut I died in 1214 and was succeeded by his son, Henri II, who fought at Bouvines on the side of Philip Augustus (160–61).

37. For evidence of his support of Otto, see *RNI*, nos. 11, 40, 90, 121; *Regesta imperii*, 5(1):57, 58, 60, 61, 64, 65, 136, 137, 142, 146–48; Guillaume le Breton, *Oeuvres*, 1:266, 287; Georges Smets, *Henri Ier, duc de Brabant (1190–1235)* (Brussels, 1908); Lejeune, "*Guillaume de Dole*," 7; and Hucker, *Otto IV.*, 377–78.

38. *RNI*, no. 59; *Regesta imperii*, 5(1):142; Lejeune, "*Guillaume de Dole*," 7. On the complexities of his situation, see Holzapfel, *Papst Innocenz III.*, 124, 189, 202–3, 207–8.

39. *Regesta imperii* 5(1):57; Lejeune, "*Guillaume de Dole*," 9.

40. Josef Fleckenstein, "Friedrich Barbarossa und das Rittertum: Zur Bedeutung der grossen Mainzer Hoftage von 1184 und 1188," *Festschrift für Hermann Heimpel zum 70. Geburtstag* (Göttingen, 1972), 2:1023–41; Arno Borst, ed., *Das Rittertum im Mittelalter*, Wege der Forschung 349 (Darmstadt, 1976), 392–401.

41. Holzapfel, *Papst Innocenz III.*, 54; Hucker, *Otto IV.*, 410–11.

42. *Regesta imperii*, 5(1):56; *RNI*, nos. 9–11, 16, 20, 26 . . . 59; Holzapfel, *Papst Innocenz III.*, 21, 24; Hucker, *Otto IV.*, 437.

43. *Reineri annales*, 658, 659; *Arnoldi chronica*, 254, 255–64; *RNI*, nos. 113, 116; *Regesta imperii*, 5(1):57, 72. See also Scheibelreiter, "Der deutsche Thronstreit," 36–40; Holzapfel, *Papst Innocenz III.*, 89, 117, 119; and Hucker, *Otto IV.*, 447–48.

44. Holzapfel, *Papst Innocenz III.*, 128, 194; Hucker, *Otto IV.*, 441.

45. On Guillaume's name, see *Arnoldi chronica*, 12. On Mathilda's residence at Argentan, where she met Bertran de Born, see Benedict of Peterborough in *The Chronicle of the Reigns of Henry II and Richard I*, ed. William Stubbs (London, 1867), 1:288, and Gérard Gouiran, *L'amour et la guerre: L'oeuvre de Bertran de Born* (Aix-en-Provence, 1985), 1:lxxvii, lxxviii. The name Elena (Helen) had become a familiar one at Henry II's court after Benoît de Sainte-Maure dedicated his *Roman de Troie* to Queen Eleanor of Aquitaine.

46. *Die Gedichte Walthers von der Vogelweide*, ed. Carl von Kraus and Hugo Kuhn (Berlin: Walter de Gruyter, 1965), I, 12, vv. 18–29.

47. For a recent discussion of Conrad's heraldry, see Anthime Fourrier, "Les armoiries de l'empereur." The major elements of the paragraph to which this endnote is affixed are provided by an extant seal of the lords of Clermont in Emile Boulet and René Wattiez, *Sceaux armoriés de Hesbaye*, Société des bibliophiles liégeois (Liège, 1985), 131–32, no. 540; drawings of Otto's heraldry in Matthew Paris, *Chronica majora*, ed. H. R. Luard (London, 1857), 2:457–58; *Historia anglorum*, ed. F. Madden (London, 1866), 2:65; Suzanne Lewis, *The Art of Matthew Paris in the Chronica Majora* (Berkeley: University of California Press, 1987), 255–56; Marie's seal in *Die Siegel der deutschen Kaiser und Könige von Pippin bis Ludwig den Bayern*, ed. Otto Posse (Dresden, 1909), vol. 2, plate 26, no. 3; and Otto's coins in *Die Münzen der Welfen seit Heinrich dem Löwen*, ed. Gerhard Welter (Braunschweig: Klinkhardt and Biermann, 1971–73), 18–29, especially no. 186 for the rampant lion and the *Reichsdoppeladler*. See also Arthur Suhle, *Deutsche Münz- und Geldgeschichte von*

den Anfängen bis zum 15. Jahrhundert, 2d ed. (Berlin: Deutscher Verlag der Wissenschaften, 1964), 92, 149, and Winkelmann, *Otto IV. von Braunschweig*, 498, 499.

Since Clermont-en-Hesbaye was held by the counts of Duras, the lords could also have been known as counts (*Actes de princes-évêques de Liège*, xxiv, xxvii). The most recent and complete discussion of Otto's heraldry is Hucker's *Otto IV.* (578–87), which adds the evidence of the Mauritius sword and the Quedlinburger casket as well as lesser testimony. Hucker is doubtful about whether problems of heraldry can be resolved by numismatic evidence because of the great variety of Otto's coinage (579). Since the major evidence does not agree whether the three lions were to the right or to the left (in Matthew Paris's manuscript and on Marie's seal they were to the left, on the Mauritius sword and the Quedlinberger casket to the right), it is pointless to try to determine how Jean and Walther saw the arrangement of their shields. Moreover, it is difficult to determine from the visual evidence if the three beasts are full-grown lions or small lions/leopards. Matthew Paris's and the Quedlinberger casket's three lions are gold on a field of red; Jean Renart's single lion is gold on a field of azure. I am grateful to Brigitte Bedos-Rezak and Michel Pastoureau for help on these questions.

48. On the family, see DuChesne, *Histoire de Chastillon*, 47–54. Gaucher's royal connections were also known to Aubry de Trois-Fontaines (*Chronica Alberici*, 846). For Bouvines see Guillaume le Breton, *Gesta*, 1:278–80. (Guillaume le Breton, however, reported a rumor that Gaucher might favor the enemy: *Gesta*, 1:276.) Robert de Châtillon, Gaucher's brother, was also at Bouvines as the bishop-elect of Laon.

49. *Registres de Philippe Auguste*, 322, 334; *Documents relatifs au comté de Champagne et de Brie, 1172–1361*, ed. Auguste Longnon (Paris, 1901), 1:437; *Registres de Philippe Auguste*, 201. In 1223 they both attended the royal judgment concerning the succession of Beaumont (*Registres de Philippe Auguste*, 530–31).

50. Ego Sophia, domina de Nantolio, notum facio, presentibus et futuris, quod ego, saluti propriae consulens, religiosorum hominum consilio, concessi ecclesiae de Longua Aqua, ut ipsa possideat pacifice, sive vivam, sive moriar, elemosinam illam quae ipsi ecclesiae facta fuit mariti mei et meo assensu, quando ipse peregrinacionem adversus Albigenses hereticos [word missing]. Concessi quidam quantum ad me pertinet, attendens debilitatem corporis mei, et maxime aegritudinis eminens periculum, quoniam in prima concessione, quum dominus meus viam, sicut praedictum est, arripuit quandiu viverem, ipsa elemosina ad ecclesiam devenire non poterat, unde rogo dominum et maritum meum, ut amore dei et pauperis ecclesie istud sine molestacione ecclesie teneat. Actum postquam dominus meus recessit pro via Albigensium, anno domini MCCIX, mense julio.

[I, Sophia, lady of Nanteuil, inform those present and future that I, mindful of my own salvation, by the advice of monks, concede to the church of Langueau that it peacefully have possession, whether I am alive or dead, of those alms which were given to that church by my husband and with my consent when he {departed on} the crusade against the Albigensian heretics. Taking heed of the weakness of my body and especially the approaching danger of illness, I concede, as much as pertains to me, because in the first concession when my lord began his journey those alms could not be available to the church as long as I was living. Hence I ask my lord and husband that for the love of God and the poor church that this {gift} be held by the church without disturbance. Done after my lord departed on the route to the Albigensians in the year of the Lord 1209, the month of July.] Cartulary of the Priory of Longueau, Arch. dép. Marne 72 H, fol. 13r.-v.

In June 1209 Gaucher with the consent of his wife Sophie and his brothers Guillaume and André came to an agreement with and made donations to the poor house of Hautvilliers (Arch. dép. Marne 2 G 1099, fol. 1r). In a charter of May 1224, Sophia, then deceased, was designated as "comitissa de Chiviniaco" [countess of Chevigny] (Cartulary of the Priory of Longueau, Arch. dép. Marne 72 H 2, fol. 13r). See Pellot, *Cartulaire du prieuré de Longueau*, 169, 338.

After the assassination of the papal legate, Pierre de Castelnau, in 1208, the pope called for a crusade against the Albigensian heretics. Meeting with his barons at Villeneuve-sur-Yvonne in May 1209 to discuss the matter, Philip Augustus decided to let them participate in the crusade, although he could not commit himself because of the threat of Otto and Jean. Among those barons at Villeneuve were Gaucher de Châtillon, who later proceeded south to Lyon with "many others too numerous to name." Gaucher de Nanteuil undoubtedly accompanied his cousin. See Pierre des Vaux de Cernay, *Hystoria Albigensis*, ed. Pascal Guébin and Ernest Lyon, Société de l'histoire de France 412 (Paris, 1926), 1:73–74, 81–84; Anonymous of Béthune, *Chronique française des rois de France*, ed. L. Delisle, *RHF*, 24:763; *Layettes*, vol. 1, no. 875; and Alexander Cartellieri, *Philipp II. August, König von Frankreich* (Leipzig, 1899–1922), 4:266–70.

51. *Testamentum domini Galcheri de Nantholio quondam mariti domine Aelidis de Betunia.* Galcherus de Nantolio universis presentes litteras inspecturis in domino salutem. Noverint univeris quod ego laborans in extremis ordinavi testamentum meum in hunc modum: Legavi ecclesie Igniacensi omni prata que habebam. . . . Inde debitur pitancia cum vino conventui Igniacensi in anniversario meo et uxoris mee. . . . Hec supradicta legavi ecclesie Igniacensi salvo iure ecclesie de Longa Aqua super legato quod dicitur esse factum eidem ecclesie a prima uxor[e] mea. Actum anno domini M CC XIII, mense maio.

    [The testament of Gaucher, lord of Nanteuil, former husband of lady Aleyde de Béthune. Gaucher de Nanteuil {sends} greetings in the Lord to all who examine the present letter. Let it be known to all that I, on my deathbed, draw up my testament in this manner: I bequeath to the church of Igny all meadows which I have. . . . From this is owed the pittance with

> wine to the convent of Igny in my anniversary and that of my wife. . . . I bequeath these aforesaid items to the church of Igny reserving the rights of the church of Longueau in the legacy which is reported to be made to the same church by my first wife. Done in the year of the Lord 1213, the month of May.] Cartulary of Igny, Paris B.N. lat. 9904, fol. 242v.-243.

The scribe of the cartulary added the rubric some time after Gaucher's death; hence the notation *quondam mariti.* In 1214 he also bequeathed to Igny bedding, cooking utensils, and table vases except for gold and silver: "Aelidis quoque uxor mea ad maius robur et minime non coacte sed spontanea suum fecit apponit" [Also Aleyde my wife assigns and made her {gift} in corroboration and in least coercion but of her own will]. Actum 1214. Arch. dép. Marne 19 H 52, no. 5.

52. "Ego Galterus de Nantolio et Aelidis uxor mea. . . ." 1215 May [I, Gaucher de Nanteuil and Aleyde my wife], *Cartulaire de l'abbaye de Saint-Cornelle de Compiègne,* ed. E. Morel, Société historique de Compiègne (Mondidier, 1904), 1:440–41; "Ego Galcherus dominus Nantholi. . . . et dilecta mea Aelidis. . . ." 1222 [I, Gaucher lord of Nanteuil . . . and my beloved Aleyde], Arch. dép. Marne 49 (1), Cartulary of Igny fol. 235r.; "Galcherus dominus de Nantolio et Aelidis uxoris eius. . . ." 1222 [Gaucher, lord of Nanteuil and Aleyde, his wife], Arch. dép. Marne 19 H 49(2), Cartulary of Igny, fol. 241v.-242r.; "Ego Gaucherus de Nantolio notum facio . . . quod ego assensu et voluntate Aelidis dilectae uxoris mea et Galcheri dilecti filii mei dedi. . . . 1224 May" [I, Gaucher de Nanteuil, give notice . . . that I gave with the assent and the will of Aleyde, my beloved wife, and Gaucher, my dear son], Cartulary of Longueau, Arch. dép. Marne 72 H 2, fol. 14r.-v.

The tomb effigy of Gaucher de Nantueil, dated 1229, was copied by Gaignières from the church of Nantueil (*Les tombeaux de la collection Gaignières: Dessins d'archéologie du XVIIe siècle,* ed. Jean Adhémar and Gertrude Dordor, Extrait de la Gazette des beaux-arts, July-September [Paris, 1974], no. 128). André DuChesne (*Histoire généalogique de la Maison de Béthune* [Paris, 1693], preuves 13), reads an epitaph on the tombs of Gaucher, Helvide his mother, and Aleyde his wife at Igny:

> G. De Nantholio lapidi qui subiacet isti;
> In coeli solio requiescat munere Christi.
> Igniaci cineres, coeli sit spiritus haeres.
> Hic iacet Helwidis domina Nantholio, mater amborum.
> Hic iacet domina Aelidis de Nantholio.
>
> [G{aucher} de Nanteuil who lies under this stone;
> Let him rest in the heavenly coffin by the gift of Christ.
> {His} ashes at Igny, let his soul be heir of heaven.
> Here lies Helvide, lady of Nanteuil, mother of both.
> Here lies lady Aleyde de Nanteuil.

53. "Ego Willelmus dominus de Bethune et Teneremunde et advocatus Attrebatensis. . . . Hanc elemosinam concessit uxor mea Mathildis, Daniel, Robertus et Balduinus filii meii. Item Aelidis et Mathildis filie mee. Actum anno dominice incarnationis M C nonagesimo quarto" [I, Guillaume, lord of Béthune and Dendermonde and avoué of Arras. . . . My wife, Mathilde, and Daniel, Robert, and Baudouin, my sons, concede these alms. Also my daughters, Aelide and Mathilde. Done the year of the Lord's incarnation 1194], Cartulary of Saint-Yved de Braine, Paris AN LL 1583, 107–8. The principal genealogical studies on the family of Béthune are DuChesne, *Histoire de Béthune,* and E. Warlop, *Flemish Nobility before 1300* (Kortrijk: G. Desmet-Huysman, 1975), 1:660–63.

54. The collaboration between members of the Béthune family and the English was amply recorded by the anonymous chronicler of Béthune. For examples, see *Chronique française des rois de France, RHF,* 24:756–57, and especially *Histoire des ducs de Normandie et des rois d'Angleterre,* ed. F. Michel, Société de l'histoire de France (Paris, 1840), 88, 92, 97, 99–100, 128–30, 140–41, 152–54. For Jean, bishop of Cambrai, see *Gallia christiana,* 3:34, 35, and Hucker, *Otto IV.,* 102, 128–29, 214, 340, 437–38. For his reputation as *prévôt* of Seclin, see *Die Register Innocenz' III.,* ed. O. Hageneder and A. Haidacher (Graz and Cologne, 1964), I: nos. 109, 110; *PL* 214:927–29; *PL* 211:531–32; Potthast nos. 115, 116, 186, 1071. For a sample of evidence for his support of Otto, see *RNI,* nos. 54, 124, 133, 138, 150, 172. At Otto's death in 1218 it was revealed that he had secretly taken the cross from the bishop of Cambrai after the coronation at Rome in 1209 (*Thesaurus novus anecdotorum . . . ,* ed. Edmond Martène [Paris, 1717] 3:1375). For his peace mission, see *Registres de Philippe Auguste,* 509, and Holzapfel, *Papst Innocenz III.,* 140, 180–84.

55. *Rotuli chartarum in Turri Londoniensi asservati,* ed. Thomas D. Hardy (London, 1837), 1(1):133; Holzapfel, *Papst Innocenz III.,* 103–5; Hucker, *Otto IV.,* 212.

56. Baldwin, *Government of Philip Augustus,* 284, 285. Milon was *prévôt* in 1207, when the chapter agreed to come to the defense of the crown and realm (like all other chapters in France) whenever summoned by the king (*Layettes,* vol. 1, no. 827 bis). *Reineri annales,* 663, states that the fortifications were raised "ut credimus propter metum Ottonis imperatoris auxilium patruo suo regi Anglie ferre volentis" [as we believe on account of fear of the determination of the Emperor Otto to bring aid to his uncle, the king of England].

In 1218, when Milon was guardian of Reims and the allies had been defeated, the citizens of Reims wrote to Pope Honorius III and complained that, because Reims was on the marches between the kingdom and the empire, it was subject to harassment by enemies both near and far (Marlot, *Histoire de Reims,* 3:785–86). At midcentury these troubles were still remembered (Pierre Varin, *Archives administratives de la ville de Reims,* 1[2]:868–69).

57. Aubry de Trois-Fontaines was aware of distant connections between the house of Châtillon and the family of Hugues de Pierrepont. Milon's great-grandfather, Hugues de Cholet, was the grandfather of the wife of Hugues de Pierrepont's brother.

(To be precise, Aubry knows of Gaucher, Milon's father, and Gaucher de Nanteuil, Milon's brother.) See *Chronica Alberici,* 823, 824, and DuChesne, *Histoire de Chastillon,* 614–18.

58. *Chronica Alberici,* 884. On the family of Perche, see M. A. P. Oeillet des Murs, *Histoire des comtes du Perche de la famille des Rotrou de 943 à 1231* (Nogent-le-Rotru, 1856), 431, 451–52, 492.

59. On Guy's activities in behalf of Otto, see *Reineri annales,* 656, 657; *Chronica Alberici,* 877; *RNI,* nos. 30, 33; Winkelmann, *Philipp von Schwaben,* 205–23; and Werner Maleczek, *Papst und Kardinalskolleg von 1191 bis 1216: Die Kardinäle unter Coelestin III. und Innocenz III.,* Publikationen des historischen Instituts beim österreichischen Kulturinstitut in Rom. 1, 6 (Vienna, 1984), 133–34.

60. In 1201 Guy met Hugues at Montpellier and remitted the debts he incurred in the disputed election to Liège (*Reineri annales,* 655, 657).

61. Baldwin, *Government of Philip Augustus,* 284–85.

62. *Layettes,* vol. 1, no. 827 bis, p. 567.

63. Hilpert, "Zwei Briefe," 137–40; *Registres de Philippe Auguste,* 509 (the text has been damaged); Holzapfel, *Papst Innocenz III.,* 137–40, 170–81; Pierre des Vaux de Cernay, *Hystoria Albigensis,* 1:73–74. See n. 50 above.

64. C. 18 in J. D. Mansi, *Sacrorum conciliorum nova et amplissima collectio* (Florence and Venice, 1759–93), 22:1006–7. See John W. Baldwin, "The Intellectual Preparation for the Canon of 1215 against Ordeals," *Speculum* 36 (1961): 613–26.

65. For a summary of his later career, see Baldwin, *Government of Philip Augustus,* 200–202, 207–8, 211–13, 215, 217–19.

66. Composition could plausibly have occurred before Otto's excommunication in November 1210 or before his defeat at Bouvines in July 1214, but not after. In a technical sense Otto's position as king and later as emperor was uncontested from November 1208 (the death of Philip of Swabia) and September 1212 (the arrival of Frederick in Germany). See Zinsmaier, *Die Urkunden Philipps von Schwaben und Ottos IV.,* 59. This concurs with Lejeune's conclusions (1208–10) proposed in 1974 ("*Guillaume de Dole,*" 22).

67. Another problem treated by both the romances was that of the role of *ministeriales* in imperial government. This issue deserves a separate study.

68. Mais deu ceptre vous di jou bien,
Et deu cor et de la corone
Dont l'apostoiles le corone
K'il n'[en] estoit nule si riche.

[But I tell you all about the scepter
And the headpiece and crown
With which the pope crowns him
That there was none so splendid.]
(*L'escoufle,* vv. 8950–53)

At the coronation of 1209, Otto IV also wore a miter (*cor*). See Hucker, *Otto IV.*, 595–96.

69. Ses atours passoit sa biauté
Et li ors qui ert el biface
Respont al vermel de la face
De celi qui la ert enointe.

[Her beauty surpassed her finery,
And the gold which was in the rich, reversible cloth
Answers the rosy hue of the face
Of her who was annointed there.]
(*L'escoufle*, vv. 8960–63)

70. Guillaume le Breton (*Philippidos*, 111–12) proposed that, at the death of Frederick Barbarossa in 1191, Henry VI had not succeeded by hereditary right but by election of the clergy and princes.

71. *De Glorioso rege Ludovico*, in *Vie de Louis le Gros par Suger*, ed. Auguste Molinier (Paris, 1887), 147–49. On Capetian dynasticism, see Andrew W. Lewis, *Royal Succession in Capetian France: Studies on Familial Order and the State* (Cambridge, Mass.: Harvard University Press, 1981).

72. The Champenois chronicler Aubry de Trois-Fontaines, the sole contemporary to trace the parentage of the family of Nanteuil, affirms ("ut dicitur") that Milon's great-grandfather Hugues de Cholet, count of Roucy, had married the sister of the emperor Conrad III of the Staufen family (*Chronica Alberici*, 823). This connection was noticed by Louis-André Vigneras, "Sur la date de 'Guillaume de Dole'," 87. On the Welf aversion to the Staufen name Konrad, see Hucker, *Otto IV.*, 5.

73. At least one bastard claimed him as father. For the story of the warning of a hermit, see Roger de Hoveden, *Chronica*, ed. William Stubbs, Rerum Britannicarum Medii Aevi Scriptores (London, 1870), 3:288–89. John Gillingham (*Richard the Lionheart* [New York: Times Books, 1978], 54, 161–63, 166, 282–83) sums up his marital history.

74. For Otto's matrimonial chronology, see Hansmartin Decker-Hauff, "Das Staufische Haus," *Die Zeit der Staufer*, 3:361; Hucker, *Otto IV.*, 378–79, 386–87. *Thesaurus anecdotorum*, 3:1375; *MGH, Constitutiones* 2:52, n. 42.

75. Louis had five marriageable daughters. See his complaint on the birth of Philip Augustus (Cartellieri, *Philipp II. August*, 1: Beilagen 49). Elsewhere, daughters from the royal houses of Scotland, Iceland (Ireland?), and England are offered as comparable alternatives (*Guillaume de Dole*, vv. 3530–31, 3575).

76. Jean Frappier, "Le motif du 'don contraignant' dans la littérature du moyen âge," *Travaux de linguistique et de littérature* 8.2 (1969): 7–46; Philippe Ménard, "Le don en blanc qui lie le donateur: Réflexions sur un motif de conte," in *An Arthurian Tapestry: Essays in Memory of Lewis Thorpe*, ed. Kenneth Varty (Glasgow, 1981), 37–53.

The Language of Lyric and the Language of Romance

CHAPTER 3

Lyric Insertions and the Reversal of Romance Conventions in Jean Renart's *Roman de la rose* or *Guillaume de Dole*

MAUREEN BARRY MCCANN BOULTON

The prologue to Jean Renart's *Roman de la rose,* which we commonly refer to as *Guillaume de Dole,* contains an unusually explicit description of the work: "Il conte d'armes et d'amors / et chante d'ambedeus ensamble" (vv. 24–25) [It tells of arms and love and sings of both together].[1] These lines announce not only the traditional dual subject of romance but also a technical innovation in the genre—namely, the insertion of quotations from the lyric repertoire.[2] Included in the 5,655 lines of the romance are eighteen *rondets de carole,* three *refrains,* two *pastourelles,* a *chanson historique,* six *chansons de toile,* a fragment of a *tournoi de dames,*[3] and stanzas from sixteen *chansons d'amour* as well as a *laisse* from a *chanson de geste*—a total of forty-eight quotations representing eight different genres.[4] The first work in which lyrics are systematically inserted as part of the evolving narrative, *Guillaume de Dole* is a hybrid composed of a double subject, multiple literary genres, and two different modes of articulation.[5] In addition to overt lyric borrowings, the work makes systematic use of allusions to other romances and thus constitutes a veritable *conjointure* of diverse materials.[6] In the words of Marc-René Jung, it is a form of "littérature sur de la littérature."[7] In this chapter I will explore both the implications for the work of these various elements—modes of discourse, lyric genres, poetic registers, narrative and lyric voices—and the interpretive problems created by an author who attempts to draw coherence from diversity.

In composing this seminal work, Jean Renart renewed the genre he inherited from the twelfth century by not only introducing a new technique but also altering the locus of action. Unlike the Arthurian romances of the twelfth and thirteenth centuries, the action of *Guillaume de Dole* is not set in a distant "bon vieux temps" but in a more or less contemporary and recognizable location. The court—identified as belonging to the ruler of a contemporary state (the empire) who bears the name of one of its recent rulers (Conrad)—moves from Maastricht to Mainz, and minor characters bear real titles.[8] By locating the fictional world of his romance within an apparently actual chronology and geography, Jean Renart articulates a complex interplay of historical fact and literary fiction that draws attention to the rivalry between history and literature. This tension provides the framework for, and resonates with, a more purely literary tension, which is itself fundamental to the structure of the romance. The realism of the setting, however, has no direct bearing on the evolution of the narrative. The hero shares no more than his name with Emperor Conrad III (died 1152) and his namesakes.[9] The historical characters who are incorporated into the romance appear only in group scenes, and their identity has no direct impact on the development of the plot. Although the romance creates an illusion of historical reality, the action itself has its source not in real life but in literature.

Although, as I have noted, Jean Renart announces the double subject characteristic of romance ("armes et amors," v. 24), he transforms the inherited pattern by treating the subject not through "aventure," as was normal in romances, but through the novel device of literary quotations from nonromance sources. Romance conventions do form the frame of the narrative structure: the plot is triggered by Jouglet's presentation of a "conte," and the hero's happiness at the dénouement is compared to that of other literary characters. Most of the narrative developments within that frame, however, are motivated by quotations from nonromance genres, both epic and lyric, which are collectively distinguished by their performance by a singer. Consequently, the structure of this romance is based on a series of concentric tensions: between literature and history; between romance and the sung genres collectively (or between narrating and singing); and among the different genres represented by the songs, which compete with one another for dominance of the narrative line. If the quotations from the chansons of the *trouvères* and troubadours constitute the largest and most important group of insertions, as I have already observed, many other genres are represented as well. Each lyric genre expresses a different type of love; in analyzing the role of songs in *Guillaume de Dole,* it is important to determine which, if any, of the genres invoked are validated by the narrative that incorporates them.

Perhaps the first question to arise in any discussion of *Guillaume de Dole* concerns the status of the lyric insertions, the most obvious and best-known innovation in the work. Does the incorporation of the lyrics actually imply the use of a singing voice? Critics have not agreed on this point, and the available evidence is inconclusive.[10] The prologue itself, however, is fairly clear. According to the author, the union of contrasting modes of articulation—singing and reading—not only constitutes an innovation in the genre of romance but is also one of the chief ornaments of his work. His audience, he asserts, will not grow tired of his romance (v. 18), which he introduces as "une novele chose" (v. 12). In the second line of his prologue he insists that he has "fet noter biaus chans." In the context of this line, the verb *noter* is glossed by Lecoy as "transcrire la musique."[11] Most of the forty-eight lyric insertions in *Guillaume de Dole* are signaled by a reference to the change in discourse and mode of communication required by the quotations. The verb *chanter* occurs twenty-eight times,[12] while less explicit verbs such as *comencer, recomencer,* and *dire* are usually qualified by nouns such as *chant, chançon,* or *chançonete.*[13] In two instances (vv. 1300, 5211) the "son" of the lyric is mentioned, glossed by Lecoy as the "melody" of a song (227–28). On four other occasions (vv. 1844, 2234, 3402, 3418) there are references to musical accompaniment.[14] Clearly, the text itself reminds its audience that insertions—lyric and epic alike—are a different mode of expression from the octosyllabic couplets of their narrative context.

Unfortunately, this internal evidence is belied by the state of the only surviving manuscript (Vatican reg. 1725), which lacks any musical notation.[15] Whether this omission signals a general disinterest in the music of the quoted songs[16] or merely a shortage of trained music scribes[17] is a question that cannot be resolved without an authoritative manuscript. Even if the romance readers had lost interest in music by the time the Vatican manuscript was copied (late thirteenth century), the characters themselves nevertheless preserve the author's musical taste through their performances in the text.

If we take the author at his word, the inserted elements in his romance constitute a significant disruption of the narrative. The sung melody of the lyric portions displaces the linear movement, the spoken voice, and the octosyllabic meter of the narrative frame. In meters of five, seven, nine, ten, and twelve syllables, the insertions break the pattern of rhymed couplets. The fact that they are also linked to the narrative text by completing the rhyme of a single introductory line only serves to highlight the rupture.

More serious than these formal disruptions, however, is the displacement of the authorial voice. Jean Renart includes in his romance the work of other writers, and his composition is irrevocably altered as a result. At the end of the prologue, he boasts of his skill in accommodating the songs to his story and claims that his audience will think that he has written both parts. In the text itself, however, he draws attention to the extraneous nature of the quotations. Jean attributes two songs to Gace Brulé (vv. 845, 3620) and others to "Renaut de Baujieu de Rencien" (vv. 1451–52), "monsegnor Renaut de Sabloeil" (vv. 3878–79), "Gautier de Saignies" (v. 5229),[18] and the Vidame de Chartres (vv. 4123–24). Six other songs are attributable to known poets, including three of Provençal origin, and all of these might well have been recognized by the audience.[19] By including not only the work but also the names of other poets, Jean multiplies the authorial voice, in effect creating a lyric chorus to respond to his own narrative voice. The contrast between the soloist and the chorus (between the principal voice and plural responses—between, as it were, stanza and refrain) is an essential element of the structure of the work, and we must examine the relationship between the romancer and his poets.

All of Jean Renart's borrowings from known authors are quotations from the genre known as the *grand chant courtois*. He uses this genre in his romance to translate the concept of *fin' amors*. The lyric quotations, particularly but not exclusively those of the *chanson courtoise*, are the sole expressions of love in the romance. The monologues and descriptive and analytical passages that were used for this purpose in earlier works are replaced in *Guillaume de Dole* by lyric insertions.[20] This technical innovation was perhaps an obvious one, for the monologues in older romances constituted a kind of lyric pause in the movement of the narrative.[21]

The romance opens with a description of the emperor Conrad, a paragon of courtly and royal virtues that are reflected in the lavish court he maintains. The description of the hero is broadened to include a description of the court and its diversions, and it is here that we encounter the first musical performances in the romance. The members of Conrad's court perform dance songs—*refrains* and *rondets de carole*—as they participate in its festivities.[22] Their songs play on the motifs of love, springtime, and joy; they are linked to the passage that incorporates them by shared references to a fountain or spring, the forest, and the month of May. Their songs are improvisations on a single theme: a love that seeks—and expects to find—pleasure and fulfillment. The pursuit of pleasure is common to both sexes: the count of Luxemburg sings, "Tenez moi, dame, por les maus d'amer" (v. 333) [Hold me, lady, for love's sorrow], and one of the ladies sings, "Se mes amis m'a guerpie, / por ce ne morrai je mie" (vv. 304–5) [If my lover has left me, / I'll hardly die of that]. These songs belong to the register designated by Paul Zumthor as "la bonne vie" (1972, 251–55) and celebrate the happy loves of Robin and Aaliz, who disport themselves near springs, in meadows, and beneath the olive tree. Finding themselves in similar settings, the aristocratic members of the imperial entourage imitate the behavior they evoke in song.

Such scenes, with variations in setting and activity, punctuate the romance: songs accompany the *carole* (vv. 492–552), a private party (vv. 1784–860), a cavalcade to a tournament (vv. 2223–431), a May festival (vv. 4110–80), and a wedding (vv. 5422–70).[23] Accounting for twenty-one quotations in such passages, the *rondet de carole* is the genre that occurs most frequently in the romance.[24] Collectively these scenes provide a background for the appearance of the emperor, who is also characterized by his setting. This court passes its time in flirtation, and it does so with the connivance of the emperor, who lures jealous husbands away on hunting expeditions before slipping back to join in the amorous dalliance of his courtiers. Conrad's skill in this area is stressed by a reference to the Tristan legend: "onques voir, puis le tens roi Marc, / empereres ne sot vuidier / si bien pavellon d'encombrier" (vv. 170–72) [never, indeed, since the time of King Mark, has an emperor known so well how to rid pavilions of nuisances].

After the long opening description, with its lyric incantation of the good life, Jean Renart gives voice to the conventions of the romance genre. Despite the brilliance of his court and his success in amorous conquests, Conrad is bored and seeks diversion in narrative. His minstrel begins a story about a valiant knight who "loved a lady in France" (v. 665). This minimalist narrative provokes the emperor to object that there are no longer such knights and ladies, but the minstrel presents Guillaume de Dole and his sister Lïenor as embodiments of the virtues of courtly fiction.[25] Here we have the characters who personify the double subject—arms and love—announced in the prologue. While the love interest of the romance centers on Lïenor, it is Guillaume who embodies the knightly virtues and displays them to good effect during the tournament at Maastricht.

The introduction of this pair of characters creates a triangle susceptible to two configurations. Because they are siblings and not lovers, Guillaume and Lïenor can act as a family unit, and it is therefore possible for Conrad to fall in love with Lïenor. In this light, we see Guillaume go to court in his sister's stead and win favor with the emperor by his valor in the tournament. By living up to the fictional ideal of the minstrel's little tale, he proves his own worth and implies that his sister is equally desirable. In this way, Guillaume acts as his sister's deputy. In a reversal of the romance convention, his prowess wins for her the love of the emperor. Where the conventions of romance required a knight to win his lady's love through deeds of valor, here the lady wins for herself a husband thanks to the prowess of her brother.[26]

It is also possible to configure the triangle of main characters differently and see the two preoccupations of romance, love and combat, divided between the two male characters. Where Guillaume is interested in feats of arms and tournaments, the emperor concentrates on thoughts of love, which he expresses by singing. Indeed, Conrad acts in the romance only through his songs. He has no adventures, defeats no enemy knights, and encounters no marvels; the plot of this romance is singularly devoid of typical romance events.[27] His response to the minstrel's story is to sing a stanza of a chanson by Gace Brulé. Inspired by his minstrel's idea of love, Conrad shifts his attention from the easy pleasures celebrated by the *rondet de carole* to the more difficult ideal of love celebrated in the *grand chant courtois.* Into the self-indulgent and pleasure-seeking context of the imperial court, Conrad suddenly, and with the slightest of literary (narrative) provocations, inserts the *chant courtois* and its ideology of *fin' amors.*

The romance contains sixteen quotations from the repertoire of troubadour and *trouvère* chansons, and these constitute the largest body of inserted material in the work.[28] Not only is this genre particularly important in terms of its sheer bulk, but twelve of the sixteen chanson fragments are sung by (or at the request of) Conrad. These quotations all belong to the register of the "requête amoureuse," which contrasts markedly with that of "la bonne vie."[29] While some of these chansons are performed in the context of court entertainment, those associated with the emperor are meant to serve as expressions of his sentiments and systematically replace love monologues. At one point, Conrad comments about a song he has just had performed: "a droiture / fu ciz vers fet por moi sanz doute" (vv. 4141–42) [truly, this song was made for me, without doubt].

Nevertheless, it is impossible to take these songs as literal expressions of the emperor's emotions because they often fail to coincide with the sentiments he could reasonably be expected to feel at such points in the story. This distance between the singer and the "je" of his song emerges clearly in the context of Conrad's second song. Having sent a messenger to summon Guillaume to his court, Conrad wonders if Lïenor will accompany her brother. He opens the window and looks at the sunlight playing on an embroidered coverlet:

> Li soleils, plus clers que puet estre,
> geta ses biaus rais par son lit;
> de sebelin et de samit
> ot covertoir a roses d'or.
> Por l'amor bele Lïenor,
> dont il avoit el cuer le non,
> a comencié ceste chançon. (vv. 916–22)
>
> [The sun as bright as it could be,
> threw its lovely rays on his bed,
> which had a coverlet of sable and samite,
> covered with golden roses.
> For love of the beautiful Lïenor,
> whose name was in his heart,
> he began this song.]

This passage is the narrative (descriptive) equivalent of the *introduction printanière* of a *chanson d'amour.* Indeed, the stanza that follows begins similarly, citing spring—the time of May trees and violets and the song of the nightingale—as the inspiration for the song. The insertion and its context thus coincide, suggesting similarities between the singer and the poet he quotes. Yet there are differences in these two evocations of spring. Where the lyric poet was inspired by a real spring, the emperor who has appropriated his song is moved by an artificial spring: golden embroidered roses rather than fragrant violets. The same distance is apparent between the emotional impetus of the poet, who is about to depart *outremer* and longs to lie with his beloved once more, and the emperor, who has nothing more than a name to cherish. A comparison between poet and performer emerges clearly, but it is one that redounds to the detriment of Conrad, who is not equal to the genre he borrows.

This sense of disparity is made explicit at other points in the romance. On an occasion when the emperor's state of mind is described as "hetiez" (v. 1443) and "liez" (v. 1449), he sings a fragment of a chanson by Renaut de Beaujeu that evokes the sorrow and pain of love. With unmistakable irony, the author remarks of his hero: "Or sachiez de fi et de voir / qu'il prent toz les maus en bons grez" (vv. 1470–71) [Know truly and certainly

/ that he accepts all this pain willingly]. These examples are characteristic of the author's treatment of the *grand chant courtois.* If he accords considerable prestige to the genre, his narrative consistently ironizes the quotations.

Because the songs are not directly expressive, there is a sense of dislocation in the manner of their performance. Conrad's appropriation of the poetry of others invites comparison with the models he aspires to emulate, yet he seems not to attain the standard. On the other hand, if Conrad's songs fail to express his own sentiments accurately, they nevertheless serve to signal his growing involvement in a love that was supposed to be no more than a diversion. Indeed, some of his songs anticipate later developments and are thus truer than he knows.

In keeping with the conventions of both lyric and romance, Conrad embarks upon an *amour lointain:* he falls in love with a lady whom he has never seen.[30] The song that is an icon for this type of love, Jaufré Rudel's "Lanquan li jorn son lonc, en may," is performed in the romance but, significantly, not by Conrad.[31] On the contrary, Guillaume de Dole himself performs a Francien version of the song (vv. 1301–7) as he rides toward the emperor's court. Supplanted by a translation, and not sung by the lover of the lady, the emblem of *amour lointain* is displaced both linguistically and by its performance in the romance. This double displacement of a song that is emblematic of the love to which Conrad aspires suggests once again his inability to attain his ideal. The suggestion is made explicit in the narrative, which diverges in important ways from the lyric model. First, the emperor's social status is much loftier than that of his chosen lady, rather than the reverse. Second, although Conrad imitates courtly lyric poets, his intentions in love are not serious. This new love is merely a game to divert a jaded flirt: "En mon roiaume n'en m'onor / n'afferroit pas q'el fust m'amie. / Mes por ce qu'el n'i porroit mie / avenir, i voel ge penser" (vv. 833–36) [Neither to my kingdom nor to my honor / is it fitting that she be my beloved. / But because it could never happen, / I wish to think about it.] Later, when he realizes that he has (despite his intentions) fallen seriously in love with the lady, his first idea is to marry her. If this decision acknowledges his social and political responsibilities (compare vv. 121–33), it is certainly not part of the repertoire of the *fin amant.* When the plot is complicated by the machinations and slanders of the seneschal, Conrad, after all his protestations of loyalty, is easily deceived by his enemy and renounces his love. These failings on the part of the emperor suggest that he is not worthy to sing the song that most clearly celebrates the type of love he has chosen. The displacement of the song implies further that, while the brother and sister are firmly rooted in a literary tradition, Conrad is not. Despite his sung declarations of adherence to an ideal of *fin' amors*, it is apparent that Conrad does not behave according to the rules. He may have found an *amour lointain*, but he does not conform to his troubadour model.

The arrangement of these initial lyric quotations suggests the opposition of two registers, but the pattern is complicated by the introduction of other genres, especially the epic *laisse*, the *chanson de toile*, and the *pastourelle*. Each new genre inserted into the romance is related to arms and love and successfully alters our understanding of that double subject.

There is some disagreement about how the *laisse* from *Gerbert de Metz* (vv. 1335–67) should be interpreted, for the context of its performance is unclear.[32] According to the French translators of *Guillaume de Dole*, the performance takes place at Conrad's court and immediately precedes the announcement of Guillaume's arrival.[33] This choice of genre appropriately anticipates Guillaume's role in the romance as exemplar of chivalric virtue, but it also shows how the warrior ethos has changed with time. The epic celebrates heroes engaged in real warfare, while Guillaume will excel in the mock warfare of the tournament, essentially an athletic event. Similarly, this single literary invocation of "armes" in the romance shows Conrad replacing the violent activity required of a knight with the fictional, sung celebration of the knightly ethos. Grace Frank, however, has suggested that the *laisse* is performed at Dole at the request of Lïenor; she argues that the choice of genre characterizes the heroine in such a way as to anticipate her active role in the dénouement of the romance.[34] Whichever interpretation is preferred, it is striking that the epic quotation should be associated with either a female singer or a female audience. This transference of a genre typically associated with a male audience is consistent with the reversals of romance conventions and the transferral of gender roles characteristic of this romance.

If the greatest significance of the epic quotation is its function as a reference to genre, the lines cited by Jean Renart nevertheless have some suggestive relevance for his romance. The passage describes a confrontation between Fromont, a member of a family synonymous with treachery, and Doon le Veneor, a deputy of the Lorrains, renowned for their loyalty.[35] When Fromont threatens his enemy—"Se dont vos vit, ja mes ne vos verra, / et, s'il vos voit, ne vos reconoistra" (vv. 1353–54) [If he saw you once, he will never see you again, / and if he does see you, he will not recognize you]—it is tempting to see a foreshadowing of the seneschal's treachery toward Lïenor and Conrad, who indeed cannot recognize that the description of the heroine is slanderous.

Once Conrad has proclaimed his new lyric allegiance, the scene shifts to Lïenor, who appears in a very different setting. She is presented with her mother, and they perform three *chansons de toile.*[36] Because the ladies are said to be embroidering, the song and its narrative context coincide. They perform in a social setting, in a way that puts musical skill on a par with needlework as a suitable feminine accomplishment. Although there is absolutely no suggestion that these songs express any inner feelings—the speakers in the songs are identified by name and are consequently differentiated from the singer—one refrain is appropriate. The lines "Hé! Hé! amors d'autre païs, / mon cuer avez et lïé et souspris" (vv. 1186–87, 1191–92) [Eh! Eh! love from another country, / you have bound and surprised my heart] describe what has happened to Conrad, if not to Lïenor.

Nevertheless, if it is true that Conrad proclaims adherence to a particular style of love through his choice of lyric genre, we should explore the type of love celebrated in the heroine's songs. The characters in the *chansons de toile*—Aude, Aye, Doe—are figures very different from the aloof, inaccessible *domna* of the courtly chanson. All of these women love—and love passionately, without restraint or disguise—in the face of opposition. With its expression of female desire and its simplicity of style, the *chanson de toile* has been described by Pierre Bec as an "antidote" to the *grand chant courtois* (1977, 1:108). If these lyric characters contrast with the *domna,* they also differ significantly from Lïenor. The heroine leads a sheltered, chaperoned life, and her affections are apparently not engaged. Unlike the women she celebrates in song, however, she will not be content to weep (v. 1188) or lament and regret (vv. 1205–6); on the contrary, she will go to court and pose as an abandoned mistress in order to expose the seneschal's slander.

The longest *chanson de toile,* quoted in its entirety (vv. 2235–94), occurs in quite different circumstances: it is sung by a knight ("uns bachelers de Normendie," v. 2231) as he rides to join in the tournament at Maastricht. Here is no woman singing at her sewing within the domestic confines of her castle. The story of Bele Aiglentine, which ends happily when the count marries his pregnant *amie,* is sung by a man in the most public of places.[37] Michel Zink categorizes this song as a parody of the genre, whose mockery is intensified by attributing it to a knight.[38] Christopher Page, however, has shown that the song may be interpreted quite differently:

> *Bele Aiglentine* is characterized not only by its narrative framework but also by its para-folkloric tone. The tone is established by the archetypal nature of the characters (a sorrowing pregnant maid, an anxious mother, a lover), and by the incremental repetition of the narrative technique. . . . This device of completing an action with the words in which the action was commanded or predicted figures in many traditional forms of narrative (English balladry provides a parallel); it contributes to an impression of the world as a place where events have a momentum of their own, largely independent of human will and choice. Yet it does so without establishing any mature sense of tragedy or even of fate. Motivation and causality become cryptic and the narrative can be pared down to its essentials, leaving the reader with a stirring sense of mystery. (1986, 36)

The displacement that we notice in the performance of this song, the lack of concordance between the lyric "je" and the singer, is a feature that we have seen in most of the other lyric insertions in the romance.[39] It is important to notice, however, that this song not only makes public the expression of female love and desire but also rewards it with the social approbation of marriage.

Whether or not this song is a parody, it is one that Lïenor could not properly have sung; yet it anticipates her actions. She will go to the court and publicly (but falsely) proclaim herself to be in a situation comparable to Aiglentine's. When the seneschal is proven innocent of her accusations, she will use the exoneration to expose his slander. Then, in a reversal of the lyric situation, the emperor will ask a question comparable to the request made by Aiglentine: "Estes vos ce, mes cuers, m'amie?" (v. 5095) [Is it you, my heart, my love?]. On a structural level, this insertion anticipates both the feigned disgrace of the heroine and the happy ending that she precipitates by means of her false accusations.[40]

The fourth lyric genre, the *pastourelle*, presents yet another image of love.[41] It enters the romance much later in the plot than do the first three. There are two quotations from this genre: the first (vv. 3403–6) is performed before Conrad, while the second (vv. 4568–83), performed as part of the *fête de mai* at Mainz, is overheard by him.[42] The first example is such a brief fragment that its significance lies more in the choice of genre than in the specific relevance of the quotation. As an image in the romance, the genre reflects the social status of the protagonists. Lïenor may not be a *vilaine* shepherdess, but her rank is clearly much inferior to that of her imperial suitor, who began his "affair" by thinking of her *because* she was so obviously ineligible. Even though the lovers of the romance have never met, there is more than a suggestion of exploitative dalliance with a social inferior in this situation. Nor does Conrad, once he falls in love, have any more intention than the knight of the *pastourelle* of contenting himself with unsatisfied desire. The difference between the action of the romance and its lyric model is that Conrad's beloved belongs to an aristocratic family and his intentions must perforce be honorable. A second feature of the *pastourelle* that finds a parallel in this romance is the violent treatment of the shepherdess, who is sometimes raped if she does not accept the knight's blandishments.[43] In *Guillaume de Dole,* sexual aggression toward Lïenor comes not from the emperor himself but from his court. His seneschal first plots to seduce her, then claims to have done so. When his slander is believed, Guillaume's nephew tries to kill Lïenor for tarnishing the family's honor. The circumstances are not those of a *pastourelle,* but it is possible to detect an echo of the genre.

The second example of the *pastourelle* is a much longer fragment. The performance of it by a female minstrel, "Bele Doete de Troies," is yet another instance of the phenomenon that Zumthor calls "transpersonnalisation," for the singer must be distinguished from the "ge" of her song. The stanza quoted by Jean Renart describes the gaiety and beauty of spring; it thus repeats elements of the narrative context, a May festival. The end of the stanza presents the beautiful shepherdess singing as she tends her sheep. This song is followed immediately by a stanza of a *chanson d'amour,* which begins: "Amours a non ciz maus qui me tormente" (v. 4587) [Love is the name of the malady that torments me]. The passage thus includes two very different expressions of male desire, both of which are overheard by the emperor. Having been obliged to renounce Lïenor when he accepted the seneschal's lies, Conrad is unhappy; and his mood contrasts strikingly with the celebrations that surround him. The author comments: "Com ses pensers estoit divers / de ciaus qu'il avoit assamblez!" (vv. 4596–97) [How his thoughts differed / from those of the people he had assembled there!]. Both of the overheard songs are performed in a celebratory context and contrast functionally with Conrad's state of mind, but their content—particularly that of the *chanson d'amour*—corresponds fairly closely.[44]

The final section of the romance dramatizes the competition among the lyric genres and their different ideologies of love, but the plot refuses to affirm any of them. This section of the work (vv. 5094–448) contains seven inserted lyrics, including a refrain, three *rondets de carole,* a *chanson de toile,* two stanzas from a *chanson d'amour* by Gautier de Saignies, as well as two stanzas from an Occitan *canso.*

When Conrad delightedly realizes Lïenor's identity and her innocence, he sings his proposal to her and supplies the answer to his own question in the *rondet* "Que demandez vos / quant vos m'avez?" (vv. 5105–6) [What do you ask for / when you have me?]. This is the first time that Conrad has sung this kind of song, and the change of genre signifies abandonment of his earlier pretensions to *fin' amors* in favor of the pleasure of requited, married love. As Jung has pointed out, the *rondet*'s renunciation of desire ("Ge ne demant rien") is the antithesis of the "requête amoureuse" of the *chanson d'amour* (45). The court sings its approval of the turn of events with an answering refrain (vv. 5113–15).

During the ensuing celebrations, the nephew of the bishop of Liège entertains the assembly with a *chanson de toile*, which reflects in miniature the action of the narrative: "Cez damoiseles i vont por caroler, / cil escuier i vont por bohorder, / cil chevalier i vont por esgarder; / vont i cez dames por lor cors deporter" (vv. 5200–5203) [These damsels go to dance the *carole*, / the squires go to joust, / the knights go to look, / and the ladies go to amuse themselves]. The song celebrates requited love in its refrain: "Guis aime Aigline, Aigline aime Guion" (vv. 5197, 5207) [Guy loves Aigline / Aigline loves Guy]. This song is interrupted; but when it is performed, the story of the heroine of *Guillaume de Dole* is already complete. The recurrence of the *chanson de toile* at the happy conclusion of the plot recalls Lïenor's songs at the beginning of the romance and shows her good fortune in contrast to the laments of Aye, Aude, and Doe. The performance of this type of song by a male singer once again bestows male approval on the heroine's success in achieving her desire.

The *chanson de toile* is not only followed by a *son poitevin* performed by a knight from Danmartin but also interrupted by the new song: "ceste n'est pas tote chantee" (v. 5208) [this one is not completely sung]. The troubadour song cuts off the articulation of requited love, reasserting the ideology of love that has guided Conrad throughout the romance. The *canso* is not a random choice but a version of one of the most famous of Bernart de Ventadorn's songs, "Quant voi l'aloete moder" (v. 5212) [When I see a lark on the wing]. Two rival ideologies are thus juxtaposed: the *chanson de femme*, expressing female desire and its effort to find fulfillment, is answered not simply by a courtly chanson but by the very language that embodied masculine aspiration toward the unattainable. But the words of the *canso* itself admit defeat. The lines "Tant cuidoie savoir / d'amor, et point n'en sai" (vv. 5220–21) [I thought I knew so much / of love, but I know nothing of it] are only too true of Conrad. This section concludes with a *trouvère* chanson that also seems applicable to the emperor: the lines "Amors doit estre si coie / la ou ele va et vient / que nuls n'en ait duel ne joie, / se cil non qui la maintient" (vv. 5248–51) [Love must be so discreet, as it comes and goes, that no one should have sorrow or joy of it except those who uphold it] describe the discretion that Conrad was unable to achieve. In the end, both masculine and feminine desire have been reconciled and transformed. The celebration of both unsatisfied male longing and passive female regret are abandoned when the *canso* and the *chanson de toile* are relegated to the role of light entertainment.

The work concludes with a description of the wedding celebrations. Lïenor, in a passage reminiscent of *Erec et Enide,* is clothed in a robe embroidered with classical figures—Helen, Paris, Hector, Priam, Achilles, and Memnon. These figures also function as allusions to the twelfth-century *Roman de Troie* and remind us of the generic framework of romance that, in *Guillaume de Dole,* becomes the new setting for the lyric insertions. But the reference to *Troie* is more than a mere reminder of genre. Benoît de Sainte-Maure's romance, like Jean Renart's, is based on literary sources. The plot—legendary (but considered historical)—serves as a setting for the double subject of arms and love.[45]

After the ceremony, the members of the court accompany their *carole* with two *rondets* in a scene that both echoes and counterbalances the beginning of the romance. The cheerful dance songs, the last insertions in the romance, juxtapose the emperor's pleasure-loving courtliness with the public celebration of his married happiness. In the repetition of this kind of scene, complete with its lyric insertions, there is a suggestion of lyric circularity. Conrad's return to the beginning suggests that the linear development of the narrative may be undermined, that the emperor has not been transformed by his experiences, and that he will return to his earlier pursuit of easy amorous conquests. This possibility is contradicted in the final lines of the romance, where the narrative conventions reemerge.

The lyric mode, of whatever genre, does not sound the last note; for the happiness of the newly married emperor is restored to a context of romance allusions:

> Quant Tristrans ama plus Yseut
> et il s'en pot miex aaisier
> et d'acoler et de baisier
> et dou sorplus qu'il i covint,
> et Lanvax, et autretex .XX.
> amant com cil orent esté,
> ce sachiez vos de verité,

ne peüst on aparellier
lor siecle a cestui de legier. (vv. 5507–15)

[When Tristan most loved Yseut
and he could best satisfy himself
with embracing and kissing
and with the other things that were fitting,
and Lanval and twenty other such lovers
as there have been,
know truly that one could not easily compare
their happiness to this.]

The reference to Tristan recalls the earlier allusion to Mark with its implicit evocation of Mark's nephew (v. 170). At the end of the romance, the emperor is not merely skilled in getting rid of jealous husbands but has, through his long (and ultimately unsuccessful) apprenticeship to *fin' amors*, become himself both a lover and a husband. Clearly implicit in these lines is the idea that Conrad's successful reconciliation of both political obligation and amorous desire far outstrips the easy dalliance of his earlier life. The altered repetition of the allusion to the Tristan legend signals the linear progression of the narrative plot and thwarts the lyric circularity suggested by the inserted songs. While the two allusions to Tristan's story mark the narrative development accomplished in the romance, Jean Renart does not use the intertext in a straightforward manner.[46] At the beginning of the work, when Conrad is flirting with married ladies, the legend is invoked by a reference to King Mark, the aggrieved husband. At the end, however, when Conrad himself has married, the legend recurs through the image of the adulterous lovers. The author's ironic vision is not confined to his treatment of lyric poetry but embraces the romance and its conventions as well.

Tristan, however, is not the only lover to whom Jean Renart alludes. The mention of Lanval and the indefinite "other lovers" widens the frame of reference and alters Conrad's relationship to his literary forebears. Conrad, who was never able to attain the ideal of *fin' amors*, has nevertheless achieved a happiness that allows him to surpass his literary predecessors.

Could Conrad's relationship to literature enact Jean Renart's response to the "anxiety of influence"? When we recall that Jean Renart explained his use of quotations by a desire to preserve them ("ramenbrance," v. 3), the systematic irony with which Conrad's songs are treated is explained.[47] The line in the prologue suggests a nostalgia for the songs of the past, but the way they are treated in the romance suggests that the older literary models have lost their effectiveness and must be transformed by the new generation of writers. The plot of the narrative dramatizes the multiplication of voices because it portrays numerous singers. If the emperor is the principal soloist, his song is answered by those of the heroine, the supporting actors, and indeed the rest of the cast, for the entire court joins in song. Thus, the lyric insertions in the romance form a kind of alternation between aria and chorus, solos and group performances. In weaving together a series of strands from the literary works of the previous century, Jean Renart has created "une novele chose" and (at least in his own opinion) outstripped his models.

The array of sung genres, epic as well as lyric, makes it easy to slip into oversimplification; for the alternation here is not simply between narrative and lyric (as is often the case) but between narrative and different sorts of lyrics and between spoken and sung narration. Each inserted genre modifies the meaning of the incorporating narrative, while each lyric genre embodies a different ideology of love. The happy ending of the romance is a narrative dénouement. While it is not an outright rejection of the lyric ideology of love, Jean Renart's plot does reaffirm the narrative model of romance. If one can both recount and sing of arms and love, one must, it appears, find a narrative and not a lyric form of closure in order to end the story. The harmony of generic combination, so successfully achieved by Jean Renart in *Guillaume de Dole,* results from the lively interaction of the various literary genres, including that of romance, which provides the framework of the story. The competition among the different genres and the ideologies they represent is played out in the context of a more or less realistic narrative setting. More important, the multiple borrowings constitute the diverse strands woven into the *conjointure* of the new romance. None of the inserted forms—neither epic nor lyric—is validated on its own terms, but each is treated as useful and valuable, a contributing factor in the creation of a new work.

Jean Renart confronted the prestige of twelfth-century literature in the boldest possible way. By quoting the works he admired, he appropriated their beauty and subordinated them to his own design. In liberating himself from the tyranny of tradition he became an important influence on successive generations of writers, and his innovation dominated literary fashion for nearly two centuries.[48]

Notes

1. Félix Lecoy, ed., *Jean Renart: "Le roman de la rose ou de Guillaume de Dole."*

2. Paul Zumthor, *Essai de poétique médiévale,* 355.

3. The *tournoi de dames* is probably a commemorative dance song; see Christopher Page, *Voices and Instruments in the Middle Ages,* 37.

4. Included in the total of forty-eight quotations is one *rondet de carole,* which occurs twice: vv. 295–99 and 2514–18. This enumeration is based on the list in Lecoy's edition (xxiii–xxix), but some uncertainty remains about the classification of certain pieces. The insertions in this romance have attracted increasing scholarly attention. See, for example, Norris Lacy, "'Amer par oïr dire'"; Maurice Accarie, "La fonction des chansons du *Guillaume de Dole*"; Maria Veder Coldwell, "*Guillaume de Dole* and Medieval Romances with Musical Interpolations"; Emmanuèle Baumgartner, "Les citations lyriques dans le *Roman de la rose*"; Michel Zink, *Roman rose et rose rouge*; Roger Dragonetti, *Le mirage des sources*; and Danièle Duport, "Les chansons dans *Guillaume de Dole.*"

5. *Galeran de Bretagne,* for many years attributed to Jean Renart but now ascribed to the otherwise unknown Renaut, seems to have anticipated Jean Renart in quoting songs but includes only two lines of lyric material—either a refrain or the beginning of a *pastourelle.*

6. On the importance of *conjointure* in romance, see Douglas Kelly, *The Art of Medieval French Romance,* especially 15–31.

7. Marc-René Jung, "L'empereur Conrad," 36.

8. See Lecoy's edition, xv; G. Servois, ed., *Le roman de la rose ou de Guillaume de Dole,* l–lxxxv; and Baldwin, chapter 2 of the present volume.

9. Charles-Victor Langlois, *La vie en France au moyen âge de la fin du XIIe siècle au milieu du XIVe siècle d'après des romans mondains du temps,* 1:73. For a reassessment of the identity of Conrad, see, however, Baldwin, chapter 2 of the present volume.

10. Douglas Kelly (*Medieval Imagination,* 256) argues that the separability of the words and music of a song emphasizes the importance of the words. In contrast, Zumthor (*Essai,* 369) assumes that the inserted songs were actually sung by the reader. See also Zink (chapter 4) and van der Werf (chapter 7) in the present volume.

11. Lecoy's edition, 220; the word was not glossed in the earlier editions by Servois or by Rita Lejeune-Dehousse. The term is discussed by Zink in chapter 4 and van der Werf in chapter 7 of the present volume.

12. Vv. 290, 326, 334, 513, 844, 1167, 1173, 1334, 1455, 1578, 1768, 1843, 2026, 2233, 2388, 2512, 3418, 3881, 4163, 4170 (porchanté), 4567, 4586 (rechante), 4652, 5112, 5187, 5231, 5426, 5447. For the contexts in which musical references occur, consult van der Werf's Appendix 2 in chapter 7 of the present volume.

13. Vv. 541, 922, 1182, 2368, 2378, 2397, 3750, 4126, 5105; other references to music are implicit in vv. 309, 522, 2519–22, 3179, 3402, and 3624.

14. See the discussion of singing and accompaniment by Page, *Voices and Instruments,* especially 31–38; van der Werf offers a different interpretation in chapter 7 of the present volume.

15. The manuscript has been described by Ernest Langlois in "Notices des manuscrits," 233ff., and by Servois, xix–xxvii.

16. Zink, *Roman rose et rose rouge,* 27.

17. John E. Stevens, *Words and Music in the Middle Ages: Song, Narrative, Dance and Drama, 1050–1350* (Cambridge: Cambridge University Press, 1986), 41.

18. Lecoy has identified this poet as Gontier de Soignies (xxiv and 191).

19. The six songs are those beginning at vv. 923 (Châtelain de Couci), 1301 (Jaufré Rudel), 2027 (Gace Brulé), 3751 (Châtelain de Couci or Roger d'Andeli), 4653 (Daude de Pradas), and 5212 (Bernart de Ventadorn). On Jean Renart's failure to attribute these songs, see Baumgartner, "Les citations lyriques," 262.

20. See Maureen Barry McCann Boulton, *The Song in the Story,* chapter 2.

21. Emil Walker, *Der Monolog im höfischen Epos: Stil und literaturgeschichtliche Untersuchungen* (Stuttgart: Kohlhammer, 1928), 40; compare Zumthor, *Essai,* 341–42.

22. For a discussion of the genres and references to older bibliography, see Pierre Bec, *La lyrique française au moyen âge* (Paris: Picard, 1977), 1:220–28; on these genres see especially Nico H. J. van den Boogaard, *Rondeaux et refrains du XIIe siècle au début du XIVe. Collationnement, introduction et notes,* Bibliothèque Française et Romane, Série D. Initiation, Textes et Documents 3 (Paris: Klincksieck, 1969).

23. For a discussion of these scenes, see Faith Lyons, *Les éléments descriptifs dans le roman d'aventure au 13e siècle (en particulier "Amadas et Ydoine," "Gliglois," "Galeran," "L'escoufle," "Guillaume de Dole," "Jehan et Blonde," "Le castelain de Couci,"* 108–25.

24. This figure includes the three *refrains,* which were probably taken from *rondets,* and the song is quoted twice (see note 4).

25. Compare Lacy, "'Amer par oïr dire'." This association between character and subject is confirmed by later allusions, where Lïenor is compared to the ladies of Arthur's court (vv. 4617–19, 4680–81) and Guillaume to Alexander and Perceval (v. 2880). It is generally understood that the tale told by Jouglet is in fact Jean Renart's own *Lai de l'ombre.* The autoreferentiality of the tale adds further complexity to Jean Renart's other narrative allusions.

26. Compare, for example, Zumthor, *Essai,* 364–65; also note Terry's comments about Guillaume and Lïenor in chapter 6 of the present volume.

27. Zumthor associates the disintegration of *aventure* with the interruption of lyric insertions but does not notice that the songs in fact replace adventurous action (*Essai,* 369).

28. There are 152 lines from chansons, 60 lines of an epic *laisse,* 114 from *chansons de toile,* 113 from *rondets de carole* and *refrains,* and 20 from *pastourelles.*

29. See Zumthor, *Essai*, 189–243, and Zink, "Troubadours et trouvères," in *Précis de la littérature française du moyen âge*, ed. Daniel Poirion (Paris: Presses Universitaires de France, 1983), 128–45; here, 131–33, 136–37.

30. This theme is discussed in some detail by Rita Lejeune-Dehousse, *L'oeuvre de Jean Renart: Contribution à l'étude du genre romanesque au moyen âge*, 37–42, and by Lacy, "'Amer par oïr dire'."

31. On the Occitan songs, see Fabienne Gégou, "Jean Renart et la lyrique occitane," and William D. Paden, "Old Occitan as a Lyric Language."

32. The *laisse* quoted in *Guillaume de Dole* does not appear in the surviving versions of the epic. See Lecoy's edition, xxiii.

33. *Jean Renart, "Le roman de la rose ou de Guillaume de Dole," roman courtois du XIIIe siècle*, trans. Jean Dufournet, Jacques Kooijman, René Menage, and Christine Tronc, 31–33: "Ce jour-là il faisait chanter par la soeur d'un jongleur." The Old French text reads: "Cel jor fesoit chanter la suer / a un jougleor mout apert / qui chante cest vers de Gerbert" (vv. 1332–34).

34. Grace Frank, "*Le roman de la rose ou de Guillaume de Dole*, ll. 1330ff.": "That day, the sister had an expert jongleur sing" (210). Frank points out that the lines "refer to the only *suer* of importance in the poem."

35. See Jessie Crosland, *The Old French Epic* (Oxford: Blackwell, 1951), 172.

36. On these songs, see Bec, *La lyrique française*, 1:107–19. Servois (xciv) attributes the fragmentary state of these songs to the negligence of the scribe. This scene is also discussed in the present volume by Jones (chapter 1), Zink (chapter 4), and Psaki (chapter 5).

37. This song has been discussed by Zumthor, *Essai*, 290–98; Bec, *La lyrique française*, 2:30–32; and Page, *Voices and Instruments*, 35–36.

38. See Zink, chapter 4 in the present volume.

39. Zumthor, commenting on Jean Renart's manipulation of the artifices of expression, describes this phenomenon as "transpersonnalisation" (*Essai*, 293).

40. This passage is also discussed by Psaki in chapter 5 of the present volume.

41. See, in addition to Bec's discussion in *La lyrique française* (1:119–36), the studies by Zink (*La pastourelle: Poésie et folklore au moyen âge* [Paris: Bordas, 1972]), and (for a later period) Joël Blanchard (*La pastorale en France aux XIVe et XVe siècles: Recherches sur les structures de l'imaginaire médiévale*, Bibliothèque du XVe Siècle 45 [Paris: Champion, 1983]).

42. This is yet another example of "transpersonnalisation," for the female singer must be distinguished from the male "ge" of her song. A similar example is the *chanson de toile* (vv. 5188–207) sung by the nephew of the bishop of Liège, discussed below, p. 97.

43. On this subject, see Kathryn Gravdal, "Camouflaging Rape: The Rhetoric of Sexual Violence in the Medieval Pastourelle," *Romanic Review* 76 (1985): 361–73, and William D. Paden, "Rape in the Pastourelle," *Romanic Review* 80 (1989): 331–49.

44. Compare Psaki, chapter 5 of the present volume.

45. For other borrowings by Jean Renart from this romance, see Lejeune-Dehousse, *Oeuvre,* 140, and Terry, chapter 6 of the present volume.

46. For additional discussion of these allusions, see Terry, ibid.

47. This desire to preserve the songs suggests that they were in danger of disappearing. But it is interesting to note that in the *Tournoi de Chauvenci,* composed more than half a century after *Guillaume de Dole* and based on an actual tournament, *refrains* of *rondets de carole* are performed exactly as they are portrayed by Jean Renart. The term *ramenbrance* is also discussed by Zink, chapter 4 in the present volume.

48. Although *Guillaume de Dole* survives in a single manuscript, one cannot use that fact to argue that the work had no influence. The romance was imitated closely by Gerbert de Montreuil (see Zink, chapter 4 in the present volume). Even if his work was not widely known, the innovation was often copied. Lyric insertions appear in more than sixty works composed before 1405. See the list in Appendix 1 of Boulton, *The Song in the Story.*

CHAPTER 4

Suspension and Fall

The Fragmentation and Linkage of Lyric Insertions in Le roman de la rose (Guillaume de Dole) *and* Le roman de la violette

MICHEL ZINK

"The lyric segments [of *Guillaume de Dole*] constitute a kind of below-the-surface conversation or parallel discourse."[1] This fine formulation by Marc-René Jung is intended by him as an approbation, as well as a nuancing of my suggestion (excessive, to be sure), that "Jean Renart composed his romance on the basis of the songs."[2] But the richness of Jung's comment goes beyond this particular issue: the metaphorization discreetly suggested by "a kind of" is full of resonance; and the "or," which links the two admirable terms "below-the-surface" and "parallel discourse," indicates not only their equivalence but, at least from a certain point of view, their reciprocal exclusion. The lyric segment constitutes a parallel discourse when, in its own language and expressive register, it happens to confirm the speech or attitude of the person who is singing it. But "below-the-surface conversation" presupposes a hidden coherence, an invisible, submerged part, of which the quoted lyric passage is the sign.

And it is certainly true that the lyric insertions in *Guillaume de Dole* and other romances that use the same technique are characterized, above all, by their fragmentary nature. This is perhaps the most perceptible difference between the procedures of collage and montage, a distinction made by Jacqueline Cerquiglini.[3] Jean Renart quotes songs that existed before he wrote his romance. On this specific point he acted no differently from Guillaume de Machaut, who reused in his *dits* lyric works that he had composed previously, and Froissart, who inserted poems by Wenceslas de Luxemburg into *Meliador.* Of course, Machaut assigned the *dit* the function of showing off the poems, whereas Jean Renart's romance holds its own and could probably do so even without the inserted songs. Let us note, however, that this is not what the prologue says and that at least one passage, where Lïenor and her mother sing spinning songs, is almost certainly the narrative reflection of the very songs that inspire the scene. The "collage" of *Guillaume de Dole* presents itself, not altogether wrongly, as a "montage"; based on this criterion at least, the distinction between the two techniques becomes blurred as soon as we examine the details.

On the other hand, fragmentary quotation is in principle excluded from consideration of the lyrics inserted into a *dit* because these are the heart of the work. Such quotation, by contrast, seems frequent—almost the rule—in *Guillaume de Dole* and analogous romances. So it seems. But here again, if one looks closely, things aren't so simple. Only an impression is real—that of the fragmentation, of the always incomplete quotation. As for the rest, this impression is produced by a variety of procedures; the corresponding aesthetic effects, in both their nature and intentions, vary as well.

One thing is certain: the context of the song is essential, not only in a general and almost metaphorical sense (the circumstances of its performance and the scene in which it is set) but also its context in the stricter sense—the lines that introduce it, the transition to the next song. Maurice Accarie has claimed that in *Guillaume de Dole* the plot and its narration, on the one hand, and the content and type of songs, on the other, are unimportant and essentially unrelated to each other.[4] The project was simply to produce a musical show with a numerically even, balanced distribution of songs. His conclusion: "That's entertainment."[5] He forgets that the romance—this very *written* romance—is not a script. Its text cannot be reduced to a screenplay. It does not vanish in performance. The songs, on the contrary, are only evocations of songs.

Let us look again at the first three lines of the romance:

Cil qui mist cest conte en romans,
ou il a fet noter biaus chans
por ramenbrance des chançons. . . .[6]

These lines are generally understood in this way: "The one who put this story into romance, / where he had beautiful melodies written down / in remembrance of songs. . . ." But what does this beginning actually mean? At first we have an impression of vague stammerings with awkward repetitions: "conte" [story] and "roman" [romance], "chans" [melodies] and "chançons" [songs]. Is Jean Renart, a virtuoso stylist, so lacking in inspiration? In fact, the meaning becomes clear as soon as we acknowledge that, on the contrary, he is not writing at random, and we pay attention to the key word *ramenbrance.* The "beautiful melodies" of the romance appear there "in memory of songs"; in other words, they are not to be confused with these songs. The author has "fait noter" these beautiful melodies in the romance. This is generally taken to mean that he has had them copied down. Félix Lecoy, Tobler-Lommatzsch, and Jean Dufournet and his collaborators all understand the phrase in this way.[7] Can one rely on this interpretation? Is it the only possible one? For the author of a romance to allude to a copyist working on his directions would be unique, it seems to me, in this context. Moreover, why would Jean Renart indicate here that he has had the melodies copied, as distinct from the whole romance? Because, as Félix Lecoy suggests in his glossary, he is thinking of a copyist who specializes in musical scores? But as it happens, the unique manuscript of the romance has no scores.

Furthermore, if such is the meaning of the phrase, the distinction being made between "chans" [melodies] and "chançons" [songs] is the opposite of what one would expect. *Chant* refers to the music itself and to the performance or vocalization, whereas *chanson,* of course, refers to the lyric piece in its entirety, text as well as melody. Because the latter vanishes in the text, Jean Renart should have said that he "has had songs written down in memory of beautiful melodies" rather than the opposite. Certainly the nuance that seems to me to separate "chan" from "chançon," hardly debatable in modern French, would need to be established and verified in Old French. I do, however, believe it is justified. Old French speaks of *chants d'oiseaux,* never *chansons d'oiseaux* (birds sing without words or else with incomprehensible ones, their "Latin"); conversely, in Old French it is *chanson de geste* and never *chant de geste* (speech here wins out over melody). One makes songs from "matières," from subjects, according to the well-known prologue of the fabliau *La vieille truande,* while the musical notes serve to make "les sons noviaus" [new sounds].[8] Jean Renart himself refers a little later in the prologue to "moz des chans" (v. 28)—that is, to the words that accompany the melodies. And when Froissart writes of a poem inserted in *L'espinette amoureuse*—"Ce virelays fis en otant / D'espasse qu'on l'iroit notant" (vv. 1046–47) [I made this virelay in the same / space one would use for notating it]—he obviously wants to say that he has not spent more time composing it than one would spend *singing* it, not *copying* it. This is also the way the editor of the text, Anthime Fourrier, defines it in his glossary. I admit, at least provisionally and in the absence of a systematic search, that "chan" and "chançon," taken separately, can sometimes be interchangeable. But I maintain that when they appear together, they differ in the way I have indicated.[9]

For all these reasons, one could prefer to see in the "noter" of v. 2 not the verb derived from *notare* but the one derived from the noun *nota*—that is, *noter*, meaning "to sing, to interpret musically" —and understand that the implicit subject of "noter" is not the copyist but those who, within the romance ("where" being understood not materially but diegetically), sing the beautiful melodies. "Ou il a fet noter biaus chans" would then mean "where he had beautiful melodies sung by the characters," "where he has placed beautiful melodies in the mouths of characters." At the very least one can claim without risk of error that, for a thirteenth-century reader or listener, the commonly used expression *noter un chant* meant first of all, and quite naturally, "to sing, to interpret a melody musically" and that if, in the particular context of this prologue, the meaning "to copy a melody" could also come to mind, it was secondarily and as word-play.

The absence of melodies in the manuscript is therefore not a lacuna, a slip, an error, an accident. The music belongs to the scene described by the narrative, but the narrative, of course, is not to be confused with it. The music does not arise from the narrative but from its referent. The narrative limits itself to describing and showing characters who are singing, to having them sing beautiful melodies. But the melody of parchment beings has no more substance than the pâté or the wine they are tasting. Nevertheless, just as the evocation of pâté and wine can make one's mouth water, so can the evocation of beautiful melodies bring to mind the memory of the songs and make them resonate there.

One might object that Jean Renart foresaw a musical interpretation, a performance based on the romance and its lyric insertions, for he stresses that:

Ja nuls n'iert de l'oïr lassez,
car, s'en vieult, l'en i chante et lit,
et s'est fez par si grant delit
que tuit cil s'en esjoïront
qui chanter et lire l'orront,
qu'il lor sera nouviaus toz jors. (vv. 18–23)

[No one will ever tire of hearing it,
because if one wants to, one can both
  sing and read in it.
And it was composed with such great skill

that it will seem endlessly new
to all those who will take pleasure in it,
in singing and reading it.]

But the choice implied by "s'en vieult" (v. 19), the possibility of perpetual renewal that is cleverly suggested by v. 23, "qu'il lor sera nouviaus toz jors," presents the actualization of the songs through performance and interpretation as an alternative to the reading of the romance or as its optional complement rather than as a necessity.

The real ambiguity and false redundancy of "noter biaus chans / por ramenbrance des chançons" are so clear that the first line, "Cil qui mist cest conte en romans," already provides a corresponding statement, an equivalent, an anticipation. The first French romances, as we know, present themselves as works "put into romance" [mises en roman], as translations from Latin into a romance language. Jean Renart uses this expression "to put into romance" but without mentioning the Latin model and substituting in it the term *conte.* Nevertheless, *conte* and *roman* are almost synonymous. Jean Renart thus seems to be saying that he has translated a Latin work, but that is not what he is saying. He seems to be saying that he has "drawn from an adventure story" something more complex, but that isn't what he is saying either, for he is careful not to speak of a "très belle conjointure" [a very beautiful conjoining]. He seems to say quite simply, but with an awkward pleonasm, that he is writing a romance, but that isn't exactly what he's saying either; for he plays with this apparent pleonasm in order to introduce into the tiny interstice that separates story and romance—by means of the deceptive echoes of translation or of the enrichment of meaning—the depths of writing itself, suggesting that no depths are involved but only translation, drifting, an imperceptible lateral slipping that makes the transition from story to romance, that makes the rose slip onto the thigh, which, as has been noted elsewhere, wholly anchors this romance in trompe-l'oeil.[10] To this trompe-l'oeil is added a *trompe-l'oreille,* pointed out immediately after and with the same stratagem: the romance is crammed full of songs, but these songs are sung by imaginary creatures and therefore resonate only in the imaginary. These are melodies that reverberate only within the fiction of the romance but that call to mind the memory of actual songs, exactly as lines 2 and 3 state.

Because these actual songs are only evoked, the quotations of them in the romance can be fragmentary. And when they are not fragmentary, they must give the impression that they are in order to increase the effect of resonance, which is precisely the effect of any quotation. This is why (to return to my argument after a long but necessary clarification) the immediate context surrounding the songs deserves careful attention. It is here that we find the key to this fragmentation effect and, even more important, the secret of the immediate presence and the remote absence that are united in these songs, as they are by the romance itself, which situates contemporary, real characters in the faraway time of an imaginary emperor.

These effects, contrary to appearances, are unique to *Guillaume de Dole. Le roman de la violette* lacks them, even while carefully specifying its predecessor and imagining it is exactly reproducing the technique launched by *Guillaume de Dole.* The two romances begin with evocations of merrymaking accompanied by dancing; they quote *rondeaux* and *refrains* that are being sung. The resemblance seems complete; the difference is profound. Jean Renart stresses that, in the excitement of the celebration, where everyone competes in gaiety, they begin each song before the preceding one has ended (v. 293, v. 305), before it has "really begun" (v. 300), or before the dance "has lasted three rounds" (v. 528). He thus creates an impression of playfulness, lightening the possible heaviness of even an apt quotation. But above all, as his first lines lead us to expect, he shows the disparity between the melody of the characters in the scene he allows us to imagine and the recension of the songs offered by the text of the romance.

There is nothing like this in Gerbert de Montreuil, who limits himself to the platitude of enumeration—the term *platitude* being less a value judgment than the designation of a style of writing that does not attempt to give the text any kind of depth through perspective by suggesting (above and beyond itself) everything it allows to escape. He names a lady, even reveals her identity, evokes her beauty, shows (when appropriate) her love situation, quotes the song she sings, and goes on to the next one: "La suer au conte de Saint-Pol, / Qui tant ot biel vis et biel col" (vv. 121–22) [The count of Saint Pol's sister, / who had such a beautiful face and neck], "La damoisiele de Couchi, / Cui Dex fache vraie merchi" (vv. 129–30) [The lady of Coucy, / may God show her true mercy], "Li castelainne de Nïor, / C'on apieloit Alïenor" (vv. 136–37) [The chatelaine of Nïor, / who was called Alïenor], "Une dame de Normendie, / Qui d'amors s'estoit enhardie" (vv. 143–44) [A lady of Normandy, who was made bold by love]. The presentation of the singers is much longer than the quotation of what they are singing, which slows and weighs down the scene. Jean Renart, by contrast, lightens and accelerates comparable scenes by an inverse distribution. He generally reproduces the entire *rondeau,* all the while claiming the characters have not sung it through to the end, whereas Gerbert de Montreuil often cites only one or two lines, letting it be understood that the characters have sung the entire song (vv. 102–5, 110–12, and so on). But the song, which the reader does not have in front of him or her, cannot produce an effect that is thus lost, whereas Jean Renart's reader can take delight in the song that is offered and that helps to compensate for the absent melody. Jean Renart's text, formed of an accelerated interlinking of long quotations, makes the rapidity of the scene palpable; it is a rapidity that, in its referential reality, comes from the abbreviation of the songs, as he is careful to stress. At the same time it allows the reader to become imbued with the atmosphere of these songs. The text, which stretches out the introduction of brief quotations, weighs down the scene by recounting at length what has happened quickly and deprives the reader of the effect of the songs.

Finally, in this type of scene Jean Renart is careful not to suggest each time a direct relation between the context of each song and the frame of mind of its interpreter. Gerbert de Montreuil systematically insists on doing this—a tiresome cleverness because the impression of slowness and redundancy and the absence of perspective, distance, resonance, and resounding echoes are thereby accentuated:

Une dame de Normendie,
Qui d'amors s'estoit enhardie,
Commenchié ot nouvielement.
Si amoit si tres durement,
Qu'ele ne savoit de li roi.
On disoit que c'estoit le roi.
Si s'en faisoit assés plus cointe
De chou que elle estoit s'acointe.
Lors cante et met son cant a moi:
    Ja ne lairai pour mon mari ne die
    Que mes amis n'ait un resgart de moi.

[A lady from Normandy,
emboldened by love
began once again.
So very much in love was she
that she lost all sense of proportion.
They all said it was the king she loved,
and she made herself even more attractive
for this reason.

Then she sings and puts her song in just the right way:
No matter what my husband says, I'll never stop
giving my friend sweet looks.]
(*Le roman de la violette*, vv. 143–53)[11]

The reader might object to this interpretation, believing that Jean Renart must be doing the same thing, or trying to, because he boasts in his prologue about the harmony that exists between his romance and the words of the songs he inserts into it. The use he makes of this technique has already been analyzed from various perspectives, in particular by Marc-René Jung in reference to the emperor's songs and by Emmanuèle Baumgartner, but especially by Sylvia Huot and Sarah Kay.[12] (To some extent I also have taken this approach, for in the scene with the spinning songs I have seen their narrative reflection.) Gerbert de Montreuil, who praises himself for the same thing, once again merely imitates his predecessor. But is it really the same thing? Here again, when we look closely at the texts, things are not so simple:

s'est avis a chascun et samble
que cil qui a fet le romans
qu'il trovast toz les moz des chans,
si afierent a ceuls del conte.

[it is everyone's opinion and it seems
that the one who made the romance
also wrote all the words of the songs,
so well do they go with those of the story.]
(*Guillaume de Dole*, vv. 26–29)

We read in Gerbert: "Et si est si bien acordans / Li cans au dit, les entendans / En trai a garant que di voir" (vv. 39–41) [And the melody goes so well / with the words, that I rely upon the listeners / to confirm that I am telling the truth].

Jean Renart doesn't take into consideration the melody itself, which, once again, has only a virtual existence in his romance. He establishes a parallel between "the words of the melodies" (that is, the words of the songs) and "the words of the story [conte]." And he establishes a parallel between them only to say that they maintain a satisfying, harmonious relation—that they are linked ("afierent") to each other. But the nature of this relation remains open. He doesn't at all reduce it to redundancy, to a reflection or direct echo. Such a situation can occur, but as one of many; its rarity confirms its effectiveness. Elsewhere we find other effects. The very expression used by Jean Renart, with the mixture of appropriateness and imprecision implied by the verb *afierent*, is perfectly applicable to the effects of quotation, which must adjust itself to its context and at the same time remain sufficiently distanced for the comparison to be suggestive and interesting. As I have observed elsewhere, Jean Renart strategically exaggerates the unexpected, the supposed accident, the happy encounter of such comparisons.[13]

Thus, he is careful not to make the content of the dance *rondeaux* coincide too closely with the identity and the situation of their interpreters. The exchange of refrains between the *rondeau* of the duke of Mayence's sister and the one sung immediately after by the count of Savoy could lead one to suspect a secret understanding at the expense of a jealous husband (vv. 307–22). But nothing is said about it; there is a more general harmony between the lively movements of all this attractive youthfulness and the absent old husbands, who, unlike the ones in the *rondeaux*, are not sleeping. On the contrary, they get up before everyone else to go hunting ("qui va a la chasse perd sa place" [he who goes on the chase loses his place]). And all those aristocratic dancers sing "que de Robin que d'Aaliz" (v. 548), finding it witty to place their dances and their love affairs under the trees in the context of these rustic lovers who are so different from them yet so similar. After a first *rondeau* where ladies dance "enmi les prez" [in the meadows], the following *rondeaux* evoke Mariette, Aelis, Enmelot, and "the dark, the handsome Robin" (vv. 511–47).

As for Gerbert, he posits an agreement between the melody and the words, taking as witness "les entendans" [his listeners]. What he has in mind is performance. Lines 39–41, cited above, immediately follow the remark that, in this romance "on i puet lire et chanter" (v. 38), a comment that is symmetrical to the one Jean Renart develops in vv. 18–23 of his prologue but discreetly separates from his statement about the relation between "the words of the melody" and "those of the story," which is thus in his work disconnected from the idea of performance. Where Jean Renart places various words into contact with one another within the texture of the romance, Gerbert does the same with melody and words. For the textual game of quotation, which combines divergence and coincidence, he substitutes speaking and singing, whose terms are sufficiently antithetical for the difference to be obvious so that only coincidence of meaning is of interest. He therefore does not avoid redundancy because he does not view the work as a self-sufficient textual ensemble composed of the romance and the words of the songs. For him, the work is created by the performance, which consists of reading the romance and singing the songs—the performance of which Jean Renart naturally recognizes as a possibility, but only that. Gerbert's conception goes perfectly with brief quotations, most often reduced to the first two lines; in his view, the most important thing is to know which song should be inserted at which moment, not to maintain a balance between the narrative and the lyric insertions in the substance of the text. The insertion of a simple incipit has only the value of calling for the performance of a lyric piece that increases the possibilities for its interpreter, who, one can assume, sang the whole thing; for example, a "joyful and happy" young girl:

Ceste chanchon a commenchie
Que le cuer ot joli et gai:
    Ja ne mi marïerai,
    Mais par amors amerai.

[Began to sing this song,
she whose heart is sweet and gay:
    I will never marry,
    but love with true love.]
(*Le roman de la violette,* vv. 117–20)

What is true of specific scenes is also true of whole romances. As Maurice Accarie has shown, Jean Renart is careful to space the songs at regular intervals and to achieve a composition that is balanced between the narrative development and the lyric insertions. But *Le roman de la violette,* whose plot is much more elaborate, contains some long narrative episodes devoid of all song and seems more indifferent to this type of balance. This effect no doubt is due less to the exigencies of performance than Accarie imagines and more to the textuality of the work.

Up to now, we have only considered the dance scenes. But elsewhere the lyric insertions in the two romances present themselves differently, and the preceding analyses do not seem necessarily to apply. These are most often courtly songs or spinning songs, songs of lovers' meetings—that is, segments comprised of several stanzas, each of which is longer than a complete *rondeau*. The quotation, usually of one or two stanzas, is itself therefore longer; but at the same time, unlike the *rondeaux,* the piece is almost never quoted in its entirety.

Here again Jean Renart plays in his own special way with both truncated and extended quotations. By quoting only the beginning of the song, he gladly lets it be known that no more of it is sung and that at the end of this single stanza—or of these two stanzas—the performance could be considered as finished and complete:

N'orent pas chevauchié grant piece
quant uns niés l'envesque dou Liege,
qui mout se set biau deporter,
conmença cesti a chanter:
    Or vienent Pasques les beles en avril
. . . .

[They had not ridden very far
when a nephew of the bishop of Liège
who knew well how to behave charmingly
began to sing this song:
    Now in April comes beautiful Easter]
[two stanzas of this *reverdie* related to spinning songs]

Ceste n'est pas tote chantee,
uns chevaliers de la contree
dou parage de Danmartin
conmença cest son poitevin:
    Quant voi l'aloete moder
. . . .

[This song had not been sung all the way through
when a knight from the region of Danmartin
began this Poitevin song:
    When I see the lark rise]
[two stanzas from the lark song by Bernart de Ventadorn]

Quant cez .II. furent bien fenies,
des bons vers Gautier de Sagnies
resovint un bon bacheler,
si les comença a chanter:
    Lors que florist la bruiere . . .

[When these songs were quite finished,
a nice young man remembered
these lovely verses by Gontier de Soignies,
and began to sing them:
    When the heather blooms . . .]
(*Guillaume de Dole,* vv. 5184–232)

As one can see in v. 5228, the first two songs are said to be "bien fenies" [quite finished]; but when the knight of the Danmartin region begins to sing his song, that of the bishop of Liège's nephew "n'est pas tote chantee" (v. 5208) [is not sung all the way through]. One can imagine the two characters singing at once without paying attention to each other or worrying about cacophony. But this is pure speculation. By staying close to the text, we find that it is the completion of the performance that counts, even if this consists of singing just one stanza and not completing the song. Similarly, earlier in the romance, when Guillaume and Nicole are on the road, heading for court:

> entre lui et ses conpegnons,
> por le deduit des oisellons
> que chascuns fet en son buisson,
> de joie ont comencié cest son:
>   Lors que li jor sont lonc en mai
> . . . .
>
> [he and his companions
> heard the joyful sounds of little birds
> in the bushes,
> and they began to sing:
>   When the days grow long in May]
> [first stanza of the song about love from afar by Jaufré Rudel]
>
> Fet Nicole, ou mout a solas,
> quant vint a la fin de son son . . .
>
> [When he came to the end of his song
> Nicole said joyfully . . .]
> (*Guillaume de Dole,* vv. 1297–309)

"La fin de son son" indicates, assuredly, not the end of Jaufré Rudel's song but the end of the first stanza, the only one quoted and the only one he sings. It is actually this stanza alone that "le deduit des oisellons" can bring to the singer's lips.

Consequently, the only song with more than two stanzas reproduced in its entirety takes on special significance. This is "Belle Aiglentine," sung by a "bachelers de Normendie" accompanied on the vielle by Jouglet during the celebrations preceding the tournament of Saint-Trond (vv. 2235–94). Is this story of a young girl, who through a bold move succeeds in getting married, an anticipation of Lïenor's story, as Susan Miller believes?[14] It is possible, even if this young, pregnant woman can scarcely evoke the virtuous Lïenor. I more readily believe that this slightly risqué song, with its tale of a distressingly passive pregnant girl, with its flat refrain awkwardly insisting on narrativity, is a parody of the spinning song aimed at making us smile at the naïve vulgarity of both the characters and the style—in short, at the genre itself. It represents a humorous inversion of the dignified, melancholy songs of Lïenor and her mother and confirms, by means of pastiche, that spinning songs benefited from a fashion for former fashions, not to speak of an outmoded charm.

But a finished performance usually does not mean a complete song. In addition to the examples already given are others, often indicated, where the execution of the song covers the time of the narrative and the progression of the action, which, completed earlier than the song, interrupts it.

> Et si chantent ceste chançon
> en l'onor monsegnor Gasçon:
>   Quant flors et glais et verdure s'esloigne
> ....
>
> [And they sang this song
> in honor of Gace Brulé:
>   when flowers and leaves and grasses fade away]
> [first stanza of Gace Brulé's song]
>
> Ainçois qu'il l'aient dite toute,
> estoit ja li plus de la route
> el chastel, et li ostel pris.
>
> [Before they had finished,
> most of the company had arrived
> at the castle and lodgings had been taken.]
> (*Guillaume de Dole*, vv. 844–55)

This procedure is also found in *Le roman de la violette:*

> Lors cante haut, seri et cler:
>   Or aroie amouretes,
>   Se voloie demourer.
> Anchois que fausist sa canchon,
> Coisist le chastel de Mosson,
> Qui estoit sour une riviere.

[Then he sings in a strong, clear voice:
    Now I would have flirtations
    If I wanted to stay.
Before he finished his song
he saw the castle of Mousson,
which was situated on a river.]
(*Le roman de la violette*, vv. 5067–72)

Similarly (and in a clear reference to *Guillaume de Dole*), at the moment when Gerard hears the lark who will remind him of his first loves:

Pour Aiglente talens li vint
De cest son poitevin chanter:
    Quant voi la loëte moder
. . . .
Ensi vait Gerars chevalcant;
Mais ains k'il ait finé son cant,
L'aloëte ses heles joint,
Si s'est assise . . .

[He wanted to sing for Aiglentine
this Poitevine song:
    When I see the lark rise
[first stanza of the lark song by Bernard de Ventadour]
Thus Gerard rode along
but he hadn't yet finished his song
when the lark folded its wings
and alighted . . .]
(*Le roman de la violette*, vv. 4185–98)

In this last example we find once again Gerbert de Montreuil's concern for introducing a close connection between the content and the context of the song. At times this concern prevails to such an extent that it makes the song become an element in the progression of the plot—for example, when one of Gerbert's songs gives Aiglente, who is in love, false hopes that another song dispels (vv. 3236–337) or when Flourentine confesses her love by singing a refrain (vv. 3141–42).

The concern for composition, balance, rhythm, rapidity, and fluid or syncopated linkages prevails throughout the work of Jean Renart. The echoes of meaning are in his work only one element among many that contribute to this balance and rhythm. These alone, however, interest Gerbert.

In the case of Jean Renart, the fragmentation of the lyric insertions corresponds to his abrupt, elliptical, and witty style; to his concern for a taut, fragmentary textual construction that plays with displacement and disconnectedness. For Gerbert, it serves as a useful system of abbreviations. The lines quoted by Jean Renart are to be taken just as they are in relation to the text, which encompasses, introduces, and interrupts them. Those quoted by Gerbert de Montreuil are the abbreviated indication of a song that it would be too long to copy in extenso. *Guillaume de Dole* exists as a whole, with its lyric insertions in the exact form in which they figure there. It is attentive to the textual effects before considering the possibility of a performance. The lyric quotations of *Le roman de la violette* serve only the meaning, while waiting to open out—to grow longer, no doubt—in performance.

Apart from *Le lai de l'ombre,* for which we have seven manuscripts, the work of Jean Renart does not seem to have had great success in his own time if we judge by the small number of extant manuscripts: only one for *Guillaume de Dole* and one for *L'escoufle,* although a fragment of the latter also exists. How is it that the technique of inserting lyrics in romance, invented by this little-valued author, was able to achieve an immediate popularity as spectacular as it was longlasting? When we examine its use in *Le roman de la violette,* we see that this popularity is based on a misunderstanding. Gerbert de Montreuil, Jean Renart's first imitator, mimics his predecessor right down to the details and seems to be persuaded that he is doing the same thing; he is, however, doing something else. In *Guillaume de Dole* in particular, Jean Renart shows himself to be an author too subtle and unusual, too removed from habits and norms, to have been well understood. He quotes songs in such a way as to enrich his text, to complicate the texture of his romance. The characters, he thinks, will be more lively and more complex if he makes them "noter biaus chans" (assuming that my interpretation of this line is apposite); the scenes will be more lively and charged with meaning. But all this lies in the interior of the text, where it matters; thus, the limits of quotation and its placement have extreme importance in his work. For Gerbert and many others, the text is, on the contrary, a pretext; the romance invites the singing of songs. It is enough to know which ones and to indicate them. Can we be surprised about this? At the time there was only one Renart to love paradox enough to find melody more melodious without music, as it blossoms in relation to words.

Notes

This chapter was translated from the original French by Nancy Vine Durling and Patricia Terry.

1. Marc-René Jung, "L'empereur Conrad," 39.

2. Michel Zink, *Roman rose et rose rouge,* 29.

3. Jacqueline Cerquiglini, "Pour une typologie de l'insertion."

4. Maurice Accarie, "La fonction des chansons du *Guillaume de Dole.*"

5. This line appears in English in Accarie's essay (ibid., 29).

6. *Jean Renart: "Le roman de la rose ou de Guillaume de Dole,"* ed. Félix Lecoy, vv. 1–3 (hereafter cited as *Guillaume de Dole*). The translation of v. 3 depends on one's interpretation of the text, which is, of course, the topic of this chapter.

7. Lecoy glosses *noter* as "transcrire (la musique)" (220). Tobler-Lommatzsch, under *noter,* from *notare,* provide the gloss "aufzeichnen" and then cite the first five lines of *Guillaume de Dole.* See *Jean Renart: "Guillaume de Dole,"* trans. Jean Dufournet et al.: "L'auteur qui a fait de ce conte un roman où il a transcrit de beaux chants afin que demeure le souvenir des chansons courtoises. . ." (7). See also the discussion by van der Werf in chapter 7 of the present volume.

8. De fables fet on fabliaus,
Et des notes les sons noviaus,
Et des materes les canchons,
Et des dras, cauces et cauchons.
(Montaiglon-Raynaud, 5:171)

[From fables one makes fabliaux
and from notes new sounds,
and from subject matter songs,
and from fabric, hose and socks.]

9. Margaret Switten, to whom I submitted this hypothesis, was kind enough to send me a list of the occurrences of *chant* and *chanson* in the work of Raymond de Miraval, the starting point for a future inquiry, and to draw my attention to the counterexample that the first stanza of song 22 might constitute, where the symmetry of lines 1 and 9 lets one suppose an equivalence between "chant" and "chanson," "entendre un chant" and "entendre une chanson":

Chans, quan non es qui l'entenda,
No pot ren valer,
E pus luec ai e lezer
Que mon bel solatz despenda,
Ses gap si'un pauc auzitz;
Quar totz ditz es mielhs grazitz,
Quant a la fi pauz'om ben las razos,
Per qu'ieu vuel far entendre mas chansos.

(*Les poésies du troubadour Raimon de Miraval,* ed. L. T. Topsfield [Paris: Nizet: 1971], 198–99)

[A song, when no one understands {/hears} it
Cannot be worth anything,
And since I have space and leisure
To be lavish with my beautiful remarks
May one listen a little without making fun;
For every composition is more pleasing,
When one makes sure to put the meaning at the end,
That's why I want to make my songs understood {/heard}.]

But one can see here a play on meaning that separates, while pretending to conflate, the melody [le chant]—the vocal performance—which one cannot seize if one makes any noise, and the song [la chanson], the understanding of which is based on "ditz" and "razos," with a progression from the one to the other.

10. Zink, *Roman rose.*

11. *"Le roman de la violette ou de Gerart de Nevers" par Gerbert de Montreuil,* ed. Douglas Labaree Buffum (Paris: Didot Firmin [SATF], 1928), vv. 143–53.

12. Emmanuèle Baumgartner, "Les citations lyriques dans le *Roman de la rose."* Sylvia Huot shows how the static and unrequited love celebrated in lyric poems is transformed by the dynamic of the story, in which the poems are inserted into a love that leans toward marriage, procreation, and the pursuit of lineage (*From Song to Book,* 108–16). Sarah Kay stresses that the narrative portion of the romance provides criticism of the representation of sexuality and of honor in the lyrics (*Subjectivity in Troubadour Poetry,* 183–98).

13. Zink, *Roman rose,* and *Belle,* 4–11.

14. Susan Lee Snouffer Miller, "The Narrative Craft of Jean Renart." See also the comments by Boulton in chapter 3 of the present volume.

CHAPTER 5

Jean Renart's Expanded Text

Lïenor and the Lyrics of Guillaume de Dole

REGINA PSAKI

Jean Renart's *Roman de la rose* (*Guillaume de Dole*) has only recently begun to attract critical attention of a literary and theoretical, rather than a historical and strictly philological, kind. Clearly, it is the readers and their preoccupations that are changing, not the text. *Guillaume de Dole* responds vigorously to questions about genre, sexual politics, courtly ideology, and poetics; and its new prominence may well encourage scholars to look also at other less-examined thirteenth-century romances. Recent studies of *Guillaume de Dole* have tended to fall into one of two groups: those that focus on the lyric insertions and Jean Renart's experiments with genre, and those that focus on the figure of the heroine Lïenor. The lyric fragments that Jean Renart inserts into his romance are its most obviously innovative feature, and they have traditionally received the lion's share of critical attention in analyses of the work.[1] In one sense this is appropriate because the author discusses them in the prologue to the virtual exclusion of more familiar prologue agendas; his comments reflect an explicit concern with craft and an implicit concern with genre.[2] But like other recent critics writing on *Guillaume de Dole,* I find that the presence of the heroine in this text is also a central issue, in a way that sets the work apart from its romance predecessors.[3] In this chapter, I argue that Jean Renart's depiction of the heroine is inextricably linked to his experiments with genre in this lyric-narrative hybrid—that the lyrics are, in fact, one strategy among many by which Jean Renart, through his handling of Lïenor, thematizes the twin issues of truth-value and genre-based expression. I suggest that Lïenor and the lyric insertions are two sides of the same experimental coin—two aspects of Jean Renart's challenge to the assumptions and processes involving both gender and genre as expressed in the courtly romances that preceded *Guillaume de Dole.*[4]

Lyric genres shape this romance on two levels: they are topical and occasional, imbricated in their immediate narrative setting; and they are ubiquitous and diffuse because the romance itself may be viewed as a dramatization of a courtly lyric scenario. In *Guillaume de Dole,* action is attenuated in favor of emotion and discourse; it is these latter concerns that serve as generative forces and focuses in the tale.[5] Michel Zink and Norris Lacy have pointed out that the plot of *Guillaume de Dole* is motivated almost entirely by literature; Zink, Lacy, and Alberto Limentani have all emphasized the explicit intertextuality of the romance, which results in a high degree of self-reflexiveness.[6] In his remarkable study of *Guillaume de Dole, Roman rose et rose rouge,* Zink examines in detail the various literary allusions in the work and their function within the economy of the romance. He maintains that *Guillaume de Dole* is, deliberately, a self-proclaiming wish-fulfillment fantasy because, according to Jean Renart, such is the function of *all* literature (1979, 24–26). "Le cercle vicieux ou magique" [the vicious or magic circle] of literature is thus its own subject, as Jean Renart's continual references to other literary works (not only lyric) attest. In an extended meditation on *how* literature can mean and what it can say, he creates a romance "fait tout entier de substitutions et de déplacements" (62) [made entirely of substitutions and displacements]. As Zink observes, "le glissement général de l'oeuvre" [the general slippage in the work] is evident both in details (the rose on Lïenor's thigh) and in larger patterns of literary borrowing (interpolations and allusions). This lateral slippage of meaning is both the technique and the subject of the work:

> A la logique du récit . . . se substitue un foisonnement de signes particuliers, nés de ses éléments éclatés et déplacés, donnant au roman un sens qui n'est pas généralisable et qui n'est plus fondé sur l'organisation narrative. On pourrait dire . . . que les fonctions du conte sont brisées au profit des indices romanesques . . . [pour] offrir une lecture nouvelle au public des romans d'aventures, dont la *conjointure* ne livre désormais plus le *sens.* (67–68)

> [The logic of the narrative . . . is replaced by a multiplication of individual signs, born of its splintered and displaced elements, giving the romance a sense which is not generalizable and which is no longer based on its narrative organization. It could be said . . . that the functions of the tale are fractured in favor of the romance indices . . . [to] offer the audience a new reading of the *roman d'aventure,* whose *conjointure* no longer delivers its *sens.*]

Thus, the romance, concerned with what can be said and how, "est, de toutes les façons, un roman sur la littérature" (26) [is, in every respect, a romance about literature].

In addition to being a romance about literature, *Guillaume de Dole* is unmistakably a story about hearsay (Zink 1979, 23; Lacy 1981, 780). The action is generated by a tale told to keep a drowsy emperor awake. This is the first story told by Jouglet, and it is generally accepted that it refers to Jean Renart's own *Lai de l'ombre.*[7] The author therefore successfully combines hearsay and literary self-reflexiveness in this important scene. Conrad's love, awakened by hearing beauty described in a story, is discovered because of an overheard lyric chanson; it is threatened when he hears a tale born of a tale (the seneschal's invention, based on the mother's report); and it is, at last, restored by Lïenor's elaborate lie, the disproving of which disproves the seneschal's lie as well. There are no wars in *Guillaume de Dole,* no marvelous adventures, no unavoidable physical dangers; instead, it is language itself that constitutes the narrative crux. More specifically, it is the accuracy and completeness of the language *about the lady* that is in question. But is any of the language used to represent Lïenor adequate to her complexity, her physical reality, her autonomy? What are the implications of this question—enacted in *Guillaume de Dole*'s plot and its patchwork form—for the romance genre, its practitioners, and its readers?

Lïenor is clearly associated with truth-value, since the denial and reestablishment of her virginity constitute the romance's central (almost its only) action. Her purity is vitally important to Conrad, to his kingdom (female purity ensures legitimate succession), and to her brother, whose honor and advancement depend on her marriageability. (For this reason no one is allowed to see Lïenor when her brother is absent.) Lïenor's virginity—her female honor—is also, of course, important to *her;* it is the specter of lost honor that inspires her dramatic scheme to accuse the seneschal of rape. At the same time, her role as defender of her honor is deferred and occupies only the final 1,500 verses of the romance. One might argue, then, that Lïenor's chastity functions throughout most of the romance as a reflection of male honor.

In a fine analysis of Old French wager tales, Roberta Krueger shows how this plot type exposes the chivalric system's need to "contain and control the threat of female sexuality."[8] She observes of *Guillaume de Dole:* "For all the text's subversion of literary conventions and self-conscious deconstruction of courtly discourse, the romance's conclusion reinscribes Lïenor in the place to which Conrad and Guillaume's exchange had initially assigned her: as the Emperor's wife . . . . the feminine voice becomes re-assimilated to the redeemed chivalric ethic."[9] While it is true that not only the figure of Lïenor, but Jean Renart's entire romance, works to challenge or at least unveil the conventions of courtly romance (as opposed to courtly discourse, or the "chivalric system" that Krueger discusses), I argue that Jean Renart does *not* ultimately reinscribe or approve the appropriation of the female figure in romance (or in reality). His great triumph in *Guillaume de Dole* is, instead, the creation of a self-conscious romance in which both the lyrics and the lady function as reminders (and critiques) of prior narratives. If in earlier romances the passive heroine and the active hero were naturalized—that is, displayed as an inevitable and transparent feature of courtly romance—Jean Renart's inversion of this model precludes any return to a view of this most disingenuous of literary forms as innocent. That is to say, the author blends a variety of mutually glossing genres and perspectives to concoct a unique romance whose primary narrative program is to challenge, deftly and playfully, the assumptions, agendas, epistemology, and ideology of the courtly romance.[10]

The lady in courtly romance is often portrayed as the locus of male anxiety about language and reality, and it is in and through Lïenor that Jean Renart constructs his drama of literary representation.[11] At the same time, this romance, while focusing on language, also deliberately moves beyond language in its narrative modalities. It is embellished by musical performances—or, rather, evocations of them—whose topic is virtually always love.[12] In addition, the limited narrative movement is suspended time and again for a rich, lush, almost excessive description of visual beauty (which in itself paradoxically points to the intrinsic inadequacy of such description). The resolution of the narrative depends on the thwarting of word with word and on word's completion by a (putatively) visual presence: the appearance and self-proclamation of Lïenor. Jean Renart joins word, sound, and image, widening the perceptual and semantic field of the work through evocations of other areas of sensual immediacy beyond the spoken word that would have been the medium of the romance's reception by its thirteenth-century audience. This widening of sensory appeal is by no means without precedent in romance; word painting of the vivid luxuries of aristocratic life has always added color and brilliance to the genre. But the extension of the range of sensory appeal to include music, dance, and lyric poetry suggests an attempt on Jean Renart's part to move beyond his predecessors in the genre, to represent experience more completely in greater detail and variety. By invoking song in his work, he increases our awareness not only of song as a genre but also of how we experience it (in performances that are only referred to, not literally present, in this work).[13] By opening a window onto lyric poetry and music (the distinction is a later one), he admits not only the view glimpsed immediately through it—the intercalated verse itself—but also the frame of reference of that verse and the common store of lyric poetry in his audience's memory.[14] One paradox of this suggested remedy to the implied inadequacy of narrative is, of course, that it is effected *solely* through narrative: the unique manuscript of *Guillaume de Dole* is neither notated nor illustrated.

The figure of Lïenor exemplifies both the extended perceptual range afforded by the expanded text and its possible aesthetic purpose. For a central character, Lïenor is very much absent; not only is she offstage for four thousand lines of this 5,655-line work but her restricted presence is curiously oblique. Jean Renart raises the epistemological issues of perception, identity, and representation through his continual deflection of the reader's (and the characters') gaze from Lïenor to her outward signs. This deflection is enacted by the partial, limited descriptions and evocations of her by narrator and characters alike. Lïenor is presented elliptically, disjointedly, and always incompletely. Perspectives on her are multiplied and dispersed by means of various generic and narrative ploys, but she herself is rarely present until the final scenes of the romance.[15] Lïenor, with her beauty that exceeds description, her chastity that is erased and then reconstituted in speech, is a figure for the "objective reality" that language tries, always imperfectly, to capture.[16] In an expressivist theory of language, that is, experience seems to antedate and underlie its expression in language; in a constitutive theory of language, experience is constituted in language, not merely articulated in it. Jean Renart seems to be playing these two models against each other by bringing Conrad's constructed version of Lïenor (for example) up against her own irreducible existence. The deployment of Lïenor as the preexisting reality underlying the romance's abundant speech about her enables a radical questioning of both the reliability of perception and the truth-value of representation, specifically of literary representation defined and constrained by poetic tradition.

Throughout the romance Lïenor is never so much present as described "around"—replaced by traces that represent her from the various perspectives of the characters in the romance. As I have noted, the first mention of her is a displaced description by Jouglet (vv. 691–722), displaced because he is describing not her but a figure in a literary creation. This initial (indirect) presentation of her as a character in a *lai,* and as a portrait constructed according to exacting rhetorical conventions, is incomplete. Jouglet describes her hair, the white and pink of her cheeks, her eyes, eyebrows, teeth, nose, face, breast, and neck; he stops at her arms and hands (v. 716) but closes his description of her as though it were in fact finished (vv. 717–22), with a summary of her courtliness, intelligence, beauty, and transformative power.[17] The elided body of the lady parallels the elided text that Jouglet is invoking without naming (*Le lai de l'ombre*), which itself suggests the suppressed name of the *lai*'s author, this romance's own. The woman is eminently a figure for the absent reality that the text attempts to replace or represent for the reader. When Conrad laments that no woman so perfect really exists, Jouglet easily translates this paragon into a living being in his own world.[18] The portrait of Lïenor herself is suppressed, alluded to only indirectly, so that we are referred back to the twice-removed and fragmentary description of the lady in the *lai*: "Lors li a cil mout bien descrite / la gentil pucele honoree" (vv. 815–16) [Then Jouglet described for him / the noble honored girl].[19] In fact, Conrad falls in love less with the description of Lïenor's double than with the name Lïenor itself:

"Et sa suer, coment a a non,
qui si a bel et gent le cors?"
"Sirë, el a non Lïenors,
ce dit li nons de la pucele."
Amors l'a cuit d'une estencele
de cel biau non mout pres del cuer;
or li seront, sachiez, d'un fuer
totes les autres por cesti. (vv. 789–96)

["And what is the name of his sister,
who is so beautiful and noble?"
"Sire, her name is Lïenor—
that is the maiden's name."
Love struck a spark near his heart

with this beautiful name;
from now on, I assure you, all other women
would be alike to him compared to this one.]

Because the emperor has never seen Lïenor, it is the beauty of her name rather than of her person that later gives rise to his daydreaming.[20] Her name becomes effectively detached from her; it alone constitutes her reality for him: from Conrad's perspective she is frequently referred to as "the maiden with the beautiful name" (vv. 1421, 3746, 4189, and so on).

Her description displaced, her name fetishized: when Lïenor herself first appears, she is not described; rather, she enters the action as though we had already seen her. In this scene, Guillaume gives her the seal from Conrad's letter:

Sa suer, la bele Lïenors,
en ot l'or por un soen fermail.
Quant ele vit le bel cheval
et un roi tot armé deseure:
"Ha! dame, se Dex me sekeure,
fet ele, or doi mout estre lie
quant j'ai un roi de ma mesnie." (1002–8)

[His sister, beautiful Lïenor,
had the gold from it to use as a clasp.
When she saw the handsome horse
and a king in armor mounted,
"Oh! my lady, so help me God,"
said she, "I should be very happy
now that I have a king in my household."]

Within the romance, Lïenor is carefully kept from the gaze of strangers; and she is kept from our gaze as well. By veiling her from us, the author problematizes rather than simply imitates the careful direction of the reader's (listener's) gaze in courtly romance, toward the woman as the object of vision and desire. The unveiling of Lïenor will not in fact occur until the end of the romance, and then in a series of fragmentary descriptions that continue to distance her from the reader.

The deferred descriptions of Lïenor give way to the lyrics sung by her in the romance. When the emperor asks his messenger Nicole if he has seen her, Nicole answers, surprisingly:

"Tesiez . . . ne dites mes!
Nus hom, s'il n'estoit bien confés,
ne doit parler de tel merveille.
Ele fu nee sanz pareille
et de beauté et de simplece.
De son beau chanter par est ce
une tres douce melodie.
Nus ne l'oit qu'autretel n'en die." (1402–9)

["Be silent . . . say no more!
No man, if he is not newly shriven,
should speak of such a wonder.
She was born without equal
for both beauty and modesty.
Her beautiful singing is truly
a most sweet melody.
No one who heard it would say otherwise."]

Lïenor is here removed from the visual field to the aural: her beauty is not to be spoken of; instead, she is "seen" as a beautiful singing voice. The narrator textually reenacts the fact that Lïenor is not meant to be spoken of by replacing her with sung lyrics in the text—for example, the three *chansons de toile* that she and her mother sing over their needlework at Guillaume's request. When Guillaume urges his mother to sing for Nicole, she protests that "it was long ago that ladies and queens used to do their needlework and sing chansons d'histoire" (vv. 1148–51). This response is intriguing, not only because it gives us an index of the historical currency of these songs but also because it establishes their temporal disjunction from Lïenor's own narrative situation. The songs, which tell of threatened love affairs, do not reflect Lïenor's situation at the time they are sung. They describe it only prospectively, potentially and incompletely, and have the effect of collapsing present and future narrative developments into a composite (fractured) present.[21] Cumulatively, they present an inexact but suggestive reflection of Lïenor.

The only song quoted nearly as a whole in the romance, "Bele Aiglentine" (vv. 2235–94), offers an interpretive key to Jean Renart's tentative solution to the incompleteness of literary representation and convention.[22] With ten stanzas, it is the longest single lyric insertion in the poem. Instead of a partial reflection of the immediate context, suggested through a fragment of a full song, we have here a prospective reflection of the narrative crux in which Lïenor effectively forces her lover to marry her.[23] The song's heroine takes direct and self-directed action despite her mother's (and her lover's) expectation that she will be passive.[24] The refrain to this *chanson d'histoire,* "Or orrez ja / conment la bele Aiglentine esploita" [Now you will hear right away / how fair Aiglentine managed], neatly foreshadows Lïenor's inventiveness and determination. This chanson, and the other three as well, suggest the future and the character of the romance's heroine; they form an incrementally intensifying series that presents both a telescoped and a kaleidoscopic version of Lïenor's later action.

The *chansons d'histoire,* fewer and more restricted in their distribution than the *refrains* or lyric chansons, reflect Lïenor's extremely attenuated presence in the bulk of this romance. Her actual existence as an agent is downplayed in favor of Conrad's shadowy representation of her in his lyric fantasies. As Krueger has observed, "*Guillaume de Dole* makes clear that the place of woman in the knight's world is as an absent figure of his fantasy whom he contemplates in the presence of other knights, as Conrad does with Guillaume" (1989, 39). Conrad represents her to himself as the lofty lady of the *grand chant courtois* and invests himself with the qualities of a conventional lover.[25] The lyrics that he himself quotes (or has sung) actually fit his narrative situation fairly poorly, although they are said to represent, or at least suit, his feelings at the time. The choice of lyrics highlights Conrad's specifically poetic preconceptions about Lïenor and reminds us that he constructed his beloved out of suggestion and stereotype. The formal and thematic similarity of the songs—imperfectly matching the narrative setting—suggests his self-imprisonment in courtly codes, to borrow a phrase from Joan Ferrante.[26] His infatuation with a description of distant, unknown perfection, itself a topos of the lyrics he sings, argues that his paralysis within courtly conventions is of his own choosing and that his suffering, like his joy, is of his own creation. He embraces a poetic scenario that does not exist at all and that never develops in the course of the romance. Our realization of this incongruity calls into question his particular narrative pose and, by extension, that of the lyric lover.

As Emmanuèle Baumgartner has noted, the lyrics sung by Lïenor are of a more popular kind than Conrad's highly wrought, formalistic, courtly lyric frame of reference; and the aesthetic tension resulting from the meeting of the two forms of lyricism is not insignificant.[27] This tension leads Marc-René Jung to conclude that the courtly lyric embodies error and must be corrected by popular lyric values; such an interpretation, I argue, is far too inflexible an allegorization of the genres in play.[28] Jean Renart suggests, I think, that any possible truth is to be sought in the totality of representations of reality. Such truth is not a unity attaching to one genre or another but a plurality of perspectives, fragmented, distorted, and tangential. Thus, when Lïenor finally arrives at court, she does not replace or obliterate Conrad's lyric fantasy about her; rather, she brings other versions of herself to his essentially lyric conception of her, completing and resolving his view. In this romance, multiple genres are used to problematize the issue of individual perspective; they do not represent individual viewpoints. Lïenor's arrival at court effectively gathers the scattered elements of the text into a whole that is formed of multiple perspectives. The inclusion in this expanded text of other worlds, other poetic frames of reference, serves to valorize all the partial truths that add up to reality but that, taken individually, cannot adequately represent it. The dissolution of generic borders in *Guillaume de Dole* thus has a positive effect: it offers Jean Renart a strategy for enhancing the representational capacity of language, especially that of genre-based expression.

Lïenor's decentered presence in the text is maintained primarily by the lyrics sung about her and by her; but it is also evoked, in displaced form, in the constant references to her brother, her name, her physical beauty. She disappears entirely from the plot for the period occupied by her brother and the tournament. Her brother himself is an important replacement for her, and it is Conrad's and Guillaume's "exclusive and constant proximity, not Conrad's love for Lïenor, which incites the seneschal's jealousy" and leads him to slander her (Krueger 1989, 40). Once she has been accused, Conrad renounces her, still sight unseen, on the basis of yet another sign, the rose-shaped birthmark on the inside of her thigh—itself a deft, if not a particularly subtle, metonymic sign of her sex.[29] From that point on, in a set of markedly erotic descriptions, she is referred to exclusively in connection with the rose:

"Ja mes nuls hom qui parler puisse
ne verra si fete merveille
come de la rose vermelle
desor la cuisse blanche et tendre.
Il n'est mervelle ne soit mendre
a oïr, ce n'est nule doute."
La grant beauté li descrit tote
et la maniere de son grant. (vv. 3362–69)

["No man who can speak

will ever see such a wonder
as the crimson rose
on her white and tender thigh.
There is no greater marvel
to hear, without a doubt."
{The mother} describes its great beauty {to the seneschal},
and the nature of its size.]

Lïenor is thus presented as the sign of her sex—a dangerous method and one that seems to incur the author's disapproval, for the entire plot bespeaks the dangers of such one-dimensional and unsubstantiated reduction.[30]

Ultimately Lïenor, through astute and autonomous action, reclaims her compromised identity in a dramatic assertion of innocence and independence. Only with the literal unveiling of her at the end of the romance do we finally see a formal portrait of Lïenor; oddly, this portrait focuses more on her clothing than on her form and connects her to the similarly rich clothing of her retainers (vv. 4355–84). The lush costumes of the group uphold her function as a lady suited to marry an emperor, downplaying her reputation as a lovely but dubious match. The specter of Lïenor's visible sexuality, the revealed rose, yields here to the outward signs of the impeccable respectability of an escorted, protected, and inviolate lady. Her long-delayed description is completed only when she dramatically uncovers her face, form, and hair as she comes before the emperor. The emphasis here is clearly on the visual:

Le hordeïs et la ventaille
enporta jus o tot le heaume,
voiant les barons dou roiaume,
si que sa crigne blonde et sore
son biau samit inde li dore
par espaulles et pres dou col.
Des le tenz mon segnor saint Pol
ne fu plus bele por solas.
Ele haoit tant son solas
que ne li chaloit de trecier;
mes, por ses chevols adrecier,
ot drecié sa greve au matin
d'une branche de porc espin,
et si ot fet front de heaumiere;

s'ot chapelet a la maniere
as puceles de son païs,
s'ot flocelez aval le vis
de ses biaus chevex ondoianz.
Li chapelez li fu aidanz,
qui li fu un poi loig des iex;
et Nature, *por veoir miex*
son biau front, li ot tret arriere.
(vv. 4722–43; my emphasis)

[With the entire helmet she brought down
the barrier and the ventail,
in the sight of the lords of the realm,
so that her blonde and golden hair
gilds the beautiful blue samite
over her shoulders and along her neck.
Since the time of Saint Paul
there has never been a more lovely woman
for delight. She cared so little for her beauty
that she did not bother to braid her hair;
but, to tidy it,
she had that morning straightened her part
with a branch of buckthorn,
and she dressed her forehead like an armoress;
she had a circlet after the fashion
of the girls of her land,
and had curls of beautiful wavy hair
falling over her face.
The circlet enhanced her,
for it was high above her eyes;
and Nature, *to show better*
her lovely forehead, had pulled it back somewhat.]

The extremely vivid uncovering of Lïenor in this passage, after her fixed invisibility throughout the rest of the romance, emphasizes her arrival in a more than locative sense. The various displacements of Lïenor—Jouglet's portrait, her name, the songs she sings and inspires, the emblem of the rose—all come together in the conjoining of multiple modes of expression and perception. After Lïenor is at last revealed, the various lyric modes evoked in the romance are united.[31] The "pucele a la rose" (v. 5040) blends with the maiden standing before Conrad; the name ("ce sui ge bele Lïenors" [v. 5097] [truly I am fair Lïenor]) blends with the face. All these conflations fill in the gaps that remained in the single poetic components.

The treatment of Lïenor exemplifies both the eclecticism of Jean Renart's compositional method and his critique of the original forms he juxtaposes in *Guillaume de Dole.* He fragments both his text and its heroine, interrupting each form of discourse with another because singly these forms report too little of the variety of both actual experience and representations of that experience. To expand this scope, the author calls various literary frames of reference into play—the courtly romance, the courtly lyric, popular dance and genre pieces. He then underpins this generic opening out with a similar expansion of perceptual fields, adding music and image to text. The resulting richness of *Guillaume de Dole* suggests that he succeeded. We can also see, however, that the author succeeded most spectacularly in disguising the obstinately one-dimensional world of the word, whose possibilities and limitations he set out to explore.

Is it fair, then, to say of *Guillaume de Dole*—as so many have said about so many texts, medieval and modern—that it is "a text seen *as* text, literature about literature"?[32] It is fair, if not exhaustive: scrutinizing the value of literary genres is one of Jean Renart's aesthetic agendas and in my view the most visible one. But such an agenda also serves to dismantle the scenario in which the female is the passive object of the male gaze and to install a narrative model of active female refusal of passivity.

In Jean Renart's prologue he notes that his genre splicing is something new, incomprehensible to the uncourtly, effecting such a renewal of the romance genre that a listener will never tire of hearing *Guillaume de Dole:* it will remain "nouviaus toz jors" (v. 23) [always new]. This "new" romance enhances the capacity of literary language to represent reality more completely and points out the perceptual and representational limits of formulaic literary forms. Within the tale, the indirect and genre-bound representations of Lïenor are incomplete and never quite accurate, and she confounds them all; the accumulation of them, however, yields a more proximate picture of her reality, a picture that is complemented in the end by her physical presence. The marriage, and the conclusion of the romance, are figures for (and results of) the inclusion of the multiple versions of the story that make up the whole. These versions—Lïenor's, Conrad's, the court's, Guillaume's, the seneschal's, the mother's—are dispersed in time and space for the protagonists in the romance but gathered up for the reader in the (linear) work. Each perspective is essential to the totality, which becomes perceptible to us thanks to our privileged position as readers. It is for this reason that the "foreign" elements—the lyric and musical intercalations; the citations from *Le lai de l'ombre, Gerbert de Metz,* and *Le roman de Troie;* and the story of Troy embroidered on Lïenor's wedding robe—are inserted into the romance.

The description of Lïenor's robe is deliberate in both content and position:

Einsi com Helaine fu nee
i estoit l'istoire portrete;
ele meïsme i fu retrete,
et Paris et ses frere Hectors
et Prians, li rois, et Mennors,
li bons rois qui toz les biens fist;
et si com Paris la ravist
i sont d'or fetes les ymages,
et si come li granz barnages
des Grieus la vint requerre aprés.
Si i fu ausi Achillés
q'ocist Hector, dont granz diels fu;
et si com cil mirent le fu
en la cité et el donjon
q'en avoit repost a larron
el cheval de fust et tapis.
En ce qu'il jut sor les tapis,
desroubee fu la navie
des Grieus . . . or n'est en vie
hom qui si biau drap seüst faire. (vv. 5332–51)

[The story of how Helen was born
was portrayed on the robe;
she herself was pictured there,
and Paris and his brother Hector
and Priam the king, and Memnon,
the good king who did all good things;
and the images of how Paris
ravished her were all done in gold;
and those of the great army
of the Greeks that came to win her back.
And Achilles was also there,
who slew Hector, which caused great grief;
and how those who had secretly

been hidden in the wooden horse,
set fire to the city
and the towers of Troy.
And while he lay inside the rug
the ships of the Greeks
disappeared . . . no man now lives
who would know how to make so beautiful a cloth.]

The narrator's long reference to the story of Troy directs a retrospective evaluation of the action and importance of *Guillaume de Dole.* While juxtaposing Lïenor's drama with the Trojan War may at first glance seem to trivialize the former, it may just as easily enhance the status of Jean Renart's romance. The two narratives share a concern for the subordination of a leader's private will to the common weal: disaster ensues when Paris abducts Helen in the story of Troy; in *Guillaume de Dole,* it pointedly does *not* ensue when Conrad denies himself his heart's desire for the public good. The end of the romance sets up a stable political continuum in which each element—emperor, bishops, lords, empress, townsfolk—accepts its assigned role. The result is political equilibrium and social tranquillity, reflected in the merciful sentence Lïenor extends to the criminal seneschal.

Beyond the literal level of the story told, however, the tale embroidered on Lïenor's robe comments still further on storytelling.[33] After all, the robe imitates not only history but also the telling of history, not only the events but also the process of communicating them. It is thus a double mediation of the actual events of Troy and implies an indefinite multiplication of intermediate retellings of the events. When we try to locate the narrator's perspective on the robe he is describing (does he claim to have seen it, or did his source describe it to him?), we find that we cannot; our inability to do so implies the existence of another, mediating version. Jean Renart's use of ekphrasis here invokes a temporal progression of perspectives on, and representations of, the events in question. From the multiplicity of occurrences that formed the Trojan War, a succession of storytellers selected those they could make into a story. The joint (female) makers of the robe (a fairy made the cloth, a queen of Apulia did the embroidery) selected and transposed the story again; Jean Renart's source (Benoît de Sainte-Maure) yet again; and Jean himself yet again. His use of ekphrasis is a static shorthand for all the infinitely various and tumultuous events that make up the "real" last referent of the sequence of stories, ungraspable and lost. Even the receding chain of narratives drawn from narratives cannot be re-created; not only do literary representations never reach the terminal point of "actual historical truth," but they do not even relate clearly to each other.

But despite (or perhaps because of) this infinite selection, reworking, and transformation, the story persists. Through stories, past events survive into the present, and experience is not wholly lost; through stories, experience is freed from an otherwise impenetrable temporal limitation. Despite the partial capacity of language to embody reality, and its cooptative tendency to transform reality into its own image (the receding chain of Troy narratives, the courtly romance itself), Jean Renart appears to give a tentative vote of confidence to storytelling at the end of *Guillaume de Dole*. His description, which partially portrays a robe that partially portrays an infinite series of preceding partial representations (the histories of Troy), gains in completeness from the very existence of the other versions. When the historical antecedents in all their richness and complexity are irrevocably lost, signs and echoes of them subsist in their literary representations. The greater the number of available perspectives, the more thorough a knowledge we can have of events (although we can never recuperate them in their immediacy or complexity).[34] The continuance of the history of Troy rests in the story's dispersal into multiple fragments. Thus, at the end of his work Jean Renart recapitulates the same poetics of multiplicity that has informed his patchwork narrative style from the beginning.

Lïenor's robe has yet another important resonance. Previously, I argued that Lïenor is a figure for the "objective reality" that language tries, always imperfectly, to represent; that each individual perspective on her is inadequate and incompletely true; and that the totality of perspectives, which were parceled out among multiple voices (a parceling reenacted in the text by different genres and even different artistic modalities) is the closest approximation of the "truth" (historical events, the phenomenal world) that we can hope to achieve. At the end, when Lïenor turns the seneschal's language against him in a communicative strategy that exploits both language and visual reality, all her scattered personae converge into one: the virtuous, beautiful woman of the inset story; the seneschal's seduced victim; the seneschal's shameless lover; the girl with the rose on her thigh; the heroine of the *chanson d'histoire*; the name Lïenor; the woman who cannot be seen; and so on. She joins all the versions of herself into one (admittedly illusory) presence, and the totality of perspectives offers the closest approximation of objective reality that language can hope to achieve. These competing versions converge to become one female body, which is then cloaked in the history of Troy. In this detail Jean Renart reenacts the concealment and re-creation of objective reality that writing inevitably effects, even while it aims to represent that reality transparently.

The intense splintering of the romance genre into a dynamic, unpredictable metagenre that is augmented by the multiplicity of genres and perceptual modalities it includes paradoxically points toward integration and completeness through that very fracturing. Ultimately the romance is disjointed in order to enhance its semantic possibilities, just as the figure of Lïenor is dispersed only to reemerge more unified and autonomous than we could have foreseen. Like Lïenor, the text unites disparate perspectives, parceled out among multiple voices, genres, and points of view, to claim for itself at least a limited validity through that plurality. And while we must not forget that the appearance of plurality is a sleight of hand on the part of a single author, something has been gained by this exploration of the expanded text. Through the fragmented woman in the text, Jean Renart frames his inquiry into the possibilities and limitations of literary language; and if his resolution in favor of multiple perspectives is illusory, and his placing of the woman as metaphor for a male textual reality problematic, he nevertheless manages to unveil and critique the enabling devices of prior French courtly romance. After Jean's manipulation of the rhetorical portrait, the chastity test, aristocratic revels, the bride quest, the testing and coming of age of the hero, and the marriage resolution, such conventions can no longer function for us as "natural" components of generic models. These devices, stretched beyond their customary functions, will carry with them an enhanced signifying capacity. Jean Renart's "dismantling of narrative,"[35] then, is less a diminution of narrativity than an augmentation, an expansion that comments not only on the existing romance canon but on the very concept of genre and genre's capacity to convey the multiplicity of experience.

Notes

1. See, for example, Emmanuèle Baumgartner, "Les citations lyriques dans *le Roman de la rose*," 260–66; Danièle Duport, "Les chansons dans *Guillaume de Dole*"; Sylvia Huot, *From Song to Book*, 108–116; Marc-René Jung, "L'empereur Conrad"; Norris Lacy, "'Amer par oïr dire'"; Félix Lecoy, introduction to *Jean Renart: "Le roman de la rose ou de Guillaume de Dole,"* xiii–xxix; Rita Lejeune-Dehousse, *L'oeuvre*; and, to a certain extent, Michel Zink, *Roman rose et rose rouge.*

2. Compare Zink, *Roman rose et rose rouge*, 26.

3. Others who have addressed the role of Lïenor include Roger Dragonetti, *Le mirage des sources*; Roberta L. Krueger, "Double Jeopardy"; Laurence de Looze, "The

Gender of Fiction"; Claude Lachet, "Présence de Liénor"; Henri Rey-Flaud, *La névrose courtoise;* and Helen Solterer, "At the Bottom of Mirage, A Woman's Body"; Professor Solterer kindly sent me her essay before its publication but after the completion of my own. Our readings dovetail in many particulars, if not in general conclusions; I note parallels as they arise.

4. Baumgartner ("Les citations lyriques," 264–65), Huot (*From Song to Book,* 111), and Sarah Kay (*Subjectivity in Troubadour Poetry,* 191, 197) have noted rightly that *Guillaume de Dole* critiques postures of courtly lyric. In Kay's words, "Jean Renart . . . shows that the subject position of the courtly lyric is shaped by self-deceiving euphemisms which are intended to safeguard desire and control perception of the love object" (197). I concentrate instead on Jean Renart's critique of the narrative conventions of courtly romance and of the epistemology implicit in that genre.

5. See, in this regard, Boulton's observation that the lyrics, in effect, replace typical romance *aventures* (chapter 3 of the present volume). Her chapter and van der Werf's (chapter 7) discuss in detail the functions of the various lyric genres represented in *Guillaume de Dole.*

6. Zink, *Roman rose;* Alberto Limentani, "Effetti di specularità" and "Jean Renart dal romanzo anti-idillico all'anti-romanzo"; Lacy, "'Amer par oïr dire'."

7. Félix Lecoy, "Sur la date du *Guillaume de Dole.*"

8. See Krueger, "Double Jeopardy," 24. "The anxiety about female chastity underlying the wager reveals the crucial role of the chaste woman as guarantor of legitimacy in primogeniture" (24–25).

9. Ibid., 43. "The romance explores the way language manipulates woman as a sign and appropriates her to the male fantasies of lyric poetry. But, at the same time that the narrative *reveals* this process to the discerning reader, it also participates in it, implicating the reader in the narrator's game" (36). Krueger also observes: "The narrator has . . . appropriated 'paroles de femme' to tease at the fibers of courtly discourse while preserving his own authority as speaker" (43). I discuss some of the implications of this statement later in this chapter.

10. Again, the collision of genres effects a similar demystification and critique of lyric forms, but to a lesser extent. Zink's insistence on the hegemony of the romance and on the fragmentation of the lyrics (chapter 4 of the present volume) supports my contention that the romance is Jean Renart's first concern. Kay and Huot disagree, emphasizing the romance's correction of lyric excesses over the lyrics' critique of romance conventions.

11. Note, for example, the pervasive textual anxiety about Enide's access to speech in *Erec et Enide* or about the truth-value of the queen's speech in Chrétien's *Chevalier de la charrete,* Eupheme's speech in *Le roman de silence,* Bisclavret's nameless wife's speech in Marie de France's *lai Bisclavret,* Iseut's speech in *Tristan et Iseut,* and others. For a recent exploration of the topic, see E. Jane Burns, *Bodytalk: When Women Speak in Old French Literature* (Philadelphia: University of Pennsylvania Press, 1993).

12. The sole exception is the fragment of a *chanson de geste* (vv. 1333f.).

13. Zink argues convincingly that actual performance of the lyric insertions or of the work as a whole is neither encouraged nor even foreseen in its prologue (chapter 4 of the present volume). Music is thus invoked only to be discarded, subordinated to the primary narrative context.

14. Jean Renart has carefully delimited that audience to exclude the uncourtly, who could not recognize his lyric insertions (v. 15).

15. Lachet enumerates the many strategies by which Jean Renart keeps the absent Lïenor present to the reader and even notes that her name is encoded in at least seven lyric insertions ("Présence de Liénor," 822–23).

16. Roger Dragonetti's reading stresses so strongly the metaphoricity of both Lïenor and her rose that it denies any literal existence to both. I would not go this far. In my reading Lïenor is not the only such figure for the phenomenal world; rather, she exemplifies the patchwork poetics by which Jean Renart attempts to evade the innumerable limitations of writing. Helen Solterer offers a shrewd critique of Dragonetti's "reduction" of Lïenor's body to the status of a "cipher, a tantalizing illusion generated by the text" ("At the Bottom of Mirage," 214). She reads *Guillaume de Dole* as playing "with the implications of *women*'s figuration" (228; my emphasis). I read it less as an inquiry into the representation of women than as one into the parameters of literary representation, in which Lïenor *among others* functions as an analogue to such representation.

17. For a discussion of the portrait conventions in place by the time of *Guillaume de Dole*'s composition, see Alice M. Colby, *The Portrait in Twelfth-Century French Literature: An Example of the Stylistic Originality of Chrétien de Troyes* (Geneva: Droz, 1965).

18. Throughout this section Jean Renart hints unmistakably at the power of the teller to create the reality he pretends only to describe (vv. 657–842).

19. All references will be to Lecoy's 1979 edition; translations are my own.

20. As Rey-Flaud notes, "A la place du corps, *Le roman de la rose* met d'abord le *nom* de la femme comme cause du désir" (*La névrose courtoise*, 89).

21. As Limentani says, the *chanson d'histoire* "partially reflects, variously refracting" its context ("Effetti di specularità," 313).

22. Even this song is abbreviated and condensed in the manuscript. On the song in general, see Paul Zumthor, "La chanson de Bele Aiglentine," in *Travaux de linguistique et de littérature* 8.1 (1970): 325–37.

23. Limentani, "Effetti di specularità," 313. See also the discussions of this song by Boulton and Zink, chapters 3 and 4 in the present volume.

24. Compare Krueger, who also refers to "a pattern of female passivity and male activity familiar to readers of romance" ("Double Jeopardy," 35).

25. Noted by Baumgartner, "Les citations lyriques," 262.

26. Joan Ferrante, "Self-Imprisonment of Man and Society in Courtly Codes," Andrew W. Mellon Lectures, Graduate School of Tulane University, 1984. On the incongruity of song and setting, see also the discussion by Boulton, chapter 3 of the present volume.

27. "On peut se demander si Léonor et Conrad ne sont pas, dans l'espace du texte, les incarnations romanesques des deux grands types de lyrisme représentés" (Baumgartner, "Les citations lyriques," 263).

28. Jung, "L'empereur Conrad," 44–46.

29. On Lïenor's rose, see Zink, *Roman rose,* 73–77; Dragonetti's reading maintains that "l'image florale emblématise la source de la parole poétique" (*Le mirage des sources,* 199).

30. De Looze notes that "Lïenor is reduced to a sign (the rose) which is prey to whatever discourse manipulates it" ("The Gender of Fiction," 602).

31. Jung and Baumgartner have emphasized the significance of the juxtaposition of the dance songs (vv. 5106–15)—declared to be Conrad's "Te Deum" (v. 5116)—and the *chanson d'histoire* ("Or vienent Pasques les beles en avril," vv. 5188–207) and the *grand chant courtois* ("Quant voi l'aloete moder," vv. 5212–27).

32. Lacy, "'Amer par oïr dire'," 786. But see also Zink, *Roman rose,* 26; Limentani, "Jean Renart," 168; and Jung, "L'empereur Conrad," 36.

33. The embroidered robe is discussed from a different but complementary angle by Jones in chapter 1 of the present volume. See also the discussion by Terry, chapter 6.

34. Dragonetti regards this romance as celebrating endless textual artifice without *any* recoverable ground in historicity. I strongly disagree; in my view, Jean Renart is attempting to mediate between artifice/representation and historicity. See my previous discussion of the complementary generic modes used to delineate Lïenor.

35. Limentani, "Jean Renart," 176.

CHAPTER 6

On the Untranslatable Surface of *Guillaume de Dole*

PATRICIA TERRY

Reading, a kind of translation in itself, evolves with the numberless re-readings inherent in the process of trying to reproduce itself in another language. Thus, says Barbara Johnson, "the more a text is worked through by the problem of translation, the more untranslatable it becomes."[1] We may come to regard our first impressions as naïve and now read the same words differently. The rather simplistic story of *Guillaume de Dole* may seem to include a variety of more sophisticated stories whose existence is, nevertheless, not quite provable. Whatever aspects of these alternative stories we find convincing should be equally potential in the words of the translation—potential but not predetermined.

While not striving to emulate Pierre Menard's carbon-copy *Quixote,* we may aspire to reproduce the *surface* of the text so that our version, too, will accommodate all legitimate readings. We will not accept, at least not consciously, George Steiner's invitation to make explicit what was implied but not stated, adding what "was already there."[2] At least we will not accept his invitation if we wish to allow the new reader of *Guillaume de Dole* the possibility of experiencing the romance as Rita Lejeune-Dehousse did. A pioneering critic of the work, she encountered little to contradict the apparent plot.[3] But she was not a translator and was thus exempt from having to make certain kinds of decisions. The problem is always to determine exactly what *is* the surface of the text, and that is the subject of this chapter.

First, let us examine some general considerations. A text's surface will be defined according to the purpose of the translation. If it is meant for readers who know the language of the original but can use assistance with a particular work, the translation should reproduce the literal meaning. A good bilingual edition intended for scholars constitutes a complete glossary, with all uncertainties acknowledged in notes. Aesthetic components—form, tone, musicality, irony—are irrelevant to a literal version. The literary experience it helps to make available remains exclusively that of reading the original text.

A literary translation must provide that experience in the *absence* of the text. Most of its readers will be undergraduates or general readers who were once undergraduates. For them the literal version serves no purpose or is counterproductive. The greater the literary work, the more its meaning lies in its style; a "trot" will not even make sense. A dull version of an interesting text is profoundly inaccurate. Jean Renart's wit and humor are an integral part of what his romance is about. We translate *Guillaume de Dole* because we enjoy reading it; that enjoyment is what our translation, then, seeks above all to reproduce: a unique enjoyment provided by *Guillaume de Dole.*[4] I now turn to the difficulties of that endeavor.

* * *

As both Rita Lejeune and John W. Baldwin have stressed, proper names, whether historical or fictional, are an irreducible part of a text's surface.[5] "Guillaume" must be Jean Renart's favorite name, for he gives it to the protagonist of *L'escoufle* as well as to Guillaume de Dole. In the latter work, however, the name loses neutrality. Guillaume, says the jongleur who describes him, was *not* being guileful when he appropriated the name of a town called Dole: "ce vient plus de sens que de guile" [literally: this comes more from good sense than from guile].[6] The emperor agrees that adopting a more distinguished name simply shows common sense.

Jouglet's comment, and the emperor's careless response, may raise questions for the reader. The very attention drawn to the name seems to suggest the opposite of Jouglet's assertion. Is there really no impropriety in taking a name not your own? A translation does not provide answers to these questions; it need only prompt them to the extent that the original does. This seems easy enough: in English we do have *guile* as well as a softer version, *beguile,* which has no French equivalent. Yet however an English-speaking reader pronounces Guillaume, the first syllable has no "guile" in it; a certain degree of emphasis is lost each time the name occurs. We also have *dole,* on which Jean Renart puns so many times. Guillaume can be "doleful," just as in Old French he was *doloros.* The idea of "on the dole" is relevant, too, since Guillaume lives so far beyond his means; but the English word will not reach as far as *doleusement* with its implication of ruse and fraud.

Lïenor's name is also very suggestive, at least in its Old French form. Most particularly she is golden Lïen*or,* but her name also includes *lié,* "linked" and "joyful." In addition, as several scholars have observed, the term *li enors* ("honor") is also inscribed in her name.[7] The names alone, however suggestive, would not be enough to change the apparent plot. But Lejeune, who saw nothing special in the name Guillaume, did note, if only in passing, that his prior relationship with the jongleur was more intimate than one might have expected (1935, 72). She also discovered that Heudes de Rades de Crouci, to whom Guillaume is favorably compared for elegance of attire, turns out to have been famous for his *lack* of elegance.[8] This is strange in itself; for Jean Renart takes great pains to show his protagonist dressed in the latest fashion, including many gold-embroidered coats of arms to which he was presumably not entitled. The fame of Heudes—along with the author's possible oblique disparagement of him—is available to modern readers only in the obscurity of a footnote. But perhaps among the words of praise for Guillaume's dress, one or two less unequivocally admiring words might slip in—unconsciously, as it were.

Scholarly readings have the great advantage of being cumulative. Critics of *Guillaume de Dole* after Lejeune became increasingly aware of possible subtexts. All the more recent critics (except, I suppose, the Freudian Rey-Flaud) understand Jean Renart to be exceedingly aware of his own craft.[9] Roger Dragonetti believes that the protagonists, including Guillaume's mother, were also crafty, deliberately plotting to achieve their goals. In our translation, Nancy Vine Durling and I follow Dragonetti's conspiracy theory a short way: we believe that Guillaume and Jouglet conspired to bring Guillaume and his sister to Conrad's attention. They were relatively impecunious minor noblefolk who wanted to rise in the world. Their success is accompanied by quite a bit of *invraisemblance,* which Michel Zink sees as a means through which literature is made to triumph over life.[10] Our own reading, however, emphasizes the *rose rouge* rather than the *roman rose:* when Jean Renart puts pimples on otherwise conventional portraits, when he adds a snide comment to a series of flattering remarks, we see him pointing to life as it resists even the transformations of art.

The difference between a reader and a translator is that the latter is involved in thousands upon thousands of judgments and decisions. Readers make judgments, too, of course, but can usually afford to be more vague. For example, the reader of *Guillaume de Dole* will encounter several times the expressions "gent sanz anui" and "li anuis": Guillaume wants "genz sans anui" to accompany him to Conrad's court; Conrad wants people "sanz anui" around him when he is bled; "gent sanz anui" watch the tournament preparations; "li anuis" leave the palace after dinner before the minstrels arrive. *Anui* is readily understandable as something we don't want to have or to be.

Lacking one word with the range of *anui,* a translation will necessarily limit its meaning, will have to decide what the most important aspect of that meaning actually is in the context, decide this on inadequate evidence. It seemed to us that what Guillaume needs for his journey is good company, men who can hold their own in court society. Conrad wants congenial people around him. Uncongenial people, in whatever ways they can be more precisely defined, are not invited to stay for the entertainment. The people going up to watch the tournament from balconies are not so much congenial or uncongenial as cheerful, although they might also have been people who don't cause *anui* to others—socially acceptable people, one might say.[11]

The judgments made by Jean Renart's translators may involve more delicate considerations. On the morning after the new empress's wedding night, noblemen come to plead with her on behalf of the seneschal. The author tells us that "ne l'avoit pas si blecie / la nuit, Deu merci, l'emperere / . . . / qu'ele n'en seüst bien respondre / sanz vilonie" (vv. 5561–65). This seems to suggest that the emperor, had he been less considerate toward his bride, would have left her either inclined toward vulgar speech or morally degraded. But "vilonie" here refers to the content of the response rather than its language and to the lack of generosity that can be a response to one's own unhappiness. Thus, our translation reads: "The emperor—thank God—had not caused her such suffering during the night that she couldn't respond as she should, without vindictiveness" (93).

To reproduce the surface of the text doesn't always require one to know exactly what that surface is made of. When Jean Renart says that Conrad was such a fair-minded judge that he wouldn't take even a thousand-mark bribe (20), we don't really have to know, in order to translate the passage, whether or not this meant that a larger bribe might possibly have been welcome. When people, at what seems a touching moment, weep "even if [they have] to borrow the tears" (73–74), translation does not require that we know the importance of that comment. But our reaction to such statements, and to many others like them in *Guillaume de Dole,* will color the text as we read it, will influence our decisions about what is important to preserve, when that has to be a choice.

For example, the first time we hear the name Lïenor, the jongleur/author deftly suggests by a rhyme the nature of Conrad's attraction to the unknown beauty, not idealizing but lustful. The emperor asks, literally, "What's the name of his sister, who has such a fine and beautiful body?" [Et sa suer, coment a a non, / qui si a bel et gent le cors? / —Sirë, el a non Lïenors] (vv. 789–91). Without the rhyme *Lïenors/cors,* a literal version seems unduly crude. On the other hand, Dufournet and his colleagues' translation ("Comment se nomme sa soeur qui est si belle et si gracieuse?") doesn't even hint at a sexual intention.[12] The suggestion seems to us important. Although we are told that what Conrad loves is the *name* Lïenor, the many allusions to a more physical attraction culminate, when Conrad finally *sees* Lïenor, in the author's comment: "Ahi! plus tire cus que corde" (v. 5300), conservatively translated as "Sex pulls harder than a rope." For Conrad's initial, abstract encounter with Lïenor, we at first tried to imitate the deftness of the rhyme by translating "bel et gent le cors" as "ravishing." Later, the text's insistent physicality persuaded us to adopt an unmediated reference to Lïenor's body.

Proverbial expressions are plentiful in *Guillaume de Dole,* and their intentions are often unclear because some aspect of the abridged reference is no longer available to us. During Guillaume's first meeting with Conrad, Jouglet whispers to Guillaume that he should not talk of his pedigree but rather of arms and love [d'armes et d'amors]; these happen to be the very words the author used to state the subject of his romance (v. 24). Jouglet thus skillfully ensures that the forthcoming tournament will have a place in the conversation, much as Jean Renart ensures that it will be a part of the romance. The jongleur's adroitness is described by a proverb: he knows "com las bués marge" (v. 1643). Unfortunately, we do not know if Jouglet knew how things were going, knew what the ox's particular way of moving signified about its own condition, or knew how to *make* an ox move. We opted for this last interpretation: "Jouglet, who knew how to move an ox," but would have preferred a more ambiguous expression.

Perhaps the most intriguing example of a proverbial expression involves a "mervelleus" young minstrel called Cupelin who was "plus tendres d'un herenc" [more tender than a herring] (v. 3400). "Tendres" has been interpreted by Lejeune to mean "thin" and the minstrel thus agile and quick. Dufournet adopts Lejeune's reading in his translation. He also suggests an ironic play on "tendre," meaning that Cupelin was the opposite, dry and hard (1988, 70, n. 1). The context includes the information that the king was very fond of Cupelin, whom he summoned every morning to play the following song:

> I gave her the white fur-lined vest,
> but it was Thierion she loved best.
> Ha! Ha! just as I thought!
> To me that shepherdess no pleasure brought. (65)

The emperor was secretly in love at the time, so the attraction of this ditty had to depend on the charm of the performer, although the author may have chosen it as a warning against optimistic expectations. As far as herring is concerned, much depends on personal experience. We were irresistibly tempted by "good enough to eat."

Guillaume de Dole relies on the distinction between narrative verse and lyrics—the latter, as Michel Zink reminds us, playing their part "below the surface."[13] Although no musical notation accompanies the poems in the extant manuscript, many of the songs were no doubt familiar; in any case, the lyric poems are nothing if not the music of their words. The rhymes quoted in the preceding paragraph suggest the naïve quality of Cupelin's song. Elsewhere in the text, sophisticated poets sing of love's sorrow even as their melodic language consoles. If this cannot at least be alluded to in the translation, their poems will have been in effect omitted.

It seemed to Nancy Durling and me that Jean Renart's narrative verse, with its vivid descriptions of courtly life and ambiguous irony, would best be served by prose.[14] My previous practice in translating verse had always been to reproduce the form, and I was astonished to discover that this actually makes it easier to stay close to a literal version. Led on by the energy, the momentum of rhyme, and the abstract structure imposed on ordinary language, the reader is likely to find unremarkable certain characteristics of medieval style that in prose seem either burdensome or quaint: frequent and redundant exclamations, arbitrary changes of tense, names of canonical hours.

Here is a typical sentence: "La dame et sa fille ont esté / au mengier a mout grant deduit" (vv. 1811–12). Literally translated, it would read: "The lady and her daughter have dined with the very greatest delight." Absolute superlatives (such as *molt, trop, tres*) are used so frequently in Old French texts that they have no chance to function by contrast. It can thus be argued that they don't function as superlatives at all but are at the most intensifiers and often less significant than unqualified nouns. We readily become accustomed to this stylistic convention in Old French, but in English our best option is to translate superlatives according to what seems to be their actual effect. Our sample sentence might read: "The lady and her daughter have enjoyed a very good dinner."[15] Similarly, when the vassals of the emperor Conrad lament his disinclination to take a wife, they say, "if he . . . dies without an heir, we are all dead . . . nothing will ever give us joy again," phrases for which reasonable equivalents might be "If he dies without an heir, we're lost . . . our happy days are over." The colloquial quality of such a translation seems to capture the conversational style of the context.

In other circumstances it seemed that a more literal version, however eccentric it might appear, was the better option. A type of understatement that occurs from time to time in *Guillaume de Dole* owes more to Jean Renart's personal style than to literary conventions of the time. When we read that a messenger's horse was "neither sore nor lame" and the messenger himself "neither a fool nor drunk," the phrases mean approximately that the horse was swift and the messenger well chosen for his task. But to translate only the meaning would be a reduction, a smoothing out of what may be intentional roughness. In such expressions, as in the proverbs that refer to oxen, cabbages, goats, and herring, Jean Renart includes aspects of life that before his time were not at home in romance.

This also applies to his portraits. A classic enumeration of Lïenor's features concludes with the remark that her neck, "par reson," has no sores or wrinkles. This isn't just an equivalent for the usual "her neck is white and smooth." *Par reson* means something like "of course"—the "reason" being that Lïenor is the heroine of a book. The Old French words have adequate equivalents in English, but our literal version risks seeming more odd than effective. The author's phrase slips by in the charm of its rhyme: *sanz fronce/selon ce.* Such images occur in other texts but not with the same insistence. *Le roman de Troie* tells us that Polixena is not round-shouldered, but Jean Renart says that Lïenor is neither a hunchback nor deformed.[16] The handsome face of Guillaume as he rides toward the tournament is not covered with blemishes. It is interesting that Guillaume de Lorris's Oiseuse, also "par reson" had neither "bube ne malan," a phrase glossed by Stephen Nichols as "ni postule ni verrue."[17]

These may or may not be intertextual references. Many other references in the work are, although they often are not apparent to the non-specialist reader. A translation may, and should, communicate irony perceived to be on the surface of the text; but it cannot build in a response to a reference. Yet Jean Renart considers his major innovation to be quotations from other writers, specifically the lyric poems, which are analyzed elsewhere in the present volume. The importance of the quotations, he says, is their unity with his own work: one will scarcely be able to believe they were not all written by himself (vv. 1–29). The allusions within what actually *is* his own text function similarly: they make us wonder what we are reading.

The earliest overt reference to another work is so familiar that even a footnote seems superfluous; it is strange for the same reason. The emperor, the better to enjoy his summertime festivities, takes all the jealous, ill-natured old men out hunting and leaves them in the woods: "onques voir, puis le tens roi Marc, / empereres ne sot vuidier / si bien pavellon d'encombrier" (vv. 170–72) [literally: No emperor since the time of King Mark has been better able to rid his tents of obstacles in the way].[18] The easiest interpretation, which emphasizes the *time* of King Mark, may be the best. Yet, as so often when we read Jean Renart, we are left with an uneasy feeling. King Mark, once evoked, will not go away. He attaches himself to Conrad innocently because they are both the senior royal personages of their stories; King Mark, however, *was* the obstacle who was eluded by the lovers. Conrad joins the younger knights in their sports; but he, again like King Mark, decides to marry someone he has never seen and does so. The real lovers, Tristan and Iseut, cannot marry. Would it be going too far to speculate about the fact that Guillaume and Lïenor, who speak of each other with such intensity of feeling (vv. 3046–51, 5266–67), cannot marry either?

King Mark and Tristan, on the surface of a translation, can still evoke appropriate responses if the reader pauses long enough to reflect. The most extensive allusions in *Guillaume de Dole* are familiar as well, although we know them from Homer rather than from Jean Renart's source, Benoît de Sainte-Maure's *Le roman de Troie.* When Guillaume de Dole comes to visit the emperor, Jean tells us that no knight was ever welcomed so joyfully at any emperor's court since the time of the Trojan Paris: "puis le tens Paris de Troie, / ne reçut on a si grant joie / a une cort d'empereor / chevalier a si grant honor" (vv. 1605–8). Here the reference is clearly to Paris rather than "his time," and the modern reader might well imagine that Paris, before his abduction of Helen, could indeed have been welcome anywhere. The comparison would still be rather odd because welcoming Paris proved such a poor idea. There is a similar allusion toward the end of *Guillaume de Dole* (vv. 5320–23) to "Alexander's leap" as an occasion for great rejoicing, although in the *Roman d'Alexandre* his arrival in Tyre meant doom to its citizens.[19]

Le roman de Troie gives an elaborate version of the relations between evil Greeks and virtuous Trojans well before the time of Priam and Agamemnon, the latter being specifically called the "emperor" of the Greeks. It would have been clear that *no* Trojan could have been welcome in any Greek court. Guillaume *was* welcome at the emperor Conrad's, which leaves us wondering how to understand the reference to Paris. Was Conrad making a mistake, or was Paris evoked in contrast to irreproachable Guillaume? Even in Benoît's pro-Trojan book, Paris is described as far from ideal. True, he was "sages et vertuos," but these adjectives are instantly followed by "E d'empire mout coveitos, / Seignorie mout desirot" (vv. 5451–53). In the end, twenty thousand lines later, he proves to be *so* desirous of power, at least the power of revenge, that he allows his mother to persuade him to attack Achilles in an utterly cowardly manner. With twenty warriors he waits in a temple to ambush and kill, with great difficulty, the unarmed hero and his one companion.

Le roman de Troie may well have been famous enough for Jean Renart's description of Guillaume to be recognized as referring not to Paris, as might have been expected, but to King Memnon. Lejeune points out the almost verbatim quotation from Benoît's text, including King Memnon's curly auburn hair (1935, 140). Instead of eyes that are "gros et hardis," Jean Renart characteristically prefers that Guillaume's be laughing, "riants et hardis." King Memnon also appears (with Paris) among the images of Troy embroidered on Lïenor's wedding robe. He is praised in this passage as "Mennors, / li bons rois qui toz les biens fist" (vv. 5336–37) [literally: Memnon, the good king who did so many good things]. He is further connected to Paris in the next line, whose rhyme word is "ravist"; and one would be hard put to determine any "biens" at all accomplished by Memnon in *Le roman de Troie* unless it was wounding Achilles, who then killed him.

Benoît's portrait of Paris includes his blond hair, which shone like fine gold, and like the gold (*or*) in Menn*or*s. This reminds us of Lïenor, of course, who otherwise has closer connections to Helen, whose story dominates the wedding robe.[20] Marc-René Jung notes that Benoît's description of Helen includes the idea of "graine" as a superior coloring agent, mentioned in Jean Renart's prologue as functioning in a similar way to the songs included in *Guillaume de Dole*.[21] There is also, perhaps simply by convention, a reference to roses: "Ausi com color de graine / Est mout plus bele d'autre chose, / Et tot ausi com la rose / Sormonte colors de beautez, / Trestot ausi, e plus asez, / Sormonta la beauté Heleine / Tote rien que nasqui humaine" (vv. 5124–30) [Just like the color of *graine* / is more beautiful than anything else, / and quite as the rose / surpasses {other} colors in beauty, / just so, and even more, / Helen's beauty surpassed / that of any human ever born]. Helen had a "wonder-working" mark between her eyebrows, but we are not told what it represented: "Enz el mi lieu des dous sorciz / Qu'ele aveit deugiez et soutiz / Aveit un seing en tel endreit / Que merveilles li aveneit" (vv. 5133–36) [Between her two eyebrows, / which were delicate and fine, / she had a sign in such a place / that wonders came from it].[22] Helen's image on the robe was embroidered in gold, although Benoît shows her to be, at the very least, a self-serving opportunist. In any version she brings destruction to Troy.

If the allusions to *Le roman de Troie* raise questions about the author's view of his protagonists, another reference points to the seneschal and to Jean Renart himself. Renard the Fox is mentioned a number of times, most notably when the seneschal "would have to be as clever as Renart" in order to escape death (vv. 5420–21). He *does* escape, and by the same means as the fox in a similar trap: by promising to go on a pilgrimage. The fox, of course, escapes from that fate, too, more than once, which makes one wonder about the seneschal.

The very last lines of the text conceal the author's name in a statement that he lost his name when he took religious vows: "il e*ntra* en *re*ligion." Perhaps he did not really do that any more than the fox did but took the latter's name as his own, much as Guillaume took the name Dole, with its underlying suggestion of clever deceit. It seems, as Jean Renart endlessly mystifies and misleads us, very suitable.

Notes

1. Barbara Johnson, "Taking Fidelity Philosophically," in *Difference in Translation,* ed. Joseph F. Graham (Ithaca: Cornell University Press, 1985), 146.

2. George Steiner, *After Babel: Aspects of Language and Translation* (Oxford: Oxford University Press, 1981), 423.

3. Rita Lejeune, ed., *Jean Renart,* xii.

4. *The Romance of the Rose or Guillaume de Dole,* trans. Patricia Terry and Nancy Vine Durling. Page references following English translations of *Guillaume de Dole* are to this translation.

5. Rita Lejeune-Dehousse (*L'oeuvre de Jean Renart*) was the first to study historical figures in *Guillaume de Dole.* See also Baldwin's discussion in chapter 2 of the present volume.

6. Félix Lecoy, ed., *Jean Renart: "Le roman de la rose ou de Guillaume de Dole,"* v. 787. All references to the Old French text are to this edition.

7. For a discussion, see Nancy Vine Durling, "The Seal and the Rose," 34.

8. Lejeune-Dehousse, *Oeuvre,* 120, and *Jean Renart,* 145–46.

9. Henri Rey-Flaud, *La névrose courtoise.*

10. Michel Zink, *Roman rose et rose rouge: "Le roman de la Rose ou de Guillaume de Dole" de Jean Renart.*

11. Vladimir Nabokov devotes six pages of the commentary to the translation of *Eugene Onegin* to *ennui* as defined from the seventeenth century onward (Aleksandr Pushkin, *Eugene Onegin,* Bollingen Series 72 [Princeton: Princeton University Press, 1975], 151–56). The quoted definitions include Fonsegrive's, from *La grande encyclopédie* (circa 1885), translated by Nabokov: "After having enjoyed a pleasure, the soul that reflects is suprized at finding pleasure so vapid." The emperor Conrad's court was clearly not a place for such reflections, but he himself must have been subject to them to some extent or he would not have so readily fallen in love with a beauty who was not there.

12. *Jean Renart: "Guillaume de Dole ou le roman de la rose,"* trans. Jean Dufournet et al., 20.

13. See chapter 4 of the present volume.

14. Some of the following remarks appear in the introduction to our translation of *Guillaume de Dole.*

15. In fact, in our final version these lines merged with other statements, the better to reflect the general atmosphere of gaiety and ease during Guillaume and Jouglet's visit to the inn.

16. Benoît de Sainte-Maure, *Le roman de Troie,* ed. Léopold Constans (Paris: Firmin-Didot, 1909), v. 5537.

17. Stephen G. Nicols, Jr., ed., *Le roman de la rose* (New York: Meredith, 1967), 32. It is worth noting that Oiseuse wore white gloves, as do so many of Jean Renart's elegantly dressed men and women. The dating of the two works remains a topic of debate. See Baldwin's discussion in chapter 2 of the present volume and Zink, *Roman rose et rose rouge.*

18. Boulton comments on the fact that *Guillaume de Dole* begins and ends with an allusion to the Tristan story (chapter 3 of the present volume). There is also an early reference to Troy in vv. 40–43.

19. *The Medieval French Roman d'Alexandre,* ed. E. C. Armstrong et al. (Princeton: Princeton University Press, 1937), 2:117, vv. 1965–75.

20. As Marc-René Jung has observed, the initials LN (Hélène) may be echoed in "LN + or." He notes in this context that Memnon had a sister named Helen and suggests a parallel between Guillaume-Lïenor and Memnon-Helen. See his "L'empereur Conrad," 38.

21. Jung observes, "Hélène, la rose, Hélène parée d'un *naevus* comme Liénor, Hélène *color de graine*—ne faut-il pas se souvenir du prologue du *Roman de la rose* de Jean Renart? . . . Les chansons insérées dans le texte (*dras*) font miroiter l'image séductrice de la belle Hélène du mythe littéraire" (ibid., 50).

22. Benoît and Jean Renart share an interest in eyebrows. Helen's are separated; but Benoît's source, Dares the Phrygian, describes Briseida as having "superciliis junctis" (quoted by Gilbert Highet in *The Classical Tradition* [New York: Oxford University Press, 1949], 575, n. 11). Benoît adds a note of disapproval: "Her eye-

brows were joined together, which was rather unbecoming" (vv. 5279–80). Jean Renart's description of a fictive lady, drawn from *Le lai de l'ombre* and later applied by extension to Lïenor, says that she had "long, shapely eyebrows, certainly not joined together" (vv. 707–98). This passage is also discussed by Alice M. Colby, who notes that "The *seing* 'spot' between Helen's eyebrows is the French equivalent of Dares' *nota* and is never mentioned as a mark of beauty elsewhere in twelfth-century literature" (*The Portrait in Twelfth-Century French Literature: An Example of the Stylistic Originality of Chrétien de Troyes* [Genève: Droz, 1965], 37).

Music and Performance

CHAPTER 7

Jean Renart and Medieval Song

HENDRIK VAN DER WERF

In the version that has come down to us, the tale of Guillaume de Dole, the emperor Conrad, and fair Lïenor does not contain a single melody; but Jean Renart, its probable author, has given us valuable information about medieval music in general and medieval song in particular. On some points, we can draw conclusions from what he actually wrote; on others, we learn from what he did *not* write. In the introductory verses he implies that he literally "wrote" his romance while creating it, but the arts of reading and writing play virtually no role in the life of his leading characters. Reading the story with this in mind greatly increases our awareness of the differences between not only his and our culture but also his and our choice of terms. The wide variety of songs in the tale suggests that the great songbooks of the later thirteenth century give a lopsided picture of medieval song. When he tells us precisely who performed a given song, Jean Renart may well give us more information about jongleurs and minstrels than most of us have realized. By indicating when a given song was performed, he gives us an insight into the role of song in medieval life. All of this forces us to question some widely accepted theories, especially those concerning so-called *rondets* and *refrains.* Finally, the very act of including songs for which we know the music prompts us to speculate about the manner in which a medieval story was rendered for those who could not read. This speculation, in turn, sheds light on the vexing question of whether Jean Renart managed to make songs and narrative into one unified work of art.

* * *

Twentieth-century experts on medieval prose and poetry have paid increasing attention to the question of whether a given work was produced and disseminated with or without the help of writing implements. It probably is typical of our script- and print-dominated society that terms with which to discuss written material are plentiful and adequate while our professional jargon is ill-equipped to deal with cultures in which the processes of creation and transmission are unaffected by script and notation. It is common, for example, to speak and write of *oral poetry,* but the expression *oral literature* seems to be a contradiction in terms because, when spoken, a poem does not have letters but phonemes. The expressions *oral tradition, oral composition,* and *orality* also are inadequate because the mouth is not the only human organ involved in the composition and dissemination of works of tonal and verbal arts. The terms *oral* and *orality* may be somewhat appropriate for music with text, but they do not work well for instrumental music. It would seem incongruous, for example, to write about the oral composition and the oral tradition of a piece for lute, crumhorn, and shawm.

For most of us, and perhaps especially for musicians, the verb *to compose* is virtually synonymous with *to write;* the verb can be almost misleading when it is used in reference to creating without pen and ink or, more likely, without stylus and wax tablet. The verbs *to create, to produce,* and *to make* have the advantage of being neutral, but they do not serve well when the absence of script and notation must be stressed. Like many other people, I have often used the verb *to improvise* as a simple term for notationless and scriptless composition. I have also used *to reimprovise* in reference to the performers' art of reconstructing a melody from memory without being pitch for pitch faithful to the original music. Recently, however, as if to illustrate the problems I am discussing here, one musicologist categorically condemned all studies in which those terms are used in relation to Gregorian chant.[1] In that scholar's opinion, reconstruction from memory played no role in the transmission of chant; he maintains, instead, that the singers relied upon memorization. In addition, he argues that the term *improvisation* refers exclusively to a work that is so incoherent and unorganized that it cannot be remembered. It is true that we customarily say that toccatas, fantasias, and the like are composed in an improvisatory style, which means that their style seems to have been derived from instances in which, for example, a harpist lets the fingers do the composing. During the past few centuries, organists must have improvised a multitude of toccatas that lacked coherence, but most of the ones that were written down are carefully thought out and well organized. Among organists, moreover, there is a longstanding tradition of concluding a recital with a fugue improvised on a theme provided by someone else only minutes before the improvisation is undertaken. By its nature, a fugue is far from incoherent; and, as we well know, an experienced improvisor can repeat the fugue after the recital even though such a reimprovisation is not always chord for chord and pitch for pitch identical to the original improvisation.

In the twelfth century, both script and notation were known, but they were rarely or never used in the processes of composition and dissemination of certain genres. For that reason, one can justify using the terms *scriptless* and *notationless* for those realms of medieval culture in which, for example, troubadour and *trouvère* chansons originated and flourished. In general, the songs that have come down to us were written down for the sake of compiling a collection of chansons; not only chansons but also books had become collectors' items. Nevertheless, even these simple terms have their drawbacks because the suffix *-less* may evoke pejorative associations. From our vantage point, it is easy to perceive the absence of script and notation as a deficiency. Many of us may be inclined to think that the troubadours and *trouvères* were at a disadvantage because they had not yet learned to use pen and ink in the creative process. Therefore, we may alleviate the problem by also using the terms *script-free* and *notation-free*. The latter term especially has advantages; for example, a thirteenth-century composer who knew nothing about notes and ligatures was free to sing durational patterns that could not be written down in the mensural notation of the time. In what may well be the most important aspect of cultural circles that were free of script and notation, performers were not necessarily required to sing a given chanson so that it was word for word and pitch for pitch the same from one rendition to another. Phrasing the same feature in positive terms, one may say that script-free and notation-free performers were at liberty to alter text and melody. One must immediately add a qualifier, however, and speak of a "certain" or a "limited" freedom because multiple versions of *trouvère* chansons generally show that, seven or eight centuries ago, this freedom was not without limitations. Most of those who were involved in the transmission of chansons seem to have been able to retain what to them must have been the most essential features of a given poem and its melody.

In discussions of poetry, it is customary to use the term *line* for a section that is set off by rhyme and that, in a modern edition, is printed on one line even when it does not occupy a single line in the manuscript. It is easy to forget that a poet-composer in a scriptless culture did not think of written lines when making up a chanson. On more than one occasion, I have had a minor conflict with an editor when I used the term *verse* where others wrote of a *line.* My doing so is not merely a matter of personal preference because, when discussing notational features such as clefs and flat signs, one often must distinguish between the music that stands on one line or staff and the melody for one verse. The layout of Jean Renart's romance is interesting on this point because each verse of the narrative proper occupies one line in the manuscript, while the verses of the songs are entered so that most lines are filled to capacity (see Figure 4).[2]

At first glance, my emphasizing these terminological niceties may seem pedantic; but experience has taught that attention to terminology fosters awareness of the multifaceted differences between the scriptless and notationless realms of medieval culture, on the one hand, and our print-dominated society, on the other. Despite our best efforts, we do not always manage to speak of medieval music and poetry in terms that cannot be misunderstood or misinterpreted. The term *orality* (literally meaning "mouthliness") is not sufficiently precise. Substituting *verbal* or *audible arts* for *literature* seems awkward until we realize that it is common to speak of *visual arts.* In a narrow interpretation of its Latin components, a *composition* is something that is "put together," but we can hardly escape the association with something that is written. Similarly, the term *improvisation* refers to what one has "not seen before," and *reimprovisation* may refer to "a restatement of what one has heard but not seen in writing." But depending upon one's preconceived notions, the adjective *improvisatory* may refer to a work that is marked more by spontaneity than design.

Jean Renart does not solve our terminological problems. He begins his tale in a neutral fashion with the statement "Cil qui mist cest conte en romans" (v. 1) [He who made this story into a romance {or} He who put this story into romance]. He goes on to claim that the work is innovative, "une novele chose" (v. 12) [a new thing]. To a large extent one's interpretation of the prologue to *Guillaume de Dole* depends on whether one sees it as an artistic manifesto or a clever sales pitch. Thus, we will probably never know for certain exactly what made this "roman" into "something new." The author did not commit himself on whether he produced a new story, whether he put an existing story in writing, whether he made an existing story into a new genre by incorporating songs into it, or whether he created both a new story and a new genre. Perhaps to give his creation the widest possible circulation, Jean Renart wrote that "l'en i chante et lit" (v. 19) [one sings and reads in it], thereby leaving open to interpretation

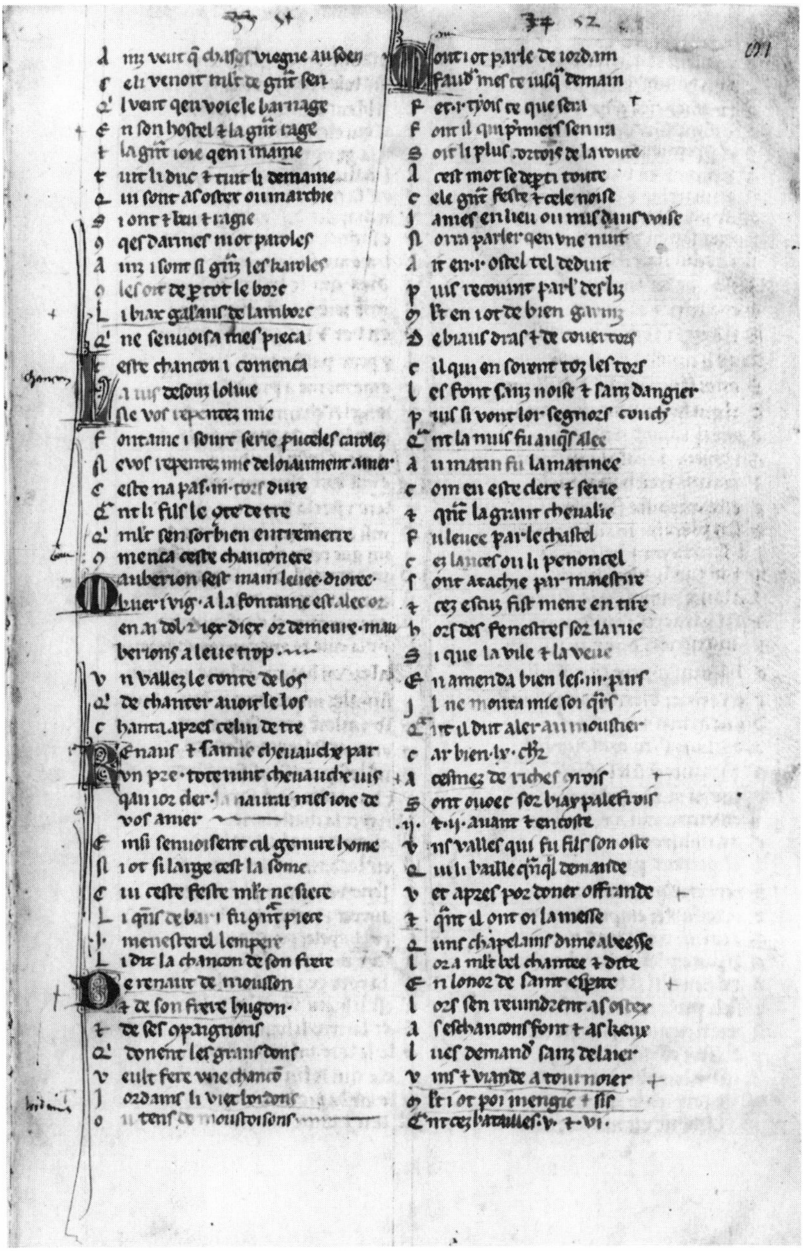

FIGURE 4. Manuscript page from *Le roman de la rose ou de Guillaume de Dole,* showing the differences in layout between narrative proper and song texts; the left-hand column contains nos. 25–27 of Appendix 2. Courtesy of the Vatican Library, Vatican reg. 1725, fol. 81r.

complex issues of simultaneity (sing *and* read), preference (one person might sing, another read in it), and performance style (sung or read aloud? sung or read silently?). But the prologue raises other questions as well. For example, should one read this work only for one's own edification? Or could one read it and retell it to listeners who themselves cannot read? If this phrase is an advertisement, it is very similar to sixteenth-century claims that the polyphonic songs in certain printed collections could be "sung or played on all kinds of instruments." One of the author's stated aims was that a certain Milon de Nanteuil might "learn about it" [l'apregne] (v. 6), but we are not told whether Milon is expected to read it himself or hear it being read.

Concerning the music of the songs, Jean Renart was equally elusive when he wrote, "ou il fet noter biaus chans / por ramenbrance des chançons" (vv. 2–3). By the beginning of the thirteenth century, writing down a French text was no longer a novelty; but extant sources with notated music suggest that, even if the art of writing down a melody had spread beyond the walls of ecclesiastical scriptoria, it still was not practiced widely. Thus, the second verse may simply mean that Jean Renart, probably an experienced scribe, did not know how to write down a melody and that someone else did it for him; the second verse might then be translated: "In which he made [someone] notate beautiful melodies."[3]

In the course of the tale itself, Jean Renart's choice of words consistently reflects a society in which script and notation play very limited roles. When the *vïelor* Jouglet is first introduced, he is said to have "oï et apris / mainte chançon et maint biau conte" (vv. 641–42) [heard and learned / many a song and many a good story], which probably means that Jouglet had learned these songs and stories from having heard (not read) them. Of similar interest are the passages in which someone remembers or recalls ("sovient," v. 3621; "sovint," v. 3879; "resovint," v. 5230) a certain song and promptly sings it. As did many others, Jean Renart used the verbs *chanter* and *dire* in such a way as to make them seem interchangeable. The only other verb to be used frequently in reference to the act of singing is *comencier* (to begin), but we do not always know whether the person concerned sang the entire text by him- or herself or whether others chimed in once the song was started.

The verbs *to write, to compose,* and the like are conspicuously absent from Jean Renart's tale. The most precise term used for any creative process seems to be the verb *to make.* At one specific point in the story, Jean Renart writes that "l'emperere . . . fist lués cez vers" (v. 3179), which may well mean that the emperor "made those verses" right then and there without either the benefit or the interference of notation and script. In the few instances in which the poet-composer of an existing song is mentioned by name, Jean Renart does not use terms such as *author, poet,* or *composer.* Similarly, syntactical practice of the time did not require him to use prepositions such as *de* or *par.* It is noteworthy that one song by Gace Brulé is said to be performed in his honor (v. 845) [en l'onor monsegnor Gasçon]. When Jouglet's description of the fair Lïenor causes the emperor Conrad to fall in love with her, the emperor instructs a clerc to "make" a letter for her brother Guillaume [que li clers fist bien e bel / les letres . . .] (vv. 876–77). The messenger who is to take it to Guillaume not only receives the actual letter but is also told of its contents (vv. 886–95); the emperor specifically states that he is asking Guillaume to come to court immediately after "il avra cest brief oï" (v. 888) [he will have heard this letter]. The subsequent passage is interesting in that the letter and its golden seal receive great attention and admiration but nobody is in a great hurry to read it. When the letter is handed to Guillaume, he is orally informed of its essential message (vv. 974–79); Guillaume repeats this information to his mother and sister, recounting the emperor's invitation to come to court. Only after some delay does one of his chevaliers actually read the letter and convey its contents to Guillaume (vv. 1014–15). Thus, we do not actually find out whether the sender, the messenger, and the addressee were able to read it; but it is clear that the letter has greater symbolic than practical value.

Letters play a role on two other occasions. The morning after his first meeting with the emperor, Guillaume "fet fere / a un cler de letres .III. paire" (vv. 1925–26) [has a clerc make three letters]: one for his mother, one for friends at home, and one for a weapons maker in Liège. After Conrad decides to marry Lïenor, he has letters made and sealed for the nobility of his realm (vv. 3121–23). On both occasions, the author is far from specific about the procedures of making and reading letters, but the audience of the romance must have been impressed with the importance of persons who send and receive letters.

To sum up, the terminology used by Jean Renart in *Guillaume de Dole* to refer to various compositional activities, while appropriate for a scriptless and notationless culture, remains noncommittal for our purposes. It may take us a long time and much effort to develop a vocabulary suitable to characterize in simple terms the creation and dissemination of the audible arts in a notation- and script-free culture. In the meantime, we ought to be tolerant and refrain from condemning other scholars' conclusions merely because of supposedly ill-suited terminology.

Recognizing the existence of scriptless and notationless realms in medieval culture has implications that are both far-reaching and hazardous, in particular because scriptless audible arts must have been in existence for centuries before Jean Renart put his pen to parchment. Thus, individual works and entire genres that existed in the scriptless areas of medieval culture but are now lost forever pose a curious problem. Speculation about presumably lost works allows one to defend any theory that is not supported by extant material; at the same time, however, systematically excluding unwritten works and genres from our scholarly deliberations is bound to lead to erroneous conclusions and faulty theories.

* * *

Several experts have concluded from Jean Renart's introductory verses that he claims to have invented a new literary genre, presumably by including preexisting songs in a newly created narrative. Was he really the first to do so? It is well known that Tristan and Ysolt frequently expressed their feelings in song. We find such a case in what is often considered to be the oldest written version of the Tristan and Ysolt narrative, in which a certain Tumas (Thomas) identifies himself as the author.[4] At one particularly sad point in the story, Ysolt "fait un lai pitus d'amor" (v. 834) [makes a piteous *lai* of love].[5] In the words of Thomas, Ysolt "chante molt dulcement / la voiz acorde a l'estrument. / Les mains sunt belles, li lais buens / dulce la voiz [e] bas li tons" (vv. 844–47) [Ysolt sings very sweetly / her voice is in accord with the instrument / Her hands are beautiful, the *lai* good / sweet the voice {and} soft {or low} the tone]. Thomas includes neither the text nor the melody of the *lai,* but things are different in the manuscripts containing prose versions of the *Tristan.* Several have seemingly complete texts of *lais* sung by either protagonist; two have music for at least some of them.[6]

When medieval authors give a label for a song composed and performed by Tristan, Ysolt, or other persons in their environment, they normally use the term *lai,* whereas Jean Renart uses by preference *chançon* and *chançonete.* It is clear that Tristan and Ysolt were not only the performers but also the poet-composers of the *lais* concerned.[7] In contrast, it seems to be generally accepted that Jean Renart's characters (with one exception) performed songs that already existed before the story took place and had been created by poet-composers who do not appear in the romance. The most obvious exception is the song made up on the spot by the emperor

(31).[8] But we cannot, in fact, be completely certain about the origin of many other songs because, except for twelve known troubadour and *trouvère* chansons (discussed later in this chapter), all of the songs in *Guillaume de Dole* are unique to that work.

A more elusive and probably more serious criterion concerns the dates for the creation not only of the works themselves but also of the extant manuscripts. Beginning with the latter, we face a curious situation: if my interpretation of Jean Renart's second verse is correct (that Jean Renart had someone else write down the melodies for the songs), his own final copy may well have contained music for all or most of the chansons and chansonnettes even though there is not a single note—not even an empty staff—in the only surviving copy. The two *Tristan* manuscripts that have music (Vienna, B.N. 2542; Paris, B.N. f. fr. 776) cannot be dated with precision, but they are neither the earliest nor the latest extant sources of Tristan stories in prose. The Vienna codex, which has the greater number of melodies, may well be more or less contemporary with the sole extant copy of *Guillaume de Dole*. More important, the two *Tristan* sources with music have different melodies for each of the three *lais* that they have in common. We therefore lack any information about the origin of the music. Concerning the two romances themselves, we lack complete certainty about the date of origin. The earliest proposed date for the prose *Tristan* is 1215; and as John W. Baldwin demonstrates in his chapter, *Guillaume de Dole* was probably written in "the years immediately following 1209."[9]

The more aware we are of the existence of a scriptless culture, the more alert we are to our lack of certainty on all points under scrutiny. We may safely accept that the tales about King Arthur and his entourage predate any written account of them. For example, even if the tale about Guillaume and Lïenor, as it stands, originated with Jean Renart, we can take for granted that Lïenor's red rose was not the first birthmark to play a crucial role in a medieval story.[10] Similarly, the ruse by which she restores her reputation and her chances for a good marriage may be no more than a variant upon a standard component of stories about persons with high aspirations. Above all, it is difficult to believe that storytellers of earlier periods never actually performed songs that played a role in an unwritten story.

Continuing in this line of thinking, let us briefly turn to the questions of how, when, and where so-called lyric song originated. Apart from the question of whether vernacular song derived from Latin song, we cannot ignore the possibility that many or all tribes of Western Europe had their own songs long before the first troubadour was born. In short, it is dangerous, perhaps even irresponsible, to presume that any extant song or any group of extant songs can represent the birth of vernacular song. It is probably just as presumptuous to hold that Occitania was the birthplace of vernacular song. The nucleus of the problem is the simple fact that we do not know how, when, and where the art of singing originated.[11]

* * *

Jean Renart's choice of songs is both interesting and instructive. By Lecoy's count, there are forty-six lyric pieces, one of which appears twice (2 and 28; see Lecoy's edition, xxii–xxix). In addition, there is an otherwise unknown excerpt from an epic about Gerbert de Metz (17). Allowing for some ambiguity of genre, Lecoy divided the lyric pieces into the following three groups: courtly chansons, narrative chansons, and dance songs. This categorization is largely in keeping with general practice; but as I will discuss shortly, one can raise serious questions about the distinction between the last two categories, especially about the characterization of all items in the third group as dance songs.

Courtly Chansons

Although we all know that the people of thirteenth-century France were familiar with a variety of songs, many of us somehow have developed the notion that those songs were primarily what we now call courtly chansons and that on the periphery of the verbal-musical arts were a few other genres of minor importance. Only sixteen of the forty-six songs in *Guillaume de Dole* belong to the category often referred to by the lofty title *grand chant courtois*. If we had reason to believe that Jean Renart's selection was representative of the entire song repertory of his time, we would have to reverse that notion and instead hold that the *grand chant* constituted a minority—albeit a large one—in a variegated repertory of secular songs. There is, however, no compelling reason to believe that Jean Renart tried to give a fair representation of early thirteenth-century song genres, so we may not have to reverse our impression completely. Conversely, we have ample reason to believe that the thirteenth-century collectors who compiled the extant *chansonniers* (song collections) concentrated on songs about *fin' amors* and basically ignored the other song genres that flourished in the notationless and scriptless realms of medieval culture. All in all, we should go slowly in assuming that the scene of twelfth- and thirteenth-century secular song was dominated by chansons about *fin' amors* created by poet-composers who officially had been accorded the title *troubadour* or *trouvère*.

Thirteen of the courtly chansons in *Guillaume de Dole* are in Old French. Nine of these appear with music in typical *trouvère* collections that were compiled later in the century (see the transcriptions in Appendix 3), while the other four (30, 31, 40, and 46) appear exclusively in *Guillaume de Dole.* It is well known that the *chansonniers* often disagree with one another on the identity of the poet-composer of a given chanson. For that reason, it is noteworthy that two of the attributions given by Jean Renart are corroborated by *chansonniers* that are generally accepted as reliable on this issue (11 and 37). For the other French chansons that also appear elsewhere, our romance is either the only source to have an author's name (18) or is one of several with conflicting attributions (8 and 36). As I have already noted, one song (31) is said to have been made by the emperor himself.

Three of the sixteen chansons are in the Frenchified form of the Old Occitan language that is well known from the troubadour songs preserved in two of the *trouvère* collections (16, 41, and 45). These three appear in typical troubadour collections as well as in one or both of the *trouvère* manuscripts that preserve some troubadour chansons. In other words, at least some of the troubadour chansons that appear in the latter collections were known in the north several decades before the earliest extant *chansonniers* are assumed to have been compiled.

Experts on medieval song tend to criticize today's performers and editors if they dare to leave out even a single strophe in their concert, recording, or anthology. But the extant troubadour and *trouvère* manuscripts often differ on the number and the order of strophes for a given poem. This type of variant suggests that the medieval performers did not worry about including all strophes in every presentation. In this regard, Jean Renart seems to have been even less scrupulous than most scribes because he makes his characters sing only one—or at the most two—of the five or six strophes we know the poem to have had.[12]

What we now call courtly love, and what medieval poets called *fin' amors,* is traditionally contemplated from the man's point of view; therefore, it is not surprising that in *Guillaume de Dole* all troubadour and *trouvère* chansons are sung by men. It is also noteworthy that the term *son,* which is used widely in Old Occitan writing in reference to either songs or melodies, is used twice by Jean Renart to refer to a troubadour chanson (vv. 1300 and 5211). Jean Renart therefore appears to have been well acquainted with the courtly chansons of his time.

Narrative Songs

Turning to the other songs in the romance, I note that all of the songs in Lecoy's second group, and most of the ones in his third, were published more than one hundred years ago by Karl Bartsch in a collection of what we may call narrative songs or short narratives (as opposed to the long narratives that go by labels such as *chanson de geste,* romance, or *lai*).[13] What for Bartsch was largely one genre is now customarily treated as several distinct genres. The narrative element in the supposed dance songs (Lecoy's third group) is ignored, and his second category is subdivided in several ways. It is regrettable that editions of narrative songs are often limited to what the editors consider to be one independent genre, such as *pastourelle* or *chanson de toile.* The introductory study of such an edition is likely to center on the decision about which songs should be included and which left out. Consequently (and sadly), we do not have an overview of the many poems that coexisted with the well-studied *grands chants.*

Dance Songs

Most of the songs in Lecoy's third group customarily are called *rondets* or little *rondeaux* even though many of them lack some or all of the features that typify the *rondeau* as we know it from fourteenth- and late thirteenth-century sources. Using capital letters for the recurrent verses, the rhyme scheme of a *rondeau* may graphically be represented as *AB a A ab AB,* with the understanding that all verses with a given rhyme have the same melody and the same number of syllables. Friedrich Gennrich, a literary historian who wrote extensively about both text and music of medieval song, stated that the *rondeau* had evolved from songs used for round dances—that is, dances in which the participants formed a circle.[14] According to Gennrich, in its earliest form the recurrent text sections were performed by a group of persons, probably all participants in the dance, while the other verses were sung by a soloist, probably the leader of the dance. At this stage (still according to Gennrich), the *rondeau* was formally the same as its full-grown descendant except that it had only six verses with the rhyme scheme *aAabAB.*

In Appendix 1, five of these early *rondeaux* are displayed to facilitate comparison of Jean Renart's practice with Gennrich's theory. In the lefthand column they are given as they appear in Lecoy's edition, in the righthand column as edited by Gennrich, with his italics for what he considered to be refrains.[15] No detailed analysis is required to justify the observation that, as preserved in their sole source, only the last of these poems corresponds to Gennrich's theory. The penultimate one comes close; but in order to give it its supposedly correct form, Gennrich had to make some emendations. In the process, he changed its assonance scheme from *aaabbb* to *aaabAb*.

Guillaume de Dole is considered to be the oldest source for early *rondeaux*; but of the eighteen pieces identified as such by Gennrich, no more than five are fairly well in keeping with the supposed rules. Seven others have some internal repetition but lack at least one of the other required features, while the other four do not even have any internal repetition.[16] Thus, if Gennrich's theory is correct, we have to draw the paradoxical conclusion that Jean Renart did not know how to make early *rondeaux*. Or if he did know, and if Gennrich's emendations restore his originals, we come to the equally paradoxical conclusion that the person who produced the extant copy did not know how to deal with *rondeaux* but did a remarkably good job on the rest of the work. We also may conclude that the author, the copyist, or both were persistent in their ignorance because both readings of the repeated song have the same formal deficiencies (2 and 28).

We also must question the theory that all so-called *rondets* are dance songs and constitute one distinct genre. Gennrich was neither the first nor the last to say so.[17] Pierre Bec, in his attempt at categorizing medieval songs, followed the unproven theory almost to the letter and added to the standard nomenclature the expression "registre lyrico-choréographique."[18] Nevertheless, the mere fact that a poem with some *rondeau*-like features occasionally is given the label *rondet de carole* does not prove that all such poems were dance songs. Similarly, the fact that a given poem is sung during a dance (7–10) does not necessarily mean that its form was dictated or influenced by the act of dancing. Furthermore, as Doss-Quinby in particular has shown, medieval authors have given varying labels to the poems under scrutiny.[19]

Johannes de Grocheio, writing in the late thirteenth century, seems to be the only medieval theorist to have made some observations about the *rondeau* and its music. With considerable justification, Gennrich, Bec, and others have accepted that what Grocheio called *cantilena rotunda* or *rotundellus* is our *rondeau*; but without any discussion they brush aside his characterization of the *rondeau* as a song that "begins and ends with the same [text and music]."[20] Nor do they pay any attention to the fact that Grocheio makes no reference to either dancing or an alternation of soloist and chorus. All in all, if the *rondets* and *rondeaux* preserved in thirteenth- and fourteenth-century sources descended from dancing songs, they had moved about as far from their original function as a scherzo in a

Beethoven symphony is removed from a minuet. Extant music from the eighteenth and nineteenth centuries allows us to reconstruct the evolution from minuet to scherzo, but we have no evidence that the *rondeau* derived from dance songs and that dance songs had a fixed form from their inception. (We shall shortly encounter more likely antecedents of not only the *rondeau* but also the *virelai* and the *ballade.*)

A few of the songs in Lecoy's third group are characterized by him as *refrains.* Current use of this term in reference to thirteenth-century poetry is marked by a number of anomalies, only some of which can be discussed here. But first we should note that, in discussions of thirteenth-century French poetry, the term *refrain* also is used in its normal meaning—namely, in reference to the text and music of a section that recurs in every strophe of a given song.[21] In this respect, Jean Renart's choice of songs is significant. Only two of the sixteen songs in Lecoy's first group have a refrain, and both are unique to *Guillaume de Dole* (31 and 46). In addition, Jaufré Rudel's song "Lors que li jor sont lonc en mai" (16) has a somewhat unusual refrain: the word *lonc* recurs at the end of the second and fourth verse of each strophe. The situation is almost the opposite for Lecoy's second group, where a refrain is given for all songs that have more than one strophe (13, 14, 15, and 23). This may well be in keeping with the general situation for the two genres because refrains appear to be more common in narrative than in lyric songs.

Great confusion has arisen from the custom of bestowing the label *refrain* upon certain short ditties (one to four verses long) that do not serve as refrains in the usual meaning of the term. The most obvious occurrence of what I call pseudo-refrains involves songs that have been given the misleading label *chansons avec des refrains* as opposed to the more typical *chansons à refrains.* About one hundred such songs have come down to us. Not all deal with courtly love; and for good reasons, about one-third of them were included by Bartsch in his collection of narrative songs. Each strophe of these songs ends with a few verses that make sense in the context of the total song but may be at odds with the song's rhyme scheme and syllable count. Thus, the verses concerned stand at the place where real refrains most often appear, but they do not recur within the song concerned. In most sources, these chansons exclusively have music for their first strophes; but in two *trouvère* manuscripts, either music or empty staffs are present for the pseudo-refrains for the second and subsequent strophes of *chansons avec des refrains.* This strengthens the notion that pseudo-refrains are not part of the strophe proper. It also suggests that each pseudo-refrain had its own music, but this suggestion is weakened considerably by the fact that many of the staffs for the pseudo-refrains for second and subsequent strophes remained empty.

In many (but far from all) cases, a pseudo-refrain of a *chanson avec des refrains* also appears in another work of verbal art, such as another *chanson avec des refrains,* a motet, a *rondeau,* or a romance. Past studies have revealed that many short ditties (we do not know how many) migrated from one work and from one genre to another.[22] These multiple occurrences have prompted some scholars to distinguish between *refrain répété* and *refrain cité.* This distinction makes the dual use of the term *refrain* more palatable, but it does not end the confusion; for as far as we now know, most of what are supposed to be *refrains cités* appear in only one work. Moreover, as Doss-Quinby has shown, the identification of *refrains cités* in motets has been far from systematic (1984, 111–33). And as I will show, many cases of multiple occurrence have systematically been excluded from the study of *refrains cités.*

The distinction between so-called *rondets* and *refrains cités* seems to be purely a matter of length. A ditty in a narrative is called a *rondet* if it has five or six verses, called a *refrain* if it has fewer verses, and likely to be called a chanson if it has seven or more verses. Thus, we have ample reason to reject the standard theories about the "other" songs of the thirteenth century. This means that we must undertake a new search for their function and origin even though that endeavor will be fraught with a number of both obvious and hidden dangers. First, these songs are likely to have their roots in the notation- and scriptless realms of medieval culture so that their antecedents are lost forever. In addition, we probably should become more circumspect in our use of the terms *courtly* and *popularizing.* Current practice has more drawbacks than benefits; for example, it seems to imply that the nobility had a monopoly on good taste and on the esoteric treatment of normal human feelings. Conversely, it suggests that commoners were the only ones to treat the facts of life in rather direct terms. If we must differentiate between social groups, we should be precise and give proper evidence for our distinctions.

In past research, little attention has been given to the distinction between actual quotations and common expressions about the pains and pleasures of love. It is regrettable, therefore, that we have music for only a small number of what are considered to be *refrains cités.* Although these snatches of melody were used by Gennrich to reconstruct the music for entire poems, they did not play a role in the formulation of the theory I am examining. With the exception of those by Gennrich, the editions of the poems rarely contain musical transcriptions; sometimes we are not even told if there is music in the manuscript from which the text was taken. It is true that those who have written about accentuation and duration in medieval music have presented diametrically opposed theories. But this should not keep us from publishing diplomatic transcriptions that adequately represent the manuscript's measured or unmeasured notation. Such transcriptions will at least tell us whether multiple occurrences of what some consider to be one poem have the same, similar, or different melodies. This, in turn, may help us distinguish between a quotation and a common expression because the former is more likely to have been preserved with identical music than is the latter.

The phrases "Main se leva bele Aeliz" and "bien se para, miex se vesti" appear, albeit with some variation, in not only the five songs in Appendix 1 but also several other poems, including two motets.[23] Despite their multiple occurrences, neither phrase appears in van den Boogaard's (or anyone else's) list of refrains. The probable reason for this exclusion is that they do not occur in positions where refrains of *rondets* and *rondeaux* are supposed to appear. This exclusion is symptomatic of an important anomaly, for the two Bele Aeliz sentences are not the only verses that appear in more than one work but have not been taken into consideration in the search for the function and origin of either the *rondeau* or the *refrain cité*.

Studied together, the Bele Aeliz poems suggest a path for renewed investigation because they conjure up a picture of a parlor game in which quick-witted players are challenged to invent on the spot a short poem that is to include a certain phrase or pair of phrases. It would be unwise to try to reconstruct the stipulations that governed this pastime in the early thirteenth century. The extant material suggests that, if there was such a game, there may not have been any rules about the placement of the quotation, the total number of verses, the rhyme scheme, and the number of syllables. Or if there were rules, they must have been less restrictive than they are for our game of making limericks, to name just one example.

At the present stage of research, prudence requires that we downplay the notion of games or competitions among versifiers; but we can safely draw some general conclusions from the extant material. In the script- and notation-free realms of medieval culture, there may have been a tradition of making new poems that contained phrases and expressions that everyone knew to have been used in other poems. Perhaps in the tradition I have just discussed, there was a practice of making short songs in which the poet was to repeat one or more phrases at least once without becoming incoherent. In the thirteenth century, these traditions and practices may have been current in scriptless circles, but they also seem to have moved into the growing literary realm. In both, they may have produced a wide variety of poems, ranging from spontaneous expressions to carefully worked out pieces of verbal art. A tour de force of the latter may be found in the song "Main se leva la bien faite Aeliz," which has three different pseudo-refrains in the course of each strophe, amounting to a total of fifteen presumed quotations.[24] In addition, the verses "Main se leva la bien fete Aeliz" and "Biau se para et plus biau se vesti" appear as the opening of strophes 1 and 2 respectively. Very different examples of a sophisticated play with recurrent verses are found in the *ballades* and especially the *rondeaux* and *virelais* of the late thirteenth and the fourteenth centuries.

Doss-Quinby has related known and supposed citations in motets of the late thirteenth century to the fourteenth-century game of making *fratas* (1984, 111–33). She may well be correct in drawing this parallel. It is also likely that various forms of using recurrent textual and musical material go back to even earlier centuries. As long as it remained in script- and notation-free surroundings, the art of playing with preexisting and internally recurrent phrases may have been practiced with great freedom; but when it moved into the area of written literature, the rules and traditions were likely to have become more restrictive. Within that development, the increasing interest in precise repetition in fixed places may have determined the form and nature of the *rondeau*, the *virelai*, and the *ballade*.[25]

As I have mentioned, Karl Bartsch had good reasons for including *rondets* and other short ditties in his collection of narrative songs because many of them tell of or hint at a loving encounter between a pretty young girl and a handsome lad. We do not know whether these short songs are excerpts from or allusions to well-known stories. Certain ones seem to leave much to the imagination of the listeners and the other participants in a game with words and verses. This feature leads to another important dimension: sexual allusions. The references to clear fountains, little streams, olives, olive trees, and green meadows may have been intended to evoke associations other than purely rustic ones. And, of course, in certain contexts, the verb *to dance* may refer to something other than simple dance steps. Such imagery occurs frequently in the seemingly incomplete ditties that begin with "down yonder" ("la jus" or "c'est la jus") and appear not only in Jean Renart's romance and similar narratives but also elsewhere in sources from the thirteenth century. In short, at least some of the *rondets* and pseudo-refrains may be delicately conceived not-so-courtly chansons.

* * *

It is risky to draw upon Jean Renart's narrative for detailed information about the function of music in medieval society, but a few generalizations seem justified. Some thirty years ago, the background information provided by Jean Renart helped me in one aspect of my research. At that time, it was generally accepted that the troubadour and *trouvère* chansons normally were executed to instrumental accompaniment, and I set out to gather information about the instruments that customarily were used for that purpose. I examined the manuscripts and the chansons as well as the Occitan *vidas* and *razos*. Much to my surprise, I did not find any evidence for the involvement of instruments, whereas I came across numerous and very clear references to the act of singing a chanson. In *Guillaume de Dole*, on two occasions, someone performs a song while Jouglet plays the vielle (21 and 23).[26] In another instance, a certain Hues is asked to sing and play(?) a certain song ("chanter en la vïele" [33]). Just previously, Jean Renart uses another curious expression in reference to the minstrel Cupelin, who performs each morning for Conrad: "il li notoit chascun matin" (v. 3402); this phrase is followed by the text of an otherwise unknown song (32). The word *notoit* may safely be translated as "performed"; but we do not know whether this performance involved Cupelin's voice, his instrument, or both. The verb *noter* appears also in the scene preceding the tournament, when it is reported that "li menesterel" have arrived and that "Li uns note un, li autres el, / cil conte ci de Perceval, / cil raconte de Rainceval" (vv. 1746–48) [One {of them} performed one, the other one another / this one relates the story of Perceval / that one tells about Roncevaux]. Here, too, we really do not know whether the minstrels sang, played, or did both. Whatever may be the proper interpretation of the verb *noter*, the following conclusion is clear: whenever a song deals with *fin' amors*, there is no reference to instrumental accompaniment; and in the cases in which instrumental accompaniment is mentioned, the song concerned does not deal with *fin' amors*. In this respect, *Guillaume de Dole* is typical of thirteenth-century narratives that contain songs.

Because my publications at that time exclusively concerned typical troubadour and *trouvère* chansons, I did not consider it necessary to present a detailed discussion of the cases in which accompaniment was mentioned. Instead, I concluded a section on the issue with this statement: "Considering the complete absence of documentary evidence for instrumental accompaniment, it seems unwise to maintain that as a rule the chansons were accompanied. Perhaps the chansons were accompanied but, in all truth, we can find no reason for this assumption other than our own wishful thinking" (1972, 21). This conclusion has not been readily accepted by musicologist-medievalists, and most authors of textbooks on medieval music have adhered to the standard theory. Richard Hoppin writes: "From both literary and pictorial evidence it seems that instruments participated in the performance of troubadour and *trouvère* songs. Unfortunately, the evidence tells us little as to the degree or manner of that participation." He continues with suggestions about how present-day performers might accompany the chansons.[27]

Charlotte Roederer goes into further detail in her discussion of the evidence, writing that songs by troubadours and *trouvères* "may have been accompanied instrumentally, but there is surprisingly little evidence to support this surmise. There is no musical notation in the *chansonniers* to indicate an accompaniment." According to Roederer, however, there are some hints that, on occasion, an accompaniment "might have been improvised. In the famous French allegory of courtly love, *Le roman de la rose* . . . , the author recounts a lady's singing of a new *chansonnette* together with a jongleur playing the *vielle,* the most popular bowed string instrument of the time. And a German literary source advises *vielle* players to join the sounds of their instruments to the songs of others."[28] Generalizing about vernacular songs from 1000 to 1300, Jeremy Yudkin writes: "The original manuscripts give only the texts of the songs and the melody, with no directions for instrumental accompaniment. There is, however, a great deal of evidence that suggests that instrumental accompaniments for the songs were invented by the musicians during performance. Descriptions of medieval celebrations and banquets often contain allusions to such performances, and some of the manuscripts themselves are decorated with pictures of a wide range of instruments."[29] Yudkin's last remark probably refers to the manuscripts with Cantigas de Santa Maria from the Iberian peninsula.

As I have pointed out elsewhere, these illustrations are likely to have allegorical meaning and do not tell us anything about the use of instruments in relation to the performance of either Cantigas de Santa Maria or any other genre of medieval monophonic song.[30] My initial findings, moreover, are fully supported by Christopher Page in his recent study of songs reported to have been accompanied (*Voice and Instruments*). Indeed, there is no evidence for instrumental accompaniment of what many habitually call courtly chansons (which I call troubadour and *trouvère* chansons and Page calls songs in the "higher style").[31] Conversely, all references to the instrumental accompaniment of a given text clearly concern songs about topics other than courtly love. It is sad that our conclusions are almost entirely negative because even Page's wide-ranging search did not turn up one single case in which the accompaniment for an extant twelfth- or thirteenth-century song has been preserved; we do not even have the melody for any song that is reported to have been accompanied.

Jean Renart provides tantalizing bits of information for yet another aspect of instrumental music. On several occasions he briefly—all too briefly—tells us that instruments are heard in the background. In the description of the picnic, reference is made to "estrumenz," "cors," and "vïeleors" who "vïelent par cez pavellons" (vv. 408, 417, and 503–4) [play vielles up and down among the tents]. The festive aspect of the tournament is marked by "flaütes et vïeles," "vïeles . . . et fleütes et estrument," "menesterex et estrumenz / et flaütes," "flaütes et . . . vïeles," and "flaütes et . . . freteles" (vv. 2295, 2348–49, 2462–63, 2555, 2640). We probably should refrain from assuming that the names of these instruments match their present meaning; it may even be unwise to take each as a generic name because *cors, freteles, flaüte,* and *vïele* do not necessarily stand for brass, reed, woodwind, and string instruments, respectively. But it is probably safe to conclude that, at the time of Jean Renart, players of various kinds of instruments joined forces for open-air performances. We would love to know more about these festive occasions—for example, what instruments the performers combined and how well they played in tune—but we do not even know whether the choice of instruments was of any concern to early thirteenth-century performers and listeners. We also would love to know what kind of music they played, but all we may conclude is that open-air repertoires as well as other genres of instrumental music flourished in the notationless realm of medieval culture. Alas, none of it appears to have been preserved in writing.

As I have pointed out, Jean Renart assigns the songs about *fin' amors* exclusively to men. Perhaps more important, these songs do not come up during the merrymaking and dancing in the beginning of the romance; instead, they appear at serious moments in the tale. In addition, nine of the sixteen are performed by the emperor, and all but one of those nine concern *fin' amors*. As one might expect, Lïenor and her mother select songs suitable to their elevated status in the story. When further evaluating the respective roles of commoners and members of the nobility, we must reckon with the fact that all major characters in the romance either belong to the nobility or are related to members of the nobility. Thus, we should probably downplay the fact that almost all singing is done by persons who in one way or another belong to the nobility: that is, we should probably not conclude that members of the lower classes sang significantly less often than more highly placed persons did. Nevertheless, the emperor's prevalent participation in the performance of songs about *fin' amors* probably indicates that such songs were especially "popular" (to use a somewhat jarring term) in upper-crust society. But beyond that observation, Jean Renart's tale shows us that, with a few subtle exceptions, just about everybody sings all kinds of songs. This conclusion is almost diametrically opposed to the old and now fading opinion of music historians that, throughout the Middle Ages, singing in public was a base occupation. In the course of the picnic scene, "une pucele," "une dame," the count of Savoy, and the count of Luxemburg sing without ever apologizing for it (3–6). During the party in the green meadow in front of the tent, "une dame," a valet, the count of Aubourg, and the duchess of Austria feel free to raise their voices in song (7–10).

This brings us to the role of minstrels and jongleurs in the dissemination of troubadour and *trouvère* chansons. As many others have done, I have often used the term *jongleur* in reference to performers of chansons. In reality, this usage is not much more than a convenient coverup for ignorance because we really do not know who were the usual performers of courtly chansons. Consequently, we do not know who were the most important participants in the unwritten transmission of troubadour and *trouvère* art. The term *jongleur* probably has undesirable associations because it implies that the task of performing the chansons was relegated to full-time professional entertainers who were members of the lower class. In this respect, it may be worth our while to survey the respective functions of Jouglet, Nicole, and Cupelin. The last is the only one to be called a "menestereuls" (v. 3397), and he is reported to sing or play ("notoit") a certain song every morning (32). But the emperor's interest in him appears primarily to concern qualities other than musical ones.

When Jouglet first appears, he is called a "vïeleor" (v. 637); he is never called a minstrel or a jongleur, unless his name is a play on the latter term. After the emperor, Jouglet is musically the most active person in the entire romance, but he does much more than provide entertainment. It is Jouglet who tells the emperor about Guillaume de Dole and his beautiful sister. It is Jouglet who is sent to welcome Guillaume when the latter arrives at the inn near the emperor's residence. On that occasion, Jouglet is first a diplomat or ambassador. A little later, he is a friend and, together with the innkeeper's daughter, an entertainer. Guillaume calls him "friend" (vv. 1481 and 1917) and even "brother" (v. 1559). On at least one occasion even the emperor calls him "friend" (v. 753). Later in the story, it is Jouglet who is with Guillaume as he despairs about his own and his sister's misfortunes. Overall, it is difficult to circumscribe Jouglet's function at the emperor's court. He is not only an entertainer but also some kind of counselor—what we might call "assistant" to the emperor.

Nicole is called either a "vallet" (without further specification) or a "valet to the emperor" (v. 1032). Although the scene remains ambiguous, toward the end of his mission, Nicole may have performed a song with Guillaume (16). But his major function clearly is to relay the emperor's all-important message to Guillaume. In this context, Guillaume calls him "friend" (vv. 1038 and 1130) and "brother" (vv. 981 and 1064), but Nicole addresses Guillaume as "sire" (v. 1043).

The word *jougleor* appears only once in the romance (v. 1333).[32] On that occasion, it is not the jongleur mentioned but his sister, who performs the next song (17, a *laisse* from a *chanson de geste*).[33] The word *menesterel,* on the other hand, appears several times in various forms (vv. 2183, 2396, 2462, 3397, and 4564), but its meaning is not absolute. It does not necessarily (or exclusively) refer to entertainers. Instead, it may well refer to servants of a relatively high level, some of whom seem to have done some entertaining.

Throughout the romance, the emperor is the most active performer of songs about courtly love; and because he is reported to have "made" one of them, we may conclude that he himself is a *trouvère.* It appears that Guillaume de Dole, Jouglet, a "vallet," a minstrel, a group of knights, a chevalier, and a "bacheler" sing one courtly chanson each (16, 22, 37, 40, 41, 45, and 46 respectively). A *bacheler* is probably a young man of noble birth who is not yet a knight, but a *vallet* clearly is a servant.[34] If we can believe Jean Renart, one did not need to be a member of the nobility nor a professional or itinerant entertainer to be accepted as a performer of songs about *fin' amors.* In addition, if we can believe Jean Renart, it was the poet-composers themselves who were the prevalent performers of chansons about courtly love. Couching these conclusions in safely vague terms, we may hold that it was not so much professional entertainers but connoisseurs, or afficionados, who most often performed and transmitted troubadour and *trouvère* chansons.

The preceding observations should make us wonder whether, in the time of Jean Renart, professional entertainers worked exclusively at their particular trade. In *Guillaume de Dole,* the term *minstrel* seems to be used to mean "servant"; it apparently refers to an employee with obligations other than domestic or agricultural ones. Judging by other uses of the term, and as discussed by other scholars, at least some of the minstrels seem to have been diplomats or administrators.[35] And it may well be that, depending upon the size of the household or court concerned, minstrels had to have many talents in order to safeguard their position. In modern terms, it probably was easier to find and retain employment as an ambassador, organizer, or administrator if one were good not only at performing those duties but also at telling and inventing stories, performing and creating songs, or playing some kind of musical instrument.

* * *

It is far from easy to characterize in one or two simple words the role of the songs in *Guillaume de Dole*. It is customary to refer to them as interpolations or insertions, which seems to imply that they are not integral parts of the total story. But most, perhaps all, of the songs perform a real function in the given scene.[36] For example, the first ten songs help to establish the atmosphere of merriment and good living in the entourage of a rich and carefree emperor. The next song clearly performs an emotional or psychological function for Conrad, who, after hearing Jouglet's description of the lovely Lïenor and her brave brother Guillaume, falls in love with Lïenor. One can defend the notion that the latter scene is unrealistic, but we cannot deny that the song itself, a chanson about courtly love, was well chosen for this sensitive turning point in the emperor's life. Admittedly, there are some curious cases, but no song is completely without rationale. Jaufré Rudel's song about the faraway beloved (16), for example, is well placed, but one may contend that it is sung by the wrong person. Both the speaker in the poem and Conrad love a lady whom they have never seen. The song occurs in the romance when the lover's expectations are high—namely, when he is about to receive his first direct word about her from her brother. It is somewhat curious, however, that it is not the lover but the brother of the beloved who sings of the faraway beloved. Clearly, subjective evaluation plays an almost decisive role in the search for an answer to the question of whether Jean Renart managed to incorporate the songs into his narrative.[37]

For instance, it is confusing to characterize all songs as lyric parts of the narrative. If the term *lyric* refers to a personal or an emotional outpouring, at least some of the songs are narrative rather than lyric. And if the term *lyric* refers to a text that is meant to be sung, calling the songs lyric inserts implies that the narrative itself is *not* meant to be sung. We cannot rule out the possibility that, in an audible presentation, a narrative was sung rather than spoken. In the case of Jean Renart's romance, the question of whether song and narrative are musically integrated is related to the distinction between poetry to be heard and poetry to be read. This issue, in turn, is related to the distinction between silent and audible reading. The former is common now; but as several scholars have pointed out, it probably was far from common then.[38] Among French-speaking people of the early thirteenth century, the arts of reading and writing were still new; and we must admit the possibility that Jean Renart's work shared characteristics with poetry to be read as well as with poetry to be heard.

As I have noted, Jean Renart clearly implies that his romance could be both sung and read. We would therefore be remiss if we did not consider the manner in which stories traditionally were presented to an audience. We have no more than incidental and rather ambiguous references to the performance of long stories. No *chanson de geste* or verse romance has been preserved with music; but past research has uncovered sufficient evidence for us to assume that at least occasionally (or at least in certain regions) the audible presentation of an epic came closer to singing than to speaking, in our current understanding of those terms.[39]

Johannes de Grocheio is the only theorist of the time to have made observations about the music of what he called the *cantus gestualis,* which almost certainly is our *chanson de geste*. One sentence in his treatise tells us that "the same melody must be reiterated for all verses" of a *chanson de geste*.[40] If "the same" is interpreted in its strictest sense, we have to assume that, in the performance of an average *chanson de geste,* one melodic sentence was repeated pitch for pitch several thousand times. Even with ample allowance for medieval patience and leisure, I find such a claim difficult to believe; but others have accepted it and find support for their position in the *chantefable* known as *Aucassin et Nicolette.* In the sole extant version of this work, dating from the thirteenth century, a musical phrase is given above the text of the first, the second, and the last verse of each verse section, or *laisse*. Essentially the same phrases are restated at the beginning and end, respectively, of each *laisse*. The manner in which the first two phrases appear over the first pair of verses allows us to assume that they were used over and over for each subsequent pair of verses. The two melodic phrases relate to one another in such a way that they may be said to form one melodic sentence. Thus, ignoring the music for the last verse of each *laisse,* one may defend the conclusion that "the same melody was repeated for all [pairs of] verses" of this *chantefable.*

Although we do not have the original melody for any extant romance or *chanson de geste,* we are not completely deprived of information about the type of music that may have been used for an audible presentation of narrative poetry in general. Certain aspects of versification justify our turning to narrative songs for the sake of learning about the music of long narratives. For example, the epic caesura is a regular feature in not only *chansons de geste* but also many narrative songs (for example, 14 and 23), while it seems to have been contrary to the traditions for songs about *fin' amors*. Almost without exception, all strophes of a song about courtly love have exactly the same number of verses, whereas the number is unstable in strophes of narrative songs, including our 15, 23, and 44. Similarly, the poet's freedom in choosing a masculine rhyme for some strophes (or *laisses*) but a feminine rhyme for others in the same work seems to have been acceptable for all narrative poetry regardless of the length of the individual work (23); however, it seems to have been anathema for the more typical *trouvère* chansons. On the other hand, the narrative songs resemble the chansons about courtly love in having strophes that are far shorter than a typical *laisse* of a *chanson de geste*.

Because Grocheio's statement about "the same melody" does not necessarily refer to one specific sequence of pitches, we could interpret it as referring to a certain type of melody that was repeated according to need. There was indeed a type of melody that could have caused Grocheio to make such a statement. At present, this type is best known from Gregorian chant, where it was used primarily for the recitation of biblical poems. In services such as matins and vespers, each verse of a psalm from the Old Testament or a canticle from the New Testament was sung so that one pitch was reiterated for as many consecutive syllables as were needed. Over the first few syllables of a verse, this recto-tono section was preceded by a melodic turn leading to the recitation pitch; over the last few syllables, it was followed by a melodic turn leading away from that pitch. What is considered to be one verse normally consisted of two so-called half-verses, and the point of division was marked by a brief departure from the recitation pitch. In at least one form of psalmody, the two parts of a verse had different recitation pitches; but the melodies for two halves of a verse always relate to one another as antecedent and consequent and thus can be said to form one musical sentence.

As I showed some twenty-five years ago, this melody type is also found in the repertory of French secular song.[41] Whether any *trouvère* chanson has a single recitation pitch for its entire strophe may depend upon one's definitions of *trouvère* chanson and recitation. But many French songs have at least some one-pitch recitation for one or two verses. As I showed at that time, multiple versions of such phrases often vary in not only the melodic turns that lead to and away from the recitation pitch but also the length of the one-pitch recitation itself. In many cases, the opening and closing passages for a given verse vary so that one version may have a brief recto-tono passage where another version has no recitation at all.[42] Such variants are important to the present discussion because they bear upon the medieval concept of "the same melody." In a very strict approach to musical analysis, one probably would have to say that those multiple versions differ from one another; but in an approach that is more appropriate for notation-free composition, one can justify calling them closely related or even essentially the same. Johannes de Grocheio seems to have been an astute observer of the music of his time, and we cannot rule out the possibility that he considered those versions "the same."

Some of the narrative songs in the aforementioned collection by Bartsch have been preserved with music. Alas, relatively few are extant in multiple versions. At present, few of these melodies are accessible in modern notation, and not much research has been done on them; therefore, we must be cautious when generalizing about the music for narrative songs. Nevertheless, it seems safe to say that a narrative song is more likely than a chanson about courtly love to contain recitation on a single pitch. It also may be true that repetition of melodic phrases is less restricted in narrative songs than in typical *trouvère* chansons. In the latter, repetition is virtually restricted to one restatement of the first two phrases, resulting in the overall form *AB AB X*, while three- or fourfold repetition of the first phrase does not seem to have been banned from narrative songs. It is not true, however, that all narrative songs have simple and syllabic tunes because the most ornate melodies of the entire French repertory of the thirteenth century are the ones preserved for the narrative songs "Belle Doette as fenestres se siet" and "En un vergier les une fontenelle" (R-S 1352 and 594).

Taking our speculation one step further, we may speak of *idem cantus* (the same melody) in a case in which an entire strophe or *laisse* (or even an entire *chanson de geste*) was sung in this recitation style but in which two or more pitches took turns functioning as the recitation pitch.[43] An interesting illustration of this phenomenon is found in one narrative song, the music of which has not yet been published.[44] Where one-pitch recitation is concerned, the total melody of this song is divided into two sections, each of which has its own recitation pitch. The multiple versions for these sections, moreover, vary not only in the manners I have just described but also in the choice of recitation pitch for a given pair of verses. If the term *cantus* in Grocheio's sentence refers to a type of melody, we may hold that, for a major part of this song, one *cantus* was reiterated for each pair of verses. Because its component features were varied more than was usual for the extant repertory of secular songs, we probably may also conclude that those who were involved in the notation-free transmission of this melody experienced it as loosely defined. Accordingly, if this type of melody was used for an audible rendition of *Guillaume de Dole,* the melodic style used for its narrative proper was more loosely defined than the tunes in Appendix 3, taken from *chansonniers* of the late thirteenth century. Regardless of the character of the other songs in the romance, the total presentation of our romance may well have vacillated between precisely and loosely defined music.

Definitive answers to our questions about Jean Renart's use of music in *Guillaume de Dole* elude us. It does seem clear, however, that the author did a remarkable job in using songs as integral constituents of a story. If he was the first to combine song and narrative, he was a genius. Of course, as I have noted, he may not have been the first to invent this combination; instead, he may have followed, and perhaps expanded upon, a generations-old tradition. In any event, his contribution to the art of combining song and story was admirable, even though we can only speculate about the relation between the songs for which we know the melodies and the music that once may have existed but is now lost forever. If the romance of Lïenor's rose was ever performed aloud by someone who had learned the story from a book, this person may well have determined the manner in which the narrative was presented. Whether, in such a performance, the songs and the narrative were musically unified may have depended upon the improvisatory abilities of this person. Accordingly, the rendition by this person may have been a stage in the long and sometimes maligned evolution of opera and oratorio.

Finally, because the only extant copy of the romance seems to have been produced late in the thirteenth century, we must conclude that Jean Renart's autograph did not survive. The mere fact that this remote copy has no music may not mean much more than that the person for whom it was made had no interest in notated melodies. Perhaps that person was one of the few who had mastered the art of silent reading and had no need for any kind of melody. But even in that case, there is the question of how a reader perceived a poem for which he or she knew a melody. Seven or eight centuries ago, connoisseurs of chansons may have been as able as we are to hear a melody mentally—that is, without uttering a single sound.

Notes

1. Kenneth Levy, "On Gregorian Orality," *Journal of the American Musicological Society* 43 (1990): 185–227.

2. In one of the troubadour manuscripts, the layout of the texts of many songs was subject to curious erasure and revision before the music was entered; see Hendrik van der Werf and Gerald A. Bond, eds., *The Extant Troubadour Melodies* (Rochester, N.Y.: published by van der Werf, 1984), 15–16. The unique extant version of *Guillaume de Dole* is found in Vatican reg. 1725.

3. As I discuss later in the chapter, the verb *noter* reappears twice (vv. 1746 and 3400). In neither case does it refer to the act of writing down a melody; but it is unclear whether it refers to singing, playing, or both. For a detailed discussion of the meaning of this phrase, see Michel Zink, chapter 4 of the present volume.

4. *Thomas of Britain: Tristan,* ed. and trans. Stewart Gregory (New York: Garland, 1991). Citations are from this edition (translations by Nancy Vine Durling).

5. The *lai* in the Tristan stories has nothing in common with the narrative *lai* of Marie de France and others. In form, it also is very different from the *lais* and *descorts* that belong to the same family of songs as the *estampie,* the Latin sequence, and the German *Leich.* Instead, the *lais* sung by Tristan and Ysolt are strophic songs with from four to thirty strophes. In most instances, a strophe has four monorhyming verses, the music of which often has the form *AABC.*

6. See Tatiana Fotitch, *Les lais du Tristan en prose d'après le manuscrit de Vienne 2542,* music discussed and transcribed by Ruth Steiner (Munich: Wilhelm Fink, 1974). The first extensive discussion of these *lais* and their melodies appeared in Jean Maillard, "Histoire, évolution et esthétique du lai lyrique des origines à la fin du XIVe siècle," Ph.D. diss., University of Paris, 1952. Maillard modified some of his interpretations in 1969; see his "Lais avec notation dans le *Tristan* en prose," in *Mélanges offerts à Rita Lejeune* (Gembloux: Duculot, 1969), 2:1347–64. See also Christopher Page, *Voices and Instruments of the Middle Ages,* 92–107.

7. Both Marie de France's *Chevrefeuille* and the prose *Tristan* itself make reference to the *lai* of "Chevrefeuille." In Marie's text, Tristan is the sole author; in the prose *Tristan* the lovers are said to have composed the *lai* together, in private.

8. Unless otherwise specified, all numbered references to the songs refer to Appendix 2.

9. Dating of the *Tristran* proposed by Philippe Ménard, *Le roman de Tristan en prose,* 5 vols. (Geneva: Droz, 1987–92).

10. The topic is discussed in some detail by Gaston Paris, "Le cycle de la gageure."

11. Because we do not yet know what kind of vocalization was produced by primeval human beings, we do not even know whether we are correct in assuming that singing derived from speaking.

12. See, however, Zink's discussion of this fragmentation effect in chapter 4 of the present volume.

13. Karl Bartsch, *Altfranzösische Romanzen und Pastourellen* (Leipzig: Vogel,

1870). The work has been translated into French under the title *Romances et pastourelles françaises des XIIe et XIIIe siècles* (Darmstadt: Wissenschaftliche Buchgesellschaft, 1967). In his introduction, Bartsch notes that he intended to write an essay about these poems and their music; alas, that study does not seem to have been published.

14. Friedrich Gennrich published his theory several times, but it is most succinctly stated in "Rondeau," in *Die Musik in Geschichte und Gegenwart*, ed. Friedrich Blume, vol. 11 (Kassel: Bärenreiter, 1963), cols. 867–68. For a more extensive presentation, see Gennrich, *Rondeaux, Virelais, und Balladen*, vols. 1 and 2.

15. From Gennrich, *Rondeaux, Virelais, and Balladen*, vol. 1, numbers 2, 3, 7, 8, and 9. In his footnotes, Gennrich generally acknowledges his emendations; but in the presentation of the texts, he is rather frugal in his use of brackets.

16. Ibid., numbers 1–18.

17. Concerning the role that dance songs are supposed to have played in the evolution of French poetry, see Alfred Jeanroy, *Les origines de la poésie lyrique en France au moyen âge: Etudes de littérature française et comparée*, 1st ed. (Paris: Hachette, 1889), and Gaston Paris, "Les origines de la poésie lyrique en France," *Journal des Savants* (November 1891): 674–88; (December 1891): 729–42; (March 1892): 155–67; and (July 1892): 407–29.

18. Pierre Bec, *La lyrique française au moyen âge (XIIe–XIIIe siècles). Contribution à une typologie des genres poétiques médiévaux. Etudes et textes* (Paris: Picard, 1977), 1:221.

19. Eglal Doss-Quinby, *Les refrains chez les trouvères du XIIe au début du XVe* (Bern: Peter Lang, 1984), 160–80.

20. Ernst Rohloff, *Die Quellenhandschriften zum Musiktraktat des Johannes de Grocheio* (Leipzig: Deutscher Verlag für Musik, 1972), 132.

21. For a critical and large-scale examination of refrains, see Doss-Quinby, *Les refrains.*

22. For a list of such cases, see Nico H. J. van den Boogaard, *Rondeaux et refrains du XIIe siècle au début du XIVe. Collationement, introduction et notes. Bibliothèque française et romane, Série D* (Paris: Klincksieck, 1969).

23. See Bartsch, *Romances et pastourelles*, 2:80–88; some of these songs appear also in Bec, *La lyrique française*, 2:150–53. To these we may add the poem "Vos n'alez pas, si comme je faz" (van den Boogaard, *Rondeaux*, rondeau 185).

24. See chanson R-S 1509, which in its sole source is attributed to Baude de la Kakerie; text edition, Bartsch, *Romances et pastourelles*, 1:17; Bec, *La lyrique française*, 2: 156–58; text and music in Rudolf Meyer, Joseph Bédier, and Pierre Aubry, *La Chanson de "Bele Aelis"* (Paris, 1904). ("R-S" refers to G. *Reynaud's Bibliographie des altfranzösischen Liedes neu bearbeitet und ergänzt erster Teil*, ed. Hans Spanke [Leiden: Brill, c. 1955.])

25. On this point see also Hendrik van der Werf, *The Chansons of the Troubadours and Trouvères* (Utrecht: Oosthoek, 1972), 68, 153, and 157–59.

26. Jouglet once is called a "vïeleor" (v. 637). In a scene with the innkeeper's

daughter he brings his fiddle along (v. 1800), and in one of the joyful scenes preceding the tournament he puts the bow to the vielle (v. 2225).

27. Richard H. Hoppin, *Medieval Music* (New York: Norton, 1978), 280.

28. Charlotte Roederer, "The Middle Ages," in *Schirmer History of Music*, ed. Léonie Rosenstiel (London: Collier Macmillan, 1982), 74.

29. Jeremy Yudkin, *Music in Medieval Europe* (Englewood Cliffs, N.J.: Prentice Hall, 1989), 331.

30. See Hendrik van der Werf, "The Raison d'être of Medieval Music Manuscripts," appended to *The Oldest Extant Part Music and the Origin of Western Polyphony* (Rochester, N.Y.: published by the author, 1993), 173–204.

31. This difference of opinion may also be related to a lack of agreement on the meaning of the terms *troubadour* and *trouvère*. Some scholars, most of them musicologists, have used these terms for virtually all poet-composers of medieval songs. For several reasons, I follow those who use the terms in reference to poet-composers of songs about *fin' amors* (van der Werf, *The Chansons*, 13–14). Admittedly, it is almost impossible to be consistent in this approach, which also yields problems with past practices. For example, the count of Poitiers is often considered to have been the first troubadour; but if we give the title *troubadour* exclusively to poet-composers of songs about *fin' amors*, he does not fit the description.

32. See Gabriel Andrieu et al., *"Le roman de la rose ou de Guillaume de Dole" de Jean Renart*.

33. The line is, however, ambiguous. For discussion of the two possible meanings, see Boulton, chapter 3 of the present volume.

34. In the course of the romance, Jean Renart uses the term *valet* in reference to unnamed servants with very general assignments, but he uses it also to indicate the personal servant of a nobleman.

35. See, for example, Maria Dobozy, "The Many Faces of the Medieval Court Minstrel in England and Imperial Germany," in *In hôhem prise: A Festschrift in Honor of Ernst S. Dick*, ed. Winder McConnell (Göppingen: Kümmerle, 1989), 31–43.

36. See, in particular, Maureen Barry McCann Boulton's discussion in *The Song in the Story*, 26–35.

37. When searching for that answer, we may want to keep in mind that exactly the same questions have been raised about the role of the chorus in ancient Greek drama and about the respective functions of aria and recitative in many operas.

38. For a recent discussion of this distinction, see Paul Saenger, "Silent Reading: Its Impact on Late Medieval Script and Society," *Viator* 13 (1982): 367–414. See also Mary Carruthers, *The Book of Memory: A Study of Memory in Medieval Culture* (Cambridge: Cambridge University Press, 1990).

39. See, especially, Friedrich Gennrich, *Der musikalische Vortrag des altfranzösischen Chanson de geste* (Halle: Niemeyer, 1923).

40. "Idem etiam cantus debet in omnibus versibus reiterari" (Rohloff, *Grocheio*, 132).

41. Hendrik van der Werf, "Recitative Melodies in Trouvère Chansons," *Festschrift für Walter Wiora: zum 30 Dezember 1966*, ed. Ludwig Finscher and Christoph-Hellmuth Mahling (Kassel: Bärenreiter, 1967), 231–40.

42. For an interesting example, see the four extant versions of the melody for "Chanterai por mon courage" (R-S 21) ibid., 236–37.

43. Compare ibid., example 2, "Amours que porra devenir" (R-S 1402).

44. "Un petit devant le jour" (R-S 1995); the text with notes about textual variants appears in Bartsch, *Romances et pastourelles*, 2:35. This piece has music in six of its eight sources, three of which clearly were copied from one exemplar so that we have essentially four versions of this melody. The textual form of its strophe was varied more than was usual for the extant repertory of secular songs. In several instances, one manuscript has more verses for a given strophe than another source; so we may wonder if we should use the term *laisse* rather than *strophe* for its subdivisions. Perhaps we may conclude that those who transmitted this song by word (and pitch) of mouth experienced not only its melody but also its text as loosely defined.

APPENDIX 1

"Bele Aeliz": A Comparison of the Lecoy and Gennrich Editions

The numbers in this appendix refer to the numbered musical references in Appendix 2.

Lecoy	Gennrich
No. 4	
Main se leva bele Aeliz,	Main se leva bele Aeliz
dormez, jalous, ge vous en pri,	*mignotement la voi venir*
biau se para, miex se vesti	bien se para, mieus se vesti
desoz le raim.	desoz le raim.
Mignotement la voi venir	*Mignotement la voi venir*
cele que j'aim!	*cele que j'aim.*
No. 5	
Main se leva bele Aeliz	Main se leva bele Aeliz
mignotement la voi venir	*"Dormez, jalous, ge vous en pri!"*
bien se para, miex se vesti	bien se para, miex se vesti
en mai.	[pour caroler] en mai
Dormez, jalous, et ge m'en-	*"Dormez, jalous, ge vous en*
voiserai	*pri*
	et je m'envoiserai"

No. 9

Main se levoit Aaliz,
J'ai non Enmelot.
Biau se para et vesti
soz la roche Guion.
Cui lairai ge mes amors,
amie, s'a vos non?

Main se levoit Aaliz,
Cui lairai ge mes amors?
biau se para et vesti
soz la roche Guion.
Cui lairai ge mes amors,
amie, s'a vos non?

No. 10

Main se leva la bien fete Aeliz,
par ci passe li bruns, li biaus Robins.
Biau se para et plus biau se vesti.
Marchiez la foille et ge qieudrai la flor.
Par ci passe Robin li amorous,

Encor en est li herbages plus douz.

Main se leva la bien fete Aeliz
par ci passe li bruns, li biaus Robins.
Biau se para et plus biau se vesti
Marchiez la foille et ge qieudrai la flor.
par ci passe li bruns, li biaus Robins;
Encor en est li herbages plus douz.

No. 19

Aaliz main se leva.
Bon jor ait qui mon cuer a!
Biau se vesti e para,
Desoz l'aunoi.
Bon jor ait qui mon cuer a!
N'est pas o moi.

Aaliz main se leva.
Bon jor ait qui mon cuer a!
Biau se vesti e para,
Desoz l'aunoi.
Bon jor ait qui mon cuer a
N'est pas a moi.

APPENDIX 2

Survey of Lyric Texts and Other Musical References

Quotations are from Lecoy's edition.

THE GOOD LIFE OF EMPEROR CONRAD AND HIS COURTIERS: HUNTING AND OPEN-AIR MERRYMAKING

(1) vv. 291–92. Preceded by "Et les dames . . . et li chevalier . . . ainz chantent ceste chançonete":

> E non Deu, sire, se ne l'ai
> l'amor de lui, mar l'acointai.

Transition to next song: "Ainz que ceste fust dite tote / conmence uns autres [chevalier?] en la route."
(2) vv. 295–99:

> La jus, desoz la raime,
> einsi doit aler qui aime,
> clere i sourt la fontaine,
> ya!
> Einsi doit aler qui bele amie a.

Transition to next song: "Ainz qu'ele fust bien conmencie / une pucele . . . / . . . / en reconmence de rechief."
(3) vv. 304–5:

> Se mes amis m'a guerpie,
> por ce ne morrai ge mie.

Transition to next song: "Ainz que ceste fust bien fenie, / une dame sanz vilonie / . . . / haut et seri et cler conmence."
(4) vv. 310–15:

Main se leva bele Aeliz,
dormez, jalous, ge vos en pri,
biau se para, miex se vesti
desoz le raim.
Mignotement la voi venir,
cele que j'aim!

Transition to next song: "Et li gentiz quens de Savoie / chante ceste tote une voie."
(5) vv. 318–22:

Main se leva bele Aeliz,
mignotement la voi venir,
bien se para, miex se vesti,
en mai.
Dormez, jalous, et ge m'envoiserai.

Transition to next song: "Et li quens de Lucelebourc / qui amoit iloec par amor / une dame de grant solaz / qui chantoit de mains et de braz / miex que dame qui fu pieça, / por l'amor de li conmença."
(6) vv. 329–33:

C'est tot la gieus, el glaioloi,
tenez moi, dame, tenez moi!
Une fontaine i sordoit.
Aé!
Tenez moi, dame, por les maus d'amer.

Followed by "Si chantant en itel meniere."

vv. 365–66: "Et quant li quens de Sagremors / ot chanté une chançonete" (no text given).
v. 408: reference to "estrumenz" and "deduit."
v. 417: reference to "la noise des cors."
vv. 503–4: reference to "Vïeleors . . . vïelent par cez pavellons."

Dance in Front of the Tent in the Green Meadow

(7) vv. 513–19. Preceded by "Main a main, em pur lor biau cors, / devant le tref, en un pré vert, / les puceles et li vallet / ront la carole commenciee. / Une dame s'est avanciee, / vestue d'une cote en graine, / si chante ceste premeraine":

C'est tot la gieus, enmi les prez,
Vos ne sentez mie les maus d'amer!
Dames i vont por caroler,
remirez voz braz!
Vos ne sentez mie les maus d'amer
si com ge faz!

Transition to next song: "Uns vallez au prevost d'Espire / redit ceste, qui n'est pas pire."
(8) vv. 522–27:

C'est la jus desoz l'olive,
Robins enmaine s'amie.
La fontaine i sort serie
desouz l'olivete.
E non Deu! Robins enmaine
bele Mariete.

Transition to next song: "Ceste n'ot pas duré .III. tours / quant li filz au conte d'Aubours / qui mout amoit chevalerie / reconmencë a voiz serie."
(9) vv. 532–37:

Main se levoit Aaliz,
J'ai non Enmelot.
Biau se para et vesti
soz la roche Guion.
Cui lairai ge mes amors,
amie, s'a vos non?

Transition to next song: "Et la duchesse d'Osteriche, / . . . / . . . / reconmença ceste chançon."
(10) vv. 542–47:

Main se leva la bien fete Aeliz,
par ci passe li bruns, li biaus Robins.
Biau se para et plus biau se vesti.
Marchiez la foille et ge qieudrai la flor.
Par ci passe Robins li amorous,
Encor en est li herbages plus douz.

Followed by "Que de Robin que d'Aaliz, / tant ont chanté que jusq'as liz / ont fetes durer les caroles."

Jouglet Tells the Emperor of Guillaume de Dole and His Sister, the Fair Lïenor

vv. 637–38: Jouglet is called a "vïeleor."
(11) vv. 846–52. Preceded by "[Conrad and Jouglet] chantent ceste chançon / en l'onor monsegnor Gasçon":

Quant flors et glais et verdure s'esloigne,
que cil oisel n'osent un mot soner,
por la froidor chascuns crient et resoigne
tresq'au biau tens qu'il soloient chanter.
Et por ce chant, que nel puis oublier,
la bon' amor dont Dex joie me doigne,
car de li sont et vienent mi penser.

See Appendix 3, Melody 11.

(12) vv. 923–30. Preceded by "Por l'amor bele Lïenor, / dont il [the emperor] avoit el cuer le non, / a comencié ceste chançon":

Li noviaus tens et mais [et violete]
et roissignox me semont de chanter;
et mes fins cuers me fet d'une amorete
un doz present que ge n'os refuser.
Or m'en doint Dex en tel honor monter,
cele ou j'ai mis mon cuer et mon penser
q'entre mes bras la tenisse nuete
ainz q'alasse outremer.

See Appendix 3, Melody 12.

Nicole, the Emperor's Valet, with Guillaume, Lïenor, and Their Mother

vv. 1144–53: "'Dame . . . une chançon / car nos dites, si ferez bien.' / Ele chantoit sor tote rien / et si le fesoit volentiers. / 'Biaus filz, ce fu ça en arriers / que les dames et les roïnes / soloient fere lor cortines / et chanter les chançons d'istoire!' / 'Ha, ma tres douce dame, voire, / dites nos en. . .'."
(13) vv. 1159–66. Preceded by "[the mother] Lors conmença seri et cler":

Fille et la mere sieent a l'orfrois,
a un fil d'or i font orïeuls croiz.

Parla la mere qui le cuer ot cortois.
Tant bon'amor fist bele Aude en Doon!
"Aprenez, fille, a coudre et a filer,
et en l'orfrois orïex crois lever.
L'amor Doon vos covient oublier."
Tant bon'amor fist bele Aude en Doon!

Followed by "Quant el ot sa chançon chantee."

(14) vv. 1183–92. Preceded by "[Lïenor] Lors conmença ceste chançon":

Siet soi bele Aye as piez sa male maistre,
sor ses genouls un paile d'Engleterre,
et a un fil i fet coustures beles.
Hé! Hé! amors d'autre païs,
mon cuer avez et lïé et souspris.
Aval la face li courent chaudes lermes,

q'el est batue et au main et au vespre,
por ce qu'el aime soudoier d'autre terre.
Hé! Hé! amors d'autre païs,
mon cuer avez et lïé et souspris.

Followed by "Quant el ot chanté haut et bien."

(15) vv. 1204–16. Preceded by "[Lïenor] Lors conmença seri et haut":

La bele Doe siet au vent;
souz l'aubespin Doon atent.
Plaint et regrete tant forment
por son ami qui si vient lent:
"Diex, quel vassal a en Doon!
Diex, quel vassal! Dex, quel baron!
Ja n'amerai se Doon non."

"Com ez chargiez, com ez floriz!
A toi me mist plet mes amis,
mes il ne veut a moi venir . . .
. . . .
"Dex, quel vassal a en Doon!
Dex, quel vassal! Dex, quel baron!
Ja n'amerai se Doon non."

Followed by "Quant el ot ceste parfenie."

Guillaume and Nicole Arrive at Lodgings near Court

(16) vv. 1301–7. Preceded by "[Guillaume] . . . et ses conpegnons, / por le deduit des oisellons / que chascuns fet en son buisson, / de joie ont comencié cest son":

Lors que li jor sont lonc en mai,
m'est biaus doz chant d'oisel de lonc.
Et quant me sui partiz de la,
menbre mi d'une amor de lonc.
Vois de ça embruns et enclins
si que chans ne flors d'aubespin
ne mi val ne qu'ivers gelas.

See Appendix 3, Melody 16.

The Emperor's Longing

(17) vv. 1335–67. Preceded by "Cel jor fesoit chanter la suer / a un jougleor mout apert / qui chante cest vers de Gerbert":

Des que Fromonz au Veneor tença,
li [bons] prevoz qui trestot escouta
tant atendi que la noise abessa.
Sor l'arestuel de l'espié s'apuia.
Ou voit Fromont, pas ne le salua.
"Fromonz, dit il, ge sui de ciaus de la.
Gerbers mis sire, qui a vos m'envoia,
par moi vos mande, nel vos celerai ja,
que li envoies Foucon que ge voi la
et Rocelin, car amdeus pris les a.
Et s'il le nient, bien est qui provera
en totes cors, la on les trovera,
ou en la toe, se sauf conduit i a."
Fouqes rougi, Rocelins embruncha.
Mal soit de cel qui onques mot sona!
Li viex Fromonz forment s'en aïra.
"Par Deu! provos, qui ça vos envoia
mout belement de vos se delivra!
Se dont vos vit, ja mes ne vos verra,
et, s'il vos voit, ne vos reconoistra.

Encor me menbre, ne l'oublierai ja,
d'un guerredon que me feïstes ja:
li rois de France un cheval me dona
voiant vos oils, .c. livres li cousta;
vos l'oceïstes, q'ainc ne se remua.
A Geronvile, au pié dou pont de ça,
uns chevaliers un tel cop m'i dona
desor mon heaume que tot le m'enbarra;
prendre me fist au col de mon cheval."
Et dit Guirrez: "Fromont, entendez ça,
ce fu mes filz qui a vos s'acointa,
mort vos eüst, mes il vos espargna.
S'il a aaise, encor i referra . . .

An otherwise unknown excerpt from an epic about Gerbert de Metz, followed by "Que que cil chante de Fromont."

Nicole Reports to the Emperor

(18) vv. 1456–69. Preceded by "[the emperor] conmença . . . a chanter":

Loial amor qui en fin cuer s'est mise
n'en doit ja mes partir ne removoir
que la dolor qui destraint et justise
samble douçor quant l'en la puet avoir.
[Nus biens d'amors ne puet petit valoir,
ainz sont tuit douz qant on les aime et prise;
ce doit chascuns bien entendre et savoir.

Tels puet dire que la morz li est prise
por bien amer, qu'il ne dit mie voir,
fals amant sont kel font par false guise,
malvais loier lor en doint Dex avoir!]
Qui en porroit morir en bon espoir,
gariz seroit devant Deu au joïse,
por ce m'en lo quant plus me fet doloir.

See Appendix 3, Melody 18.

Guillaume with Jouglet and the Innkeeper's Daughter at the Inn

vv. 1560–62. The innkeeper's daughter: "Je vos has, / Juglet, que ne chantastes puis / quë entrastes dedenz cest huis."

vv. 1565–69: "Si dit: 'Or le me pardonez.' / 'Volentiers voir, se revenez / anquenuit o tot la vïele.' / 'Volentiers voir, ma damoisele, / se nos devons fere caroles'."
(19) vv. 1579–84. Preceded by "Tuit cil de la rue et de l'estre / le resgardent a grant mervelle, / quant Juglés li chante en l'orelle":

Aaliz main se leva.
Bon jor ait qui mon cuer a!
Biau se vesti et para,
Desoz l'aunoi.
Bon jor ait qui mon cuer a!
N'est pas o moi.

Guillaume with the Emperor

vv. 1746–48. After "li menesterel" have arrived, "Li uns note un, li autres el / cil conte ci de Perceval, / cil raconte de Rainceval."
vv. 1764–65: "Et Jouglés lor a dit chançons / et fabliaus, ne sai .III. ou .IIII."
(20) vv. 1769–76. Preceded by "L'empereres, por lui esbatre, / le reveut de tant conforter / qu'il veut ceste chançon chanter":

Mout me demeure
que n'oi chanter
la tourtre a l'entree d'esté
autresi com ge soloie;
mes une amor me desvoie
et tient esgaré
ou j'ai mon pensé,
en quel lieu que onques soie.

See Appendix 3, Melody 20.

v. 1782: "qu'il fet bon boivre aprés chançons."

Jouglet and Guillaume at the Inn

vv. 1799–1800: "Li conpegnon firent porter / Juglet a l'ostel la vïele."
vv. 1813–14: "Mout pres dusque vers mie nuit / ont entr'ex chanté et ragié."
(21) vv. 1846–51. Preceded by "[the innkeeper's daughter] a chantee / ovoec Jouglet en la vïele / ceste chançonete novele":

C'est la jus en la praele,
or ai bone amor novele!

Dras i gaoit Perronele.
Bien doi joie avoir:
Or ai bon'amor novele
a mon voloir.

Guillaume with the Emperor

(22) vv. 2027–35. Preceded by "Juglet vit devant lui ester, / si li fet la chançon chanter":

Contrel tens que voi frimer
les arbres et blanchoier,
m'est pris talenz de chanter;
si n'en eüsse mestier,
q'Amors me fet comparer
ce q'onques ne soi trichier
n'onqes ne poi endurer
a avoir faus cuer legier.
Por ce ai failli a amie.

See Appendix 3, Melody 22.

Before the Tournament

vv. 2182–83: "Mout avoit de hustin laienz / de hyraus, de menestereus."
vv. 2224–25: ". . . Juglés / qui met l'arçon sor la vïele."
(23) vv. 2235–94. Preceded by "Uns bachelers de Normendie / chevauchoit la grande chaucie, / conmença cesti a chanter, / si la fist Jouglet vïeler":

Bele Aiglentine en roial chamberine
devant sa dame cousoit une chemise
. . . .
Ainc n'en sot mot quant bone amor l'atise.
Or orrez ja
conment la bele Aiglentine esploita.

Devant sa dame cousoit et si tailloit;
mes ne coust mie si com coudre soloit:
el s'entr'oublie, si se point en son doit.
La soe mere mout tost s'en aperçoit.
Or orrez ja
conment [la bele Aiglentine esploita].

"Bele Aiglentine, deffublez vo sorcot,
. . . .
Je voil veoir desoz vostre gent cors.
—Non ferai, dame, la froidure est la morz."
Or orrez ja
[conment la bele Aiglentine esploita.]

—"Bele Aiglantine, q'avez a empirier
que si vos voi palir et engroissier?
. . . .
. . . .
[Or orrez ja
conment la bele Aiglentine esploita.]

—"Ma douce dame, ne le vos pui noier:
jë ai amé un cortois soudoier,
le preu Henri, qui tant fet a proisier.
S'onqes m'amastes, aiez de moi pitié."
Or orrez ja
conment [la bele Aiglentine esploita.]

—"Bele Aiglentine, vos prendra il Henris?
—Ne sai voir, dame, car onqes ne li quis."
. . . .
. . . .
[Or orrez ja
conment la bele Aiglentine esploita.]

—"Bele Aiglentine, or vos tornez de ci,
tot ce li dites que ge li mant Henri
s'il vos prendra ou vos lera einsi.
—Volentiers, dame," la bele respondi.
Or orrez ja
[Conment la bele Aiglentine esploita.]

Bele Aiglentine s'est tornee de ci,
et est venue droit a l'ostel Henri.
Li quens Henris se gisoit en son lit.
Or orrez ja que la bele li dit.

Or orrez ja
[Conment la bele Aiglentine esploita.]

—"Sire Henri, velliez vos ou dormez?
Ja vos requiert Aiglentine au vis cler
se la prendrez a moullier et a per.
—Oïl, dit il, onc joie n'oi mes tel."
Or orrez ja
[conment la bele Aiglentine esploita.]

Oit le Henris, mout joianz en devint.
Il fet monter chevalier trusq'a .xx.,
si enporta la bele en son païs
et espousa, riche contesse en fist.
Grant joie en a
li quens Henris quant bele Aiglentine a.

vv. 2295–96: "O flaütes et o vïeles, / por veoir les joustes noveles."
vv. 2348–49: "Vïeles i sonent si cler, / et fleütes et estrument"
(24) vv. 2369–74. Preceded by "Li biax Galerans de Lamborc / . . . / ceste chançon i comença":

La jus desouz l'olive,
ne vos repentez mie,
fontaine i sourt serie:
Puceles, carolez!
Ne vos repentez mie
de loiaument amer.

Transition to next song: "Ceste n'a pas .III. tors duré / quant li fils le conte de Tré, / qui mout s'en sot bien entremetre, / conmença ceste chançonete."
(25) vv. 2379–85:

Mauberjon s'est main levee;
Dioree,
buer i vig.
A la fontaine est alee,
or en ai dol.
Diex! Diex! or demeure
Mauberjons a l'eve trop.

Transition to next song: "Un vallez le conte de Los, / qui de chanter avoit le los, / chanta aprés celui de Tré."
(26) vv. 2389–91:

Renaus et s'amie chevauche par un pré,
tote nuit chevauche jusq'au jor cler.
Ja n'avrai mes joie de vos amer . . .

(27) vv. 2398–404. Preceded by "Un menesterel de l'Empere / li dit la chançon de son frere":

De Renaut de Mousson
et de son frere Hugon,
et de ses conpaignons
qui donent les grans dons,
veult fere une chançon
Jordains, li viex bordons,
ou tens de moustoisons.

Followed by "Mout i ot parlé de Jordain."

vv. 2441–43: "et quant il ont oï la messe, / q'uns chapelains d'une abeesse / lor a mout bel chantee et dite / en l'onor de Saint Esperite."
vv. 2462–63: "menesterex et estrumenz / et flaütes i font grant noise."
(28) vv. 2514–18 (compare no. 2). Preceded by "Et Jouglés chante la chançon / entre lui et Aigret de Grame":

La gieus desoz la raime,
einsi doit aler qui aime,
clere i sort la fontaine,
ya!
Einsi doit aler qui bele amie a.

Transition to next song: "Ainz que ceste chançon faussist, / dui damoisel cui mout bien sist, / neveu au segnor de Dinant, / reconmencent el chief devant."
(29) vv. 2523–27:

Sor la rive de mer,
mignotement alez!
Un baut i ot levez.
Mignoz sui.
Mignotement alez,
dui et dui!

vv. 2554–55: "et voit la joie et oit les sons / des flaütes et des vïeles."
vv. 2640–41: "A flaütes et a freteles / l'ont einsi mené jusq'au renc."

THE EMPEROR TELLS GUILLAUME OF HIS LOVE FOR LÏENOR

(30) vv. 3107–14. Preceded by "Fet li rois: 'Savez vos cest vers?'"

"Mout est fouls, que que nus die,
qui cuide que aillors bé,
car miex aim son escondire
q'autre m'eüst cuer doné.
Et maintes gens serf [en gré],
felons plains de tricherie.
Por ce faz lor volenté
que ge cuit chascuns la voie."

(31) vv. 3180–95. Preceded by "Que qu'il sont amdui acosté / as fenestres vers un vergier / ou il oient aprés mengier / des oisillons les chans divers, / l'emperere en fist lués cez vers":

Quant de la foelle espoissent li vergier,
que l'erbe est vert et la rose espanie,
et au matin oi le chant conmencier
dou roissignol qui par le bois s'escrie,
lors ne me sai vers Amors consellier,
car onques n'oi d'autre richece envie,
fors que d'amors,
ne riens [fors li] ne m'en puet fere aïe.

Ja fine amors ne sera sanz torment,
que losengier en ont corrouz et ire.
Ne ge ne puis servir a son talent,
qu'ele me voelle a son servise eslire.
Je soufferrai les faus diz de la gent
qui n'ont pooir, sanz plus, fors de mesdire
de bone amor,
ne riens fors li ne me puet geter d'ire.

Followed by "Cez .II. vers li fist pechiez dire."

THE EMPEROR THINKING OF LÏENOR

(32) vv. 3403–7. Preceded by "[the minstrel Cupelin] li notoit chascun matin":

Quant ge li donai le blanc peliçon,
ele amast mout miex le biau Tierrion.
Hé! Hé! ge disoie bien
que la pastorele ne m'en feroit rien.

(33) vv. 3419–30. Preceded by "Cest vers de bele Marguerite, / qui si bel se paie et aquite / de la chançonete novele, / li fet chanter en la vïele":

Cele d'Oisseri
ne met en oubli
que n'aille au cembel.
Tant a bien en li
que mout embeli
le gieu soz l'ormel.
En son chief ot chapel
de roses fres novel.
Face ot fresche, colorie,
vairs oils, cler vis simple et bel.
Por les autres fere envie
i porta maint bel joël.

The Emperor after Learning of Lïenor's Loss of Virtue

(34) vv. 3625–31. Preceded by "Des bons vers mon segnor Gasson / li sovient [i.e., the emperor] . . . / . . . / . . . / Un petit le conmence en haut":

Je di que c'est granz folie
d'encerchier ne d'esprover
ne sa moullier ne s'amie
tant com l'en la veut amer,
ainz s'en doit on bien garder
d'encerchier par jalousie
ce qu'en n'i voudroit trover.

See Appendix 3, Melody 34.

(35) vv. 3751–59. Preceded by "[the emperor] Sospirant, plorant et plains d'ire, / . . . / se plaint es vers de sa chançon":

Por quel forfet ne por quel ochoison
m'avez, Amors, si de vos esloignié
que de vos n'ai secors ne garison
ne ge ne truis qui de moi ait pitié?
Malement ai mon servise emploié

c'onqes de vos ne me vint se max non.
[N'ancor, Amors, ne vos ai reprochié
mon servise], mes ore m'en plaig gié,
et di que mort m'avez sanz ochoison.

See Appendix 3, Melody 35.

(36) vv. 3883–98. Preceded by "Des bons vers celui de Sabloeil, / mon segnor Renaut, li sovint [i.e., the emperor]; / de grant cortoisie li vint / qu'il les conmença a chanter / por sa dolor reconforter":

Ja de chanter en ma vie
ne quier mes avoir corage,
ainz voeil miex qu'Amors m'ocie
por fere son grant domage;
car ja mes si finement
n'iert amee ne servie.
Por c'en chasti tote gent,
q'el m'a mort et li traïe.

Las! j'ai dit par ma folie,
ce sai de voir, grant outrage;
mes a mon cuer prist envie
d'estre legier et volage.
A! Dame, si m'en repent.
Mes cil a tart merci crie
qui atent tant que il pent,
por ce ai la mort deservie.

See Appendix 3, Melody 36.

(37) vv. 4127–40. Preceded by "[the emperor, Guillaume, and Jouglet] s'oïrent chanter un vallet / la bone chançon le Vidame / de Chartres. . . . / . . . / miex ne dist cest vers ne cest chant":

Quant la sesons del douz tens s'asseüre
que biaus estez se raferme et esclaire,
et tote riens a sa droite nature
vient et retret, se n'est trop de mal aire,
chanter m'estuet, car plus ne m'en puis taire,
por conforter ma cruel aventure
qui m'est tornee a grant mesaventure.

A ma dolor n'a mestier coverture,
si sui sospris que ne m'en puis retrere.
Mar acointai sa tres douce feture
por tel dolor ne por tel mal atrere,
qui ce me fet que nus ne puet deffere,
fors ses fins cuers dont vers moi est si dure
q'a la mort sui, se longuement m'i dure!

See Appendix 3, Melody 37.

Followed by "Fet li rois: 'Juglet, a droiture / fu ciz vers fet por moi sanz doute'."

THE MAY FESTIVAL

(38) vv. 4164–69. Preceded by "Et dui damoisel vont chantant":

Tout la gieus, sor rive mer,
conpaignon, or dou chanter!
Dames i ont bauz levez,
mout ai le cuer gai.
Conpaignon, or dou chanter
en l'onor de mai!

Followed by "Quant il l'orent bien porchanté."

THE ASSEMBLY IN MAINZ

vv. 4563–64: "l'en i chantë et sons et lais, / li menestrel de mainte terre / qui erent venu por aquerre."
(39) vv. 4568–83. Preceded by "De Troies [the minstrel?] la Bele Doete / i chantoit ceste chançonete":

Quant revient la sesons
que l'erbe reverdoie,
que droiz est et resons
que l'en deduire doie,
seuls aloie,
si pensoie
as noviaus sons
que ge soloie.
Touse gaie
o ses moutons

trovai sanz compegnons,
ou s'esbanoie
a ses chançons.
Gente ert sa façons;
chevex que venz baloie
avoit sorez et blons.

Transition to next song: "Et uns autres [minstrel?] de Chaalons, / qui ot vestu uns biaus dras vers, / rechante d'autre part cest vers."
(40) vv. 4587–93:

Amours a non ciz maus qui me tormente;
mes n'est pas teuls com les autres genz l'ont,
s'est bien resons que li miens cuers s'en sente,
qui set mout bien coment on l'en respont.
Et ge di: "Las! mi mal, quant fineront?"
Ne ja Jhesus fenir ne mes consente,
s'aprés les mauls li bien gregnor n'en sont.

Followed by "D'une chambre ou li baron sont / oï l'empereres cest vers."

Lïenor at Court

(41) vv. 4653–59. Preceded by "Cil chanteor ne lor chançon / ne la poënt esleecier; / si oï ele [Lïenor] conmencier / iceste chançon auvrignace. / Se ne fust cil . . . / qui la cuida desloiauter, / mout seüst cest vers chanter."

Bele m'est la voiz altane
del roissillol el pascor
que foelle est verz, blanche flor,
et l'erbe nest en la sane
dont raverdissent cil vergier.
Et joi m'avroit tel mestier
que cors me garist et sane.

See Appendix 3, Melody 41.

Lïenor and the Emperor Reconciled

(42) vv. 5106–11. Preceded by "De la joie qui l'en [the emperor] rehete / li est ciz chans dou cuer volez":

Que demandez vos
quant vos m'avez?
Que demandez vos?

dont ne m'avez vos?
—Ge ne demant rien
se vos m'amez bien.

Transition to next song: "Et li autre en ont tuit chanté."
(43) vv. 5113–15:

Tendez tuit voz mains a la flor d'esté,
a la flor de liz,
por Deu, tendez i!

Followed by "Ce fu *Te Deum laudamus.*"

GUILLAUME REJOINS THE COURT

(44) vv. 5188–207. Preceded by "uns niés l'envesque dou Liege, / . . . / conmença cesti a chanter":

Or vienent Pasques les beles en avril.
Florissent bois, cil pré sont raverdi,
cez douces eves retraient a lor fil,
cil oisel chantent au soir et au matin.
Qui amors a, nes doit metre en oubli.
Sovent i doit et aler et venir.
. . . .
. . . .
Ja s'entr'amoient Aigline et li quens Guis.
Guis aime Aigline, Aigline aime Guion.

Souz un chastel q'en apele Biaucler,
en mout poi d'eure i ot granz bauz levez.
Cez damoiseles i vont por caroler,
cil escuier i vont por bohorder,
cil chevalier i vont por esgarder;
vont i cez dames por lor cors deporter.
La bele Aigline s'i est fete mener,
si ot vestu un bliaut de cendel
qui granz .II. aunes traïnoit par les prez.
Guis aime Aigline, Aigline aime Guion.

Transition to next song: "Ceste n'est pas tote chantee, / uns chevaliers de la contree / dou parage de Danmartin / conmença cest son poitevin."

(45) vv. 5212–27:

Quant voi l'aloete moder
de goi ses ales contre el rai,
que s'oblie et lesse cader
par la douçor q'el cor li vai,
ensi grant envie m'est pris
de ce que voi . . .
Miravile est que n'is del sens
ne coir dont desier non fon.

Ha! las! Tant cuidoie savoir
d'amor, et point n'en sai!
Pas onc d'amar non pou tenir
celi dont ja prou nen avrai.
Tol mei lou cor et tol meismes
et soi meesme et tol le mon,
et por tant el ne m'oste rent
fors desier et cor volon.

See Appendix 3, Melody 45.
Transition to next song: "Quant cez .II. [strophes?] furent bien fenies, / des bons vers Gautier de Sagnies / resovint un bon bacheler, / si les comença a chanter."
(46) vv. 5232–52:

Lors que florist la bruiere,
que voi prez raverdoier,
que chantent en lor maniere
cil oisillon el ramier,
lors sospir en mon corage,
quant cele me fet irier
vers qui ma longue proiere
ne m'i pot avoir mestier.

Celi aim d'amor certaine
dont j'ai le cuer d'ire plain.
Las! ce m'i fet estre en paine
dont j'ai le cuer d'ire plain.

Trop vilainement foloie
qui ce qu'il aime ne crient.
Et qui d'amors se cointoie,
sachiez qu'il n'aime nïent.
Amors doit estre si coie
la ou ele va et vient
que nuls n'en ait duel ne joie,
se cil non qui la maintient.

Celi aim . . .

After the Wedding

(47) vv. 5427–34. Preceded by "Uns chanterres de vers Touart, / . . . / pensoit mout poi de son anui; / ausi fesoient ne sai quant / qui s'en vont par laienz chantant":

C'est la gieus, la gieus, q'en dit en ces prez.
Vos ne vendrez mie, dames, caroler.
La bele Aeliz i vet por joer
souz la vert olive.
Vos ne vendrez mie caroler es prez,
que vos n'amez mie.
G'i doi bien aler et bien caroler
car j'ai bele amie.

(48) vv. 5440–45. Preceded by "refet il lués, / qui vaut un mauvés entremés":

C'est la gieus, en mi les prez,
j'ai amors a ma volenté,
dames i ont baus levez,
gari m'ont mi oel.
J'ai amors a ma volenté
teles com ge voel.

APPENDIX 3

Melodies

Hendrik van der Werf

In general, the combination of song-texts from *Guillaume de Dole* with melodies taken from a typical thirteenth-century song collection posed few problems. In a few instances, however, the number of syllables did not match the number of notes and note groups; in order to make the two fit, either the text or the melody had to be adjusted. I chose the former alternative, but I suspect that close scrutiny of the song-texts in *Guillaume de Dole* (especially the Occitan ones) will yield significant information about oral tradition. In the following examples, the texts of the French songs are reproduced essentially as edited by Lecoy, but the three Occitan ones (16, 41, and 45) have been modified. In *Guillaume de Dole,* the Occitan songs are given in a Frenchified version of the original language, but not all passages fared well in the transmission from South to North. I have resolved the resulting problems by consulting other sources in which the texts appear in similarly Frenchified readings.

In the thirteenth-century *chansonniers,* the relation between text and melody is generally unambiguous. A group of notes printed in immediate succession in the transcription represents notes that, in the manuscript, are written as one notational symbol. Sharp and flat signs (represented with # and b, respectively) are given where they occur in the manuscript from which the melody is copied; an arrow marks the beginning of a new staff in the manuscript.

In the captions for each song, the abbreviation "R-S" refers to the song's number in Hans Spanke, *G. Raynaud's Bibliographie des altfranzösischen Liedes* (Leiden: E. J. Brill, ca. 1955). The abbreviation "P-C" refers to the song's number in Alfred Pillet and Henry Carstens, *Bibliographie der Troubadours* (Halle, 1933). These publications contain references to a song's sources and editions.

Short titles in captions refer to *Trouvères-Melodien I, Monumenta monodica medii aevi II,* ed. Hendrik van der Werf (Kassel: Bärenreiter, 1977), and *The Extant Troubadour Melodies,* ed. Hendrik van der Werf and Gerald A. Bond (published by van der Werf, 1984).

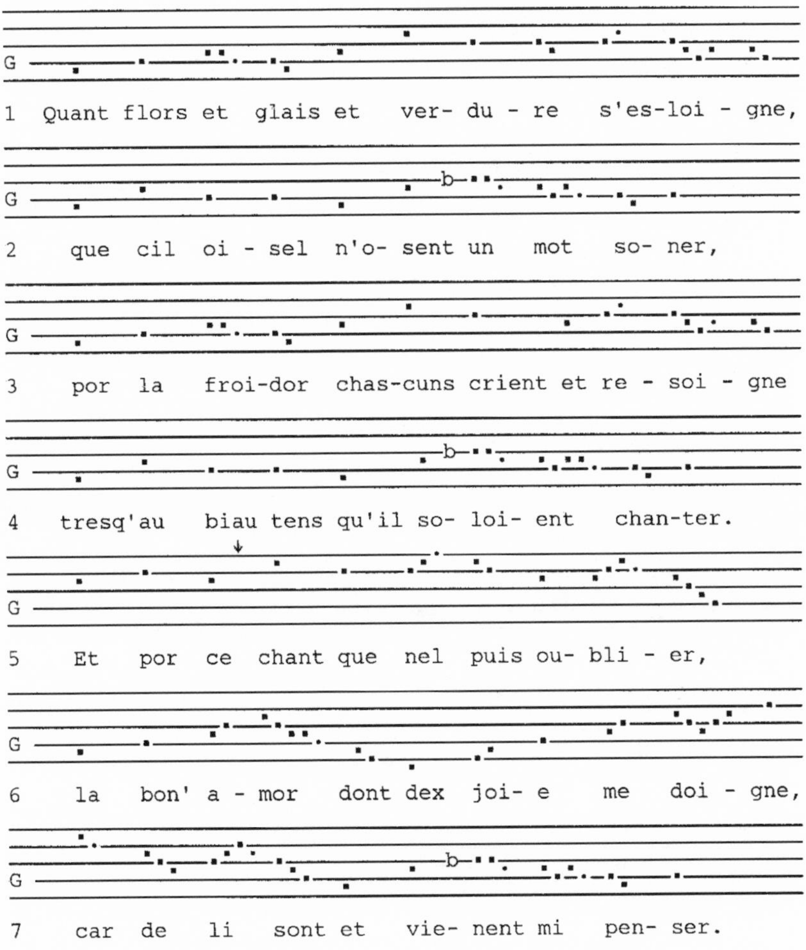

1 Quant flors et glais et ver- du - re s'es-loi - gne,

2 que cil oi - sel n'o- sent un mot so- ner,

3 por la froi-dor chas-cuns crient et re - soi - gne

4 tresq'au biau tens qu'il so- loi- ent chan-ter.

5 Et por ce chant que nel puis ou- bli - er,

6 la bon' a - mor dont dex joi- e me doi - gne,

7 car de li sont et vie- nent mi pen- ser.

Melody 11. "Quant flors et glais et verdure s'esloigne," vv. 846–52 (R-S 1779). According to MS. Paris, B.N. fr. 844, fol. 37d. In most sources, this song is attributed to Gace Brulé. For all extant versions see *Trouvères-Melodien I*, 520–26.

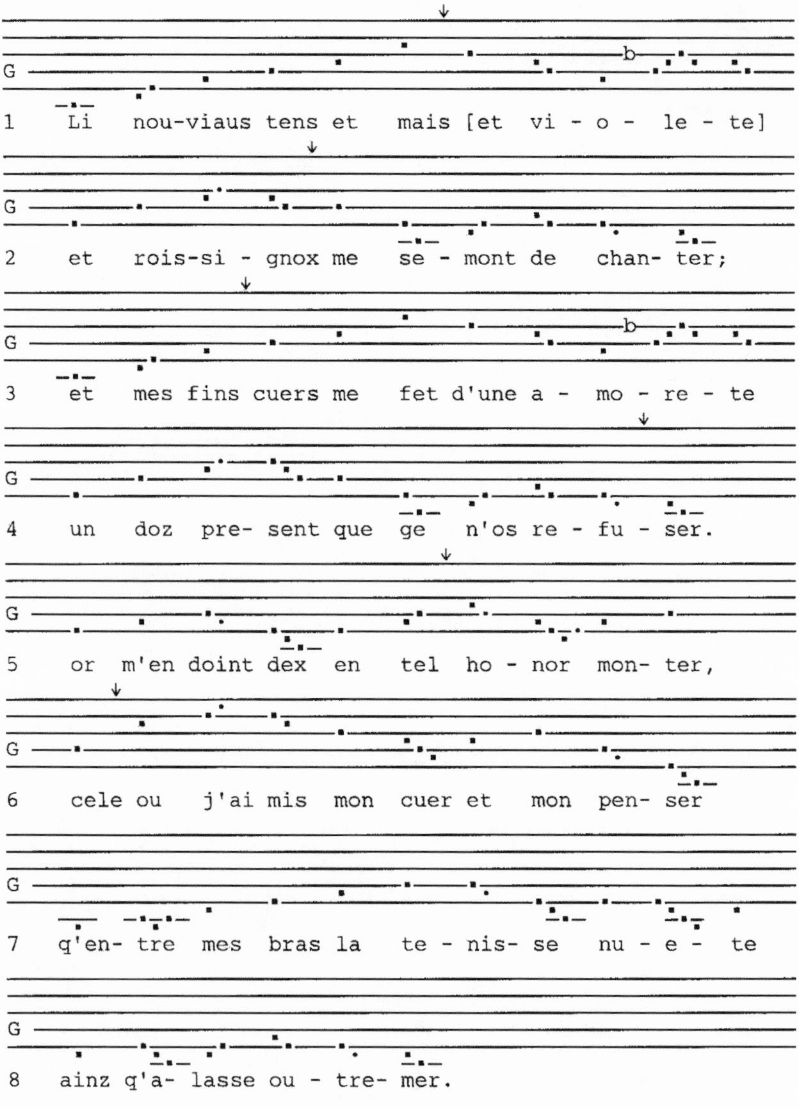

1 Li nou-viaus tens et mais [et vi - o - le - te]

2 et rois-si - gnox me se - mont de chan- ter;

3 et mes fins cuers me fet d'une a - mo - re - te

4 un doz pre- sent que ge n'os re - fu - ser.

5 or m'en doint dex en tel ho - nor mon- ter,

6 cele ou j'ai mis mon cuer et mon pen- ser

7 q'en- tre mes bras la te - nis- se nu - e - te

8 ainz q'a- lasse ou - tre- mer.

Melody 12. "Li noviaus tens et mais," vv. 923–30 (R-S 986). According to MS. Paris, B.N. fr. 844, fol. 53; for all extant versions, see *Trouvères-Melodien I*, 243–50. In most sources, this song is attributed to the Chastelain de Coucy.

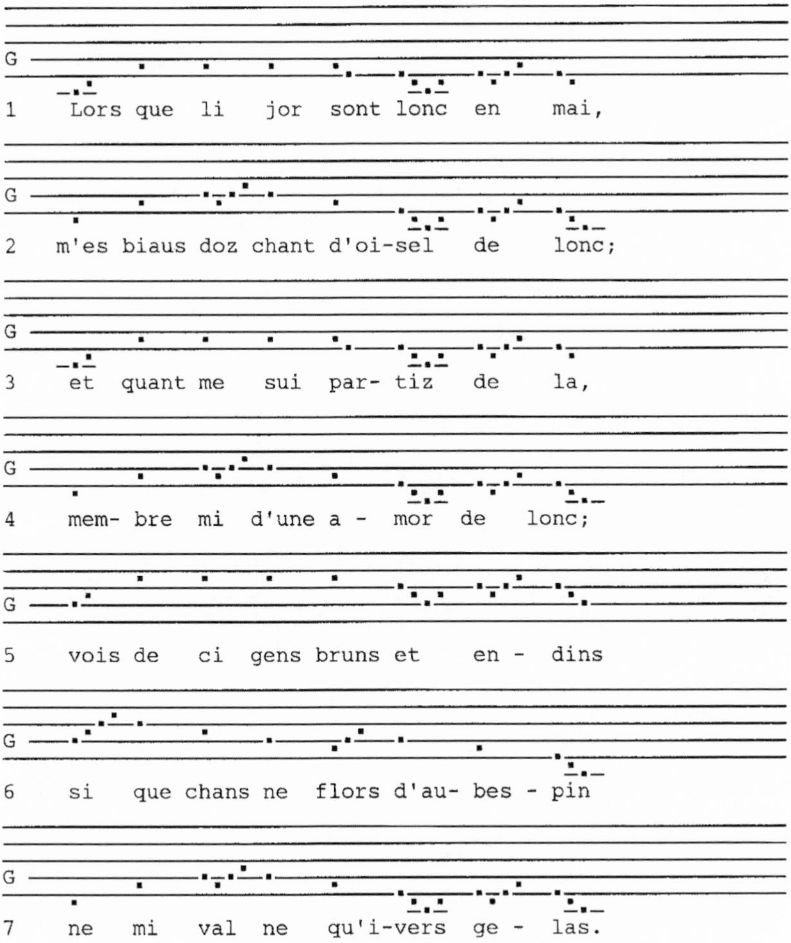

1 Lors que li jor sont lonc en mai,

2 m'es biaus doz chant d'oi-sel de lonc;

3 et quant me sui par- tiz de la,

4 mem- bre mi d'une a - mor de lonc;

5 vois de ci gens bruns et en - dins

6 si que chans ne flors d'au- bes - pin

7 ne mi val ne qu'i-vers ge - las.

Melody 16. "Lors que li jor sont lonc en mai," vv. 1301–7 (P-C 262, 2). According to MS. Paris, B.N. fr. 22543, fol. 63; for other versions, see *Troubadour Melodies,* 215*-219*. In Occitan sources this song is attributed to Jaufre Rudel.

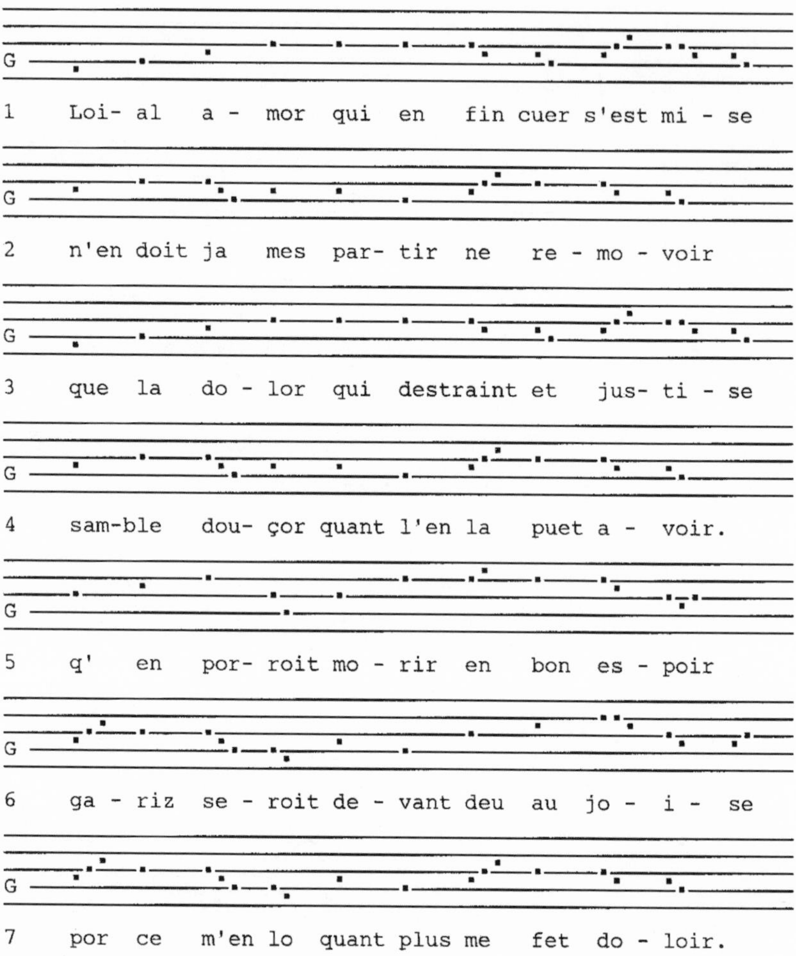

1 Loi- al a - mor qui en fin cuer s'est mi - se

2 n'en doit ja mes par- tir ne re - mo - voir

3 que la do - lor qui destraint et jus- ti - se

4 sam-ble dou- çor quant l'en la puet a - voir.

5 q' en por- roit mo - rir en bon es - poir

6 ga - riz se - roit de - vant deu au jo - i - se

7 por ce m'en lo quant plus me fet do - loir.

Melody 18. "Loial amor qui en fin cuer s'est mise," vv. 1456–69 (R-S 1635). According to MS. Paris, B.N. fr. 20050, fol. 19. With the exception of *Guillaume de Dole,* the song is anonymous in all of its sources.

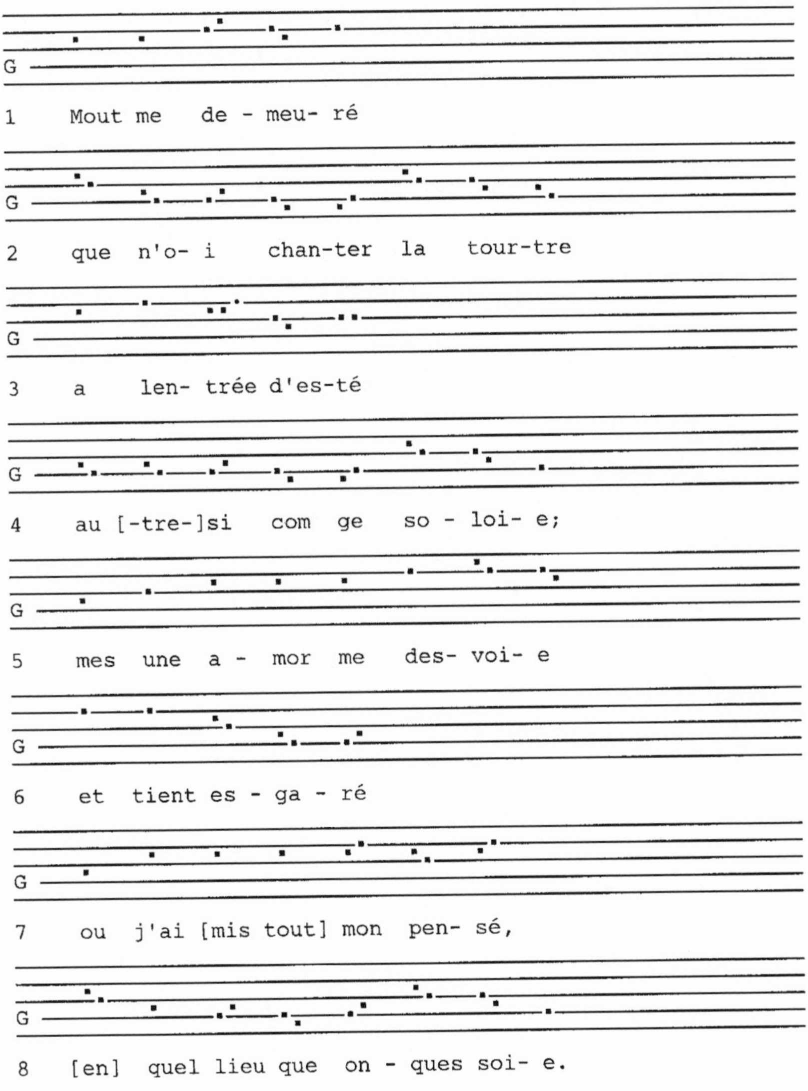

Mout me de - meu- ré
que n'o- i chan-ter la tour-tre
a len- trée d'es-té
au [-tre-]si com ge so - loi- e;
mes une a - mor me des- voi- e
et tient es - ga - ré
ou j'ai [mis tout] mon pen- sé,
[en] quel lieu que on - ques soi- e.

Melody 20. "Mout me demeure," vv. 1769–76 (R-S 420). According to MS. Paris, B.N. fr. 845, fol. 18. The song is anonymous in all of its sources.

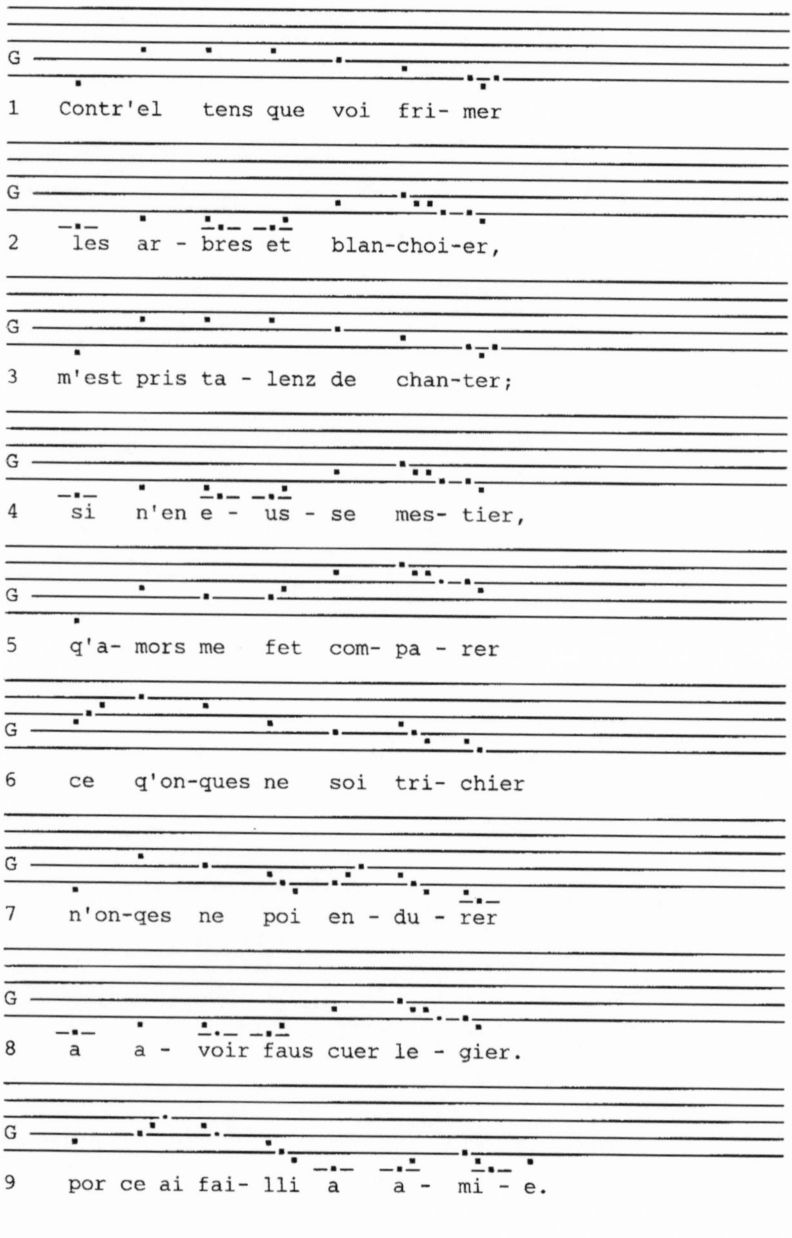

1 Contr'el tens que voi fri- mer

2 les ar - bres et blan-choi-er,

3 m'est pris ta - lenz de chan-ter;

4 si n'en e - us - se mes- tier,

5 q'a- mors me fet com- pa - rer

6 ce q'on-ques ne soi tri- chier

7 n'on-qes ne poi en - du - rer

8 a a - voir faus cuer le - gier.

9 por ce ai fai- lli a a - mi - e.

Melody 22. "Contr'el tens que voi frimer," vv. 2027–35 (R-S 857). According to MS. Paris, B.N. fr. 844, fol. 23; for all extant versions, see *Trouvères-Melodien I,* 429–37. In most sources, this song is attributed to Gace Brulé.

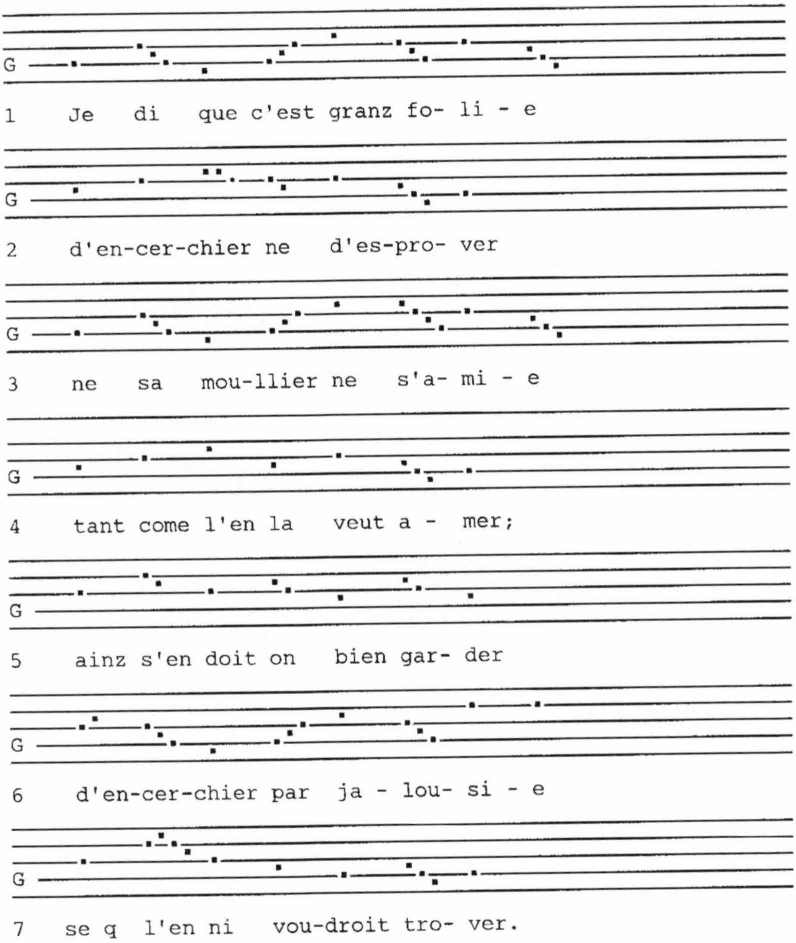

G

1 Je di que c'est granz fo- li - e

G

2 d'en-cer-chier ne d'es-pro- ver

G

3 ne sa mou-llier ne s'a- mi - e

G

4 tant come l'en la veut a - mer;

G

5 ainz s'en doit on bien gar- der

G

6 d'en-cer-chier par ja - lou- si - e

G

7 se q l'en ni vou-droit tro- ver.

Melody 34. "Je di que c'est granz folie," vv. 3625–31 (R-S 1232). According to MS. Paris, B.N. fr. 12615, fol. 109. Other sources have the above text as the second strophe of "Bien me cuidai toute ma vie," for which we have several conflicting attributions.

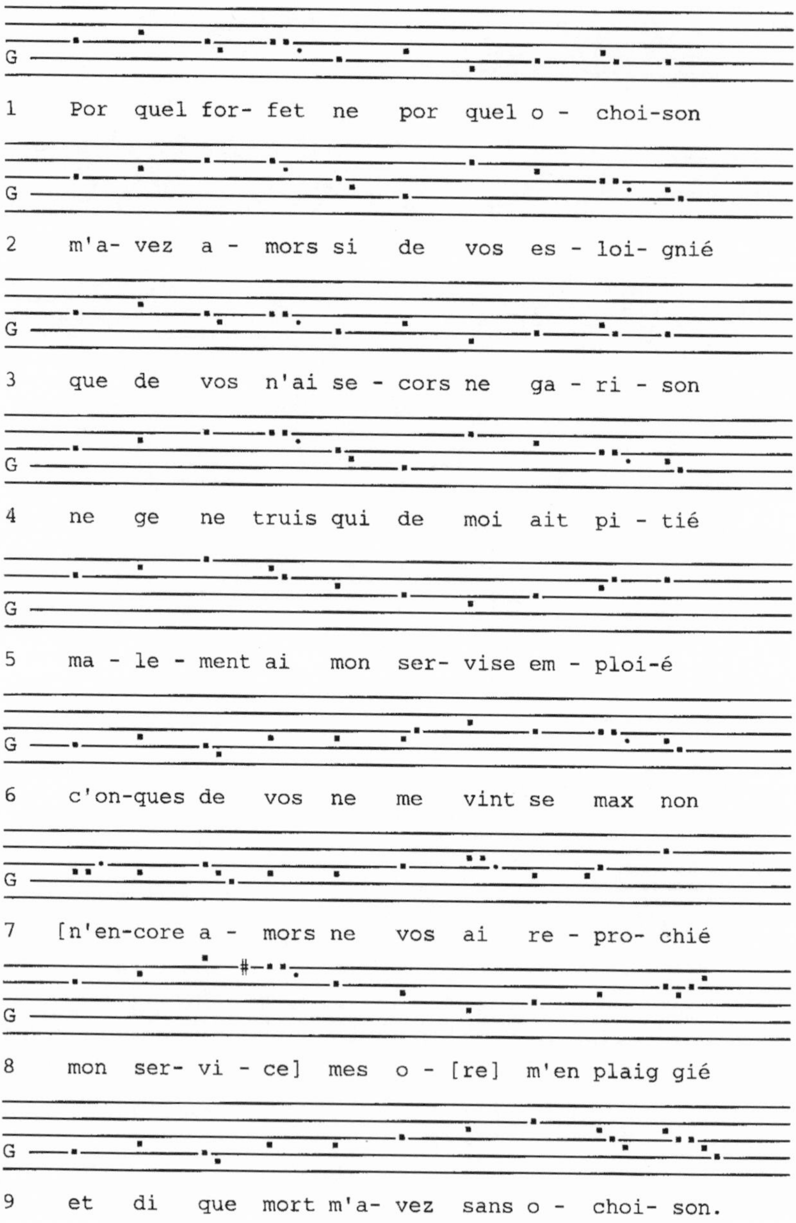

1 Por quel for- fet ne por quel o - choi-son

2 m'a- vez a - mors si de vos es - loi- gnié

3 que de vos n'ai se - cors ne ga - ri - son

4 ne ge ne truis qui de moi ait pi - tié

5 ma - le - ment ai mon ser- vise em - ploi-é

6 c'on-ques de vos ne me vint se max non

7 [n'en-core a - mors ne vos ai re - pro- chié

8 mon ser- vi - ce] mes o - [re] m'en plaig gié

9 et di que mort m'a- vez sans o - choi- son.

Melody 35. "Por quel forfet ne por quel ochoison," vv. 3751–59 (R-S 18876a). According to MS. Paris, B.N. fr. 844, fol. 170; many more versions of this song are extant, with conflicting attributions.

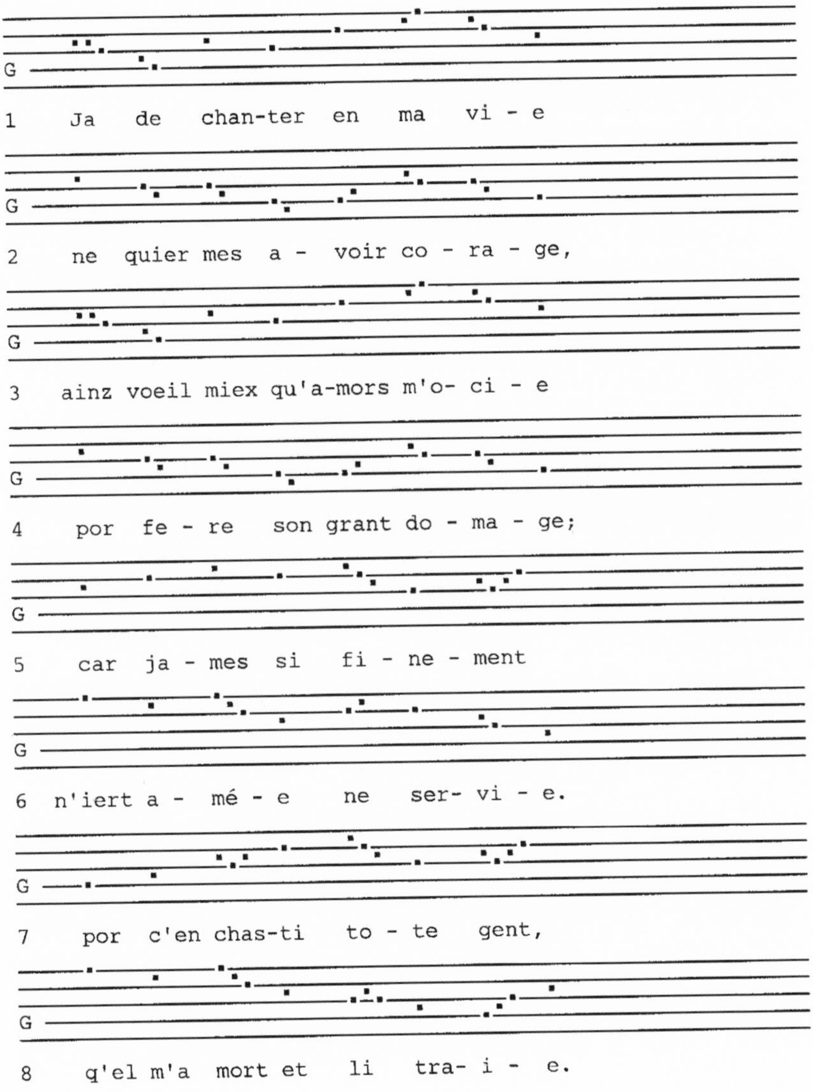

1 Ja de chan-ter en ma vi - e

2 ne quier mes a - voir co - ra - ge,

3 ainz voeil miex qu'a-mors m'o- ci - e

4 por fe - re son grant do - ma - ge;

5 car ja - mes si fi - ne - ment

6 n'iert a - mé - e ne ser- vi - e.

7 por c'en chas-ti to - te gent,

8 q'el m'a mort et li tra- i - e.

Melody 36. "Ja de chanter en ma vie," vv. 3883–90 (R-S 1229). According to MS. Paris, B.N. fr. 845, fol. 144. Many more versions of this song are extant, with conflicting attributions.

G
1 Quant la se - sons del douz tens s'as-se- u - re,
G
2 que biaus es - tez se ra- ferme et es - clai - re,
G
3 et to - te riens a sa droi-te na- tu - re
G
4 vient et re - tret se n'est trop de mal ai - re,
G
5 chan-ter m'es-tuet car plus ne m'en puis tai - re,
G
6 por con- for- ter ma cru- el a - ven- tu - re
G
7 qui m'est tor- née a grant mes- a - ven- tu - re.

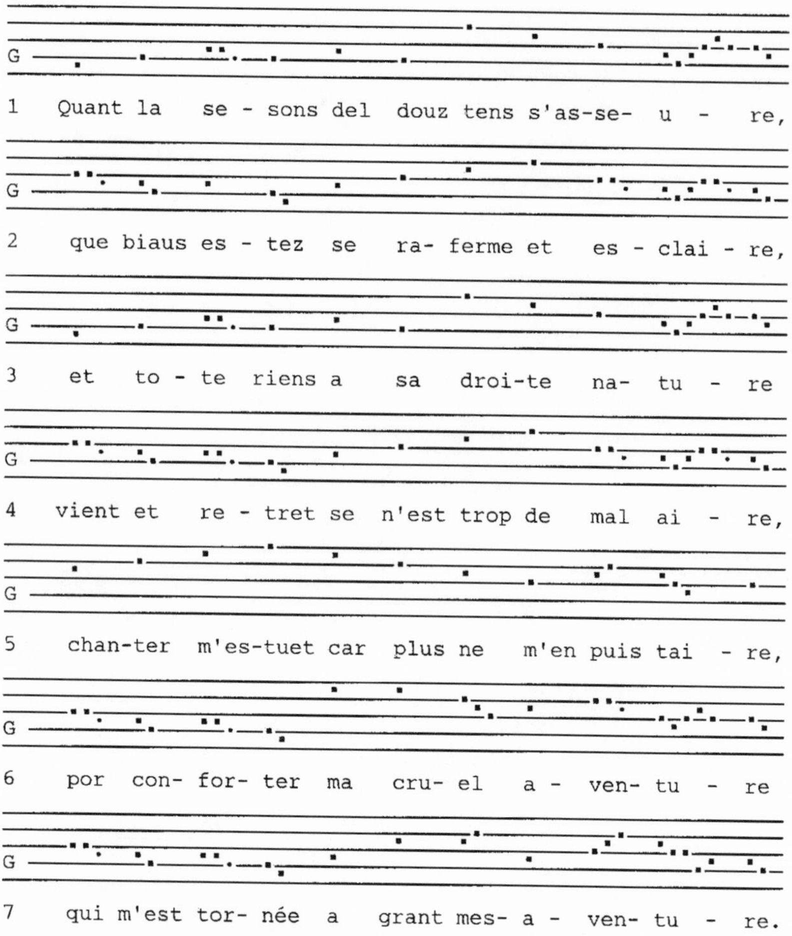

Melody 37. "Quant la sesons del douz tens s'asseüre," vv. 4127–33 (R-S 2086). According to MS. Paris, B.N. fr. 844, fol. 7. Many more versions of this song are extant, with conflicting attributions; the majority of the sources give Vidame de Chartres as author. In *Guillaume de Dole,* the first verse is hypermetric and reads: "Quant li douz tens et la sesons s'asseüre."

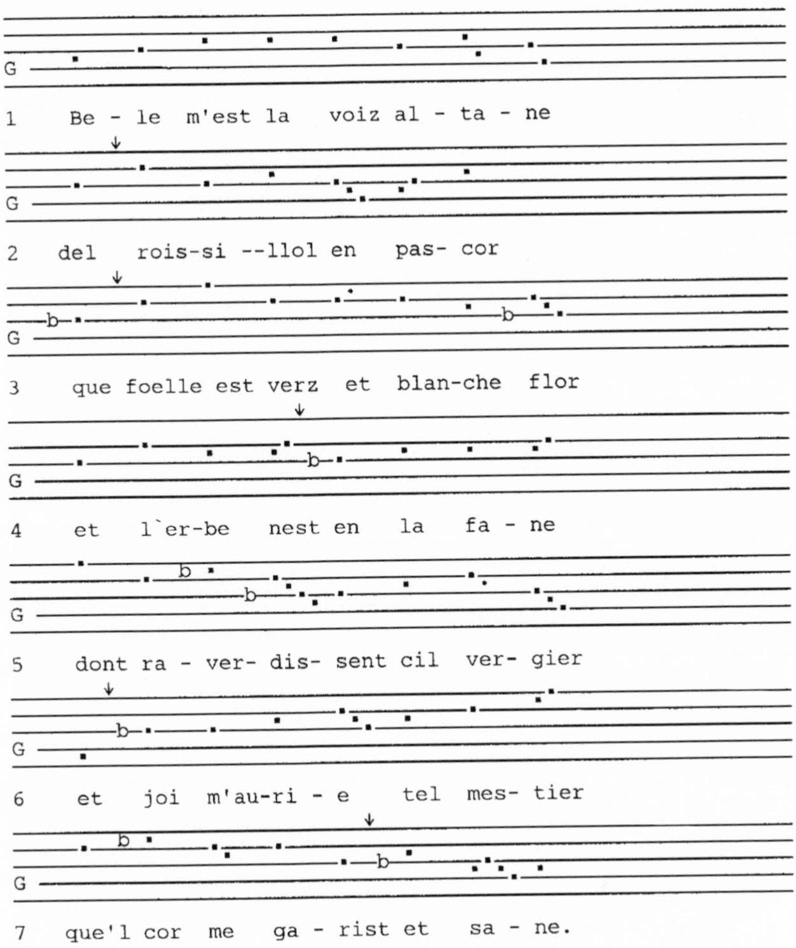

1 Be - le m'est la voiz al - ta - ne

2 del rois-si --llol en pas- cor

3 que foelle est verz et blan-che flor

4 et l`er-be nest en la fa - ne

5 dont ra - ver- dis- sent cil ver- gier

6 et joi m'au-ri - e tel mes- tier

7 que'l cor me ga - rist et sa - ne.

Melody 41. "Bele m'est la voiz altane," vv. 4653–59 (P-C 124, 5). According to MS. Paris, B.N. fr. 844, fol. 196. As discussed in *Troubadour Melodies*, p. 78*, the song probably stems from Daude de Pradas. This melody was also used for one of the "Cantigas de Santa Maria" (see Higinio Anglès, *La Música de las Cantigas de Santa María, del Rey Alfonso el Sabio III* [Deputacion Provincial de Barcelona, 1958], 3:216).

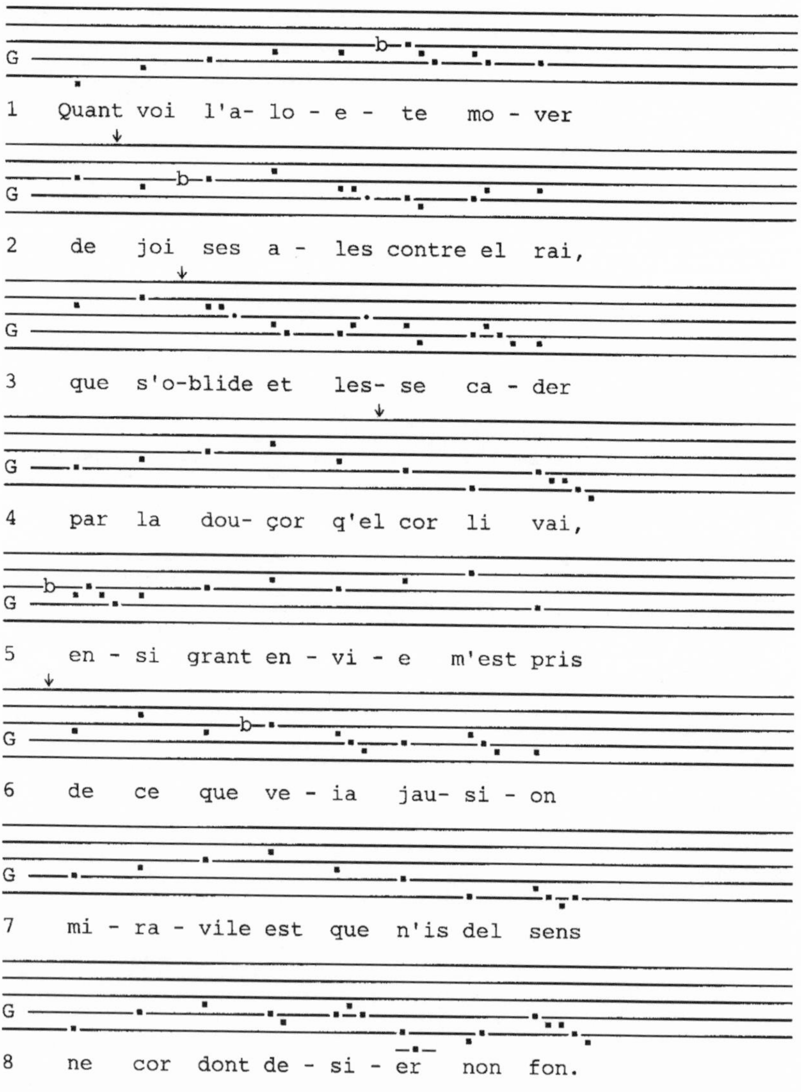

1 Quant voi l'a- lo - e - te mo - ver

2 de joi ses a - les contre el rai,

3 que s'o-blide et les- se ca - der

4 par la dou- çor q'el cor li vai,

5 en - si grant en - vi - e m'est pris

6 de ce que ve - ia jau- si - on

7 mi - ra - vile est que n'is del sens

8 ne cor dont de - si - er non fon.

Melody 45. "Quant voi l'aloete mover," vv. 5212–19 (P-C 70, 43). According to MS. Paris, B.N. fr. 844, fol. 190. In Occitan sources, this song is generally attributed to Bernart de Ventadorn. For other versions of the same melody, some with different texts, see *Troubadour Melodies*, 62*-70*.

Selected Bibliography

This bibliography is designed as a guide to research on Jean Renart's romances, with special emphasis on *Guillaume de Dole.*

Accarie, Maurice. "La fonction des chansons du *Guillaume de Dole.*" In *Mélanges Jean Larmat: Regards sur le moyen âge et la Renaissance (histoire, langue et littérature),* edited by Maurice Accarie, 13–29. *Annales de la Faculté des lettres et sciences humaines de Nice* 39 (1982). Paris: Belles Lettres, 1983.

Adams, Alison. "Jean Renart's *L'escoufle* and the Tristan Legend: Moderation Rewarded." In *Rewards and Punishments in the Arthurian Romances and Lyric Poetry of Mediaeval France: Essays Presented to Kenneth Varty on the Occasion of his Sixtieth Birthday,* edited by Peter V. Davies and Angus J. Kennedy, 1–7. Cambridge: D. S. Brewer, 1987.

———. "The Old French Tristan Poems and the Tradition of Verse Romance." *Tristania* 12.1–2 (1986–87): 60–68.

Alvar, Carlos. "Algunos Aspectos de la Lírica Medieval: El Caso de *Belle Aeliz.*" In *Symposium in honorem prof. M. de Riquer,* 21–49. Universitat de Barcelona: Quaderns Crema, 1984.

Andrieu, Gabriel, J. Piolle, M. Plouzeau. *"Le roman de la rose ou de Guillaume de Dole" de Jean Renart: Concordancier complet des formes graphiques occurentes d'après l'édition de Félix Lecoy.* Aix-en-Provence: CREL–France CUERMA, Université de Provence; Paris: Champion, 1978.

Baldwin, John W. "The Case of Philip Augustus." *Viator* 19 (1988): 195–207.

———. "The Crisis of the Ordeal: Literature, Law, and Religion around 1200." *Journal of Medieval and Renaissance Studies* 24 (1994): 327–53.

———. "Five Discourses on Desire: Sexuality and Gender in Northern France around 1200." *Speculum* 66.4 (1991): 797–819.

———. "French Chivalry Revisited: The *Guillaume de Dole* of Jean Renart." *Haskins Society Journal* 1 (1989): 182–91.

———. "Jean Renart et le tournoi de Saint-Trond: Une conjonction de l'histoire et de la littérature." *Annales ESC* 3 (1990): 565–88.

———. *The Language of Sex: Five Voices from Northern France around 1200.* Chicago: University of Chicago Press, 1994.

Baumgartner, Emmanuèle. "Les brodeuses et la ville." *50 rue de Varenne.* Supplemento italo-francese di *Nuovi Argomenti dell'Istituto Italiano di Cultura di Parigi* 43 (September 1992): 89–95.

———. "Les citations lyriques dans le *Roman de la rose* de Jean Renart." *Romance Philology* 35.1 (1981): 260–66.

Beekman, Pauline H. *Jean Renart and His Writings.* Paris: Droz, 1935.

Birkhan, Helmut. *Jean Renart, Der "Roman von der Rose oder Wilhelm von Dole," Ein Roman von Liebe und Intrige aus dem Altfranzösischen.* Vienna: Wilhelm Braumüller (*Fabulae mediaevales* 1), 1982.

Boulton, Maureen Barry McCann. *The Song in the Story: Lyric Insertions in French Narrative Fiction, 1200–1400.* Philadelphia: University of Pennsylvania Press, 1993.

Brereton, G. E. "Une règle d'étiquette royale au moyen âge." *Moyen Age* 64 (1958): 395–97.

Bruel, Andrée. *Romans français du moyen âge, essais.* Paris: Droz, 1934.

Callahan, Christopher. "The Evolution of the Lyric Insertion in Thirteenth-Century Narrative." *Essays in Medieval Studies* 7 (1990): 29–40.

———. "Interpolating the Musical Text of the Lyric Interpolations: *Guillaume de Dole* and the Trouvère Manuscript Tradition." *Essays in Medieval Studies* 8 (1991): 43–58.

Carmona, Fernando. "La narrativa lírica medieval: El roman lírico." In *Ensayos de literatura europea e hispanoamericana,* edited by Félix Menchacatorre, 73–82. San Sebastián, Spain: Universidad del País Vasco, 1990.

———. "La Obra de Jean Renart y su significación literaria en el roman en verso del siglo XIII." In *La lengua y la literatura en tiempos de Alfonso X,* 135–57. Actas del Congreso Internacional: Murcia, March 5–10, 1984. Murcia, Spain: Departamento de Literaturas Romanicas, Facultad de Letras, Universidad de Murcia, 1985.

Cerquiglini, Jacqueline. "Pour une typologie de l'insertion." *Perspectives médiévales* 3 (1977): 9–14.

Charlier, Gustave. "*L'escoufle* et *Guillaume de Dole.*" In *Mélanges de philologie romane et d'histoire littéraire offerts à M. Maurice Wilmotte,* 1:81–98. Paris: Champion, 1910. Geneva: Slatkine Reprints, 1972, 2 vols.

Chênerie, Marie-Luce. "L'épisode du tournoi dans *Guillaume de Dole:* Etude littéraire." *Revue des langues romanes* 83 (1979): 41–62.

Coldwell, Maria Veder. "*Guillaume de Dole* and Medieval Romances with Musical Interpolations." *Musica Disciplina* 35 (1981): 55–86.

Cooper, Linda. "L'ironie iconographique de la coupe de Tristan dans *L'escoufle.*" *Romania* 104.2 (1983): 157–76.

Cremonesi, Carla. *Le prime manifestazioni letterarie volgari italiane anteriori al '200: Jean Renart e il romanzo francese nel sec. XIII.* Milan: La Goliardica (Edizioni Universitarie), 1949–50.

Daremberg, Charles, and Ernest Renan. "Mission en Italie: 1er Rapport." *Archives des Missions Scientifiques,* 5e Cahier, 241–92. Paris, May 10, 1850.

Delbouille, Maurice. "Sur les traces de 'Bele Aëlis'." In *Mélanges de philologie romane dédiés à la mémoire de Jean Boutière,* edited by Irenée Marcel Cluzel and François Pirot, 199–218. Liège: Soledi, 1971.

de Looze, Laurence. "The Gender of Fiction: Womanly Poetics in Jean Renart's *Guillaume de Dole." French Review* 64.4 (1991): 596–606.

Diller, George T. "Remarques sur la structure esthétique du *Guillaume de Dole." Romania* 98.3 (1977): 390–98.

———. "Techniques de contraste dans *Guillaume de Dole." Romania* 99.4 (1978): 538–49.

Dragonetti, Roger. *Le mirage des sources: L'art du faux dans le roman médiéval.* Paris: Seuil, 1987.

Dubois, Michel. "Anc. Fr. *taleboté." Romania* 85.1 (1964): 112–16.

Dufournet, Jean. "La glorification des ménestrels dans le *Guillaume de Dole* de Jean Renart." *L'information littéraire* 32 (1980): 6–11.

Dufournet, Jean, Jacques Kooijman, René Ménage, and Christine Tronc, trans. *Jean Renart: "Guillaume de Dole ou le roman de la rose," roman courtois du XIIIe siècle.* 2d ed. Paris: Champion, 1988.

Duport, Danièle. "Les chansons dans *Guillaume de Dole."* In *Et c'est la fin pour quoy sommes ensemble: Hommage à Jean Dufournet, Professeur à la Sorbonne Nouvelle: Littérature, histoire et langue du moyen âge,* edited by Jean-Claude Aubailly, Emmanuèle Baumgartner, Francis Dubost, Liliane Dulac, and Marcel Faure, 2:513–23. Paris: Champion, 1993.

Durling, Nancy Vine. "The Seal and the Rose: Erotic Exchanges in *Guillaume de Dole." Neophilologus* 77.1 (1993): 31–40.

Färber, Ernst. "Die Sprache der dem Jean Renart zugeschriebenen Werke: *Lai de l'ombre, Roman de la rose ou de Guillaume de Dole* und *Escoufle." Romanische Forschungen* 33 (1915): 683–793.

Fauchet, Claude. *Oeuvres,* folios 483a–b, 529b, 570b, 572a–b, and 578a. Paris, 1610.

———. *Origines des chevaliers, armoiries et héraux.* 2d ed. Paris, 1606.

———. *Recueil de l'origine de la langue et poésie françaises: Réimpression de l'édition de Paris de 1581.* Geneva: Slatkine Reprints, 1972.

Ferrante, Joan M. *In Pursuit of Perfection: Courtly Love in Medieval Literature.* Port Washington, N.Y.: Kennikat, 1975.

Foulet, Lucien. "*Galeran* et Jean Renart." *Romania* 51 (1925): 76–104.

———, ed., *Galeran de Bretagne.* Paris: Champion (CFMA), 1925.

Fourrier, Anthime. "Les armoiries de l'empereur dans *Guillaume de Dole."* In *Mélanges offerts à Rita Lejeune, Professeur à l'Université de Liège,* 2:1211–26. Gembloux: Duculot, 1969.

Frank, Grace. "*Le roman de la rose ou de Guillaume de Dole,* ll. 1330ff." *Romanic Review* 29 (1938): 209–11.

Gégou, Fabienne. "Jean Renart et la lyrique occitane." In *Mélanges de langue et de littérature médiévales offerts à Pierre Le Gentil,* 319–23. Paris: SEDES, 1973.

Gennrich, Friedrich. *Rondeaux, Virelais und Balladen aus dem Ende des XII., dem XIII., und dem ersten drittel des XIV. Jahrhunderts mit den überlieferten Melodien.*

3 vols. Dresden: Gesellschaft für romanische Literatur, 1921–27. Langen bei Frankfurt, 1963.

Goddard, Eunice Rathbone. *Women's Costume in French Texts of the Eleventh and Twelfth Centuries.* The Johns Hopkins Studies in Romance Literatures and Languages 7. New York: Johnson Reprints, 1973.

Görres, [Johan] Joseph [de]. *Altdeutsche Volks- und Meisterlieder aus den Handschriften der Heidelberger Bibliothek.* Frankfurt, 1817.

Hinstorff, C. A. *Kulturgeschichtliches im "Roman de l'escoufle" und im "Roman de la rose ou de Guillaume de Dole."* Heidelberg, 1895.

Hoepffner, Ernst. "Les lais de Marie de France dans *Galeran de Bretagne* et *Guillaume de Dole.*" *Romania* 56 (1930): 212–35.

Huot, Sylvia. *From Song to Book: The Poetics of Writing in Old French Lyric and Lyrical Narrative Poetry.* Ithaca and London: Cornell University Press, 1987.

———. "Voices and Instruments in Medieval French Secular Music: On the Use of Literary Texts as Evidence for Performance Practice." *Musica Disciplina* 43 (1989): 63–113.

Jean Renart: "The Romance of the Rose or of Guillaume de Dole." Videocassette and booklets (vol. 1, script; vol. 2, commentary). Directed by Margaret Switten for "Teaching Medieval Romance through Video Performance" (project supported by the National Endowment for the Humanities and Mount Holyoke College, May 1993).

Jeanroy, Alfred. "Le roman de *Guillaume de Dole* et Gautier de Coinci." *Romania* 51 (1925): 424.

Jewers, Caroline. "Fabric and Fabrication: Lyric and Narrative in Jean Renart's *Roman de la Rose.*" *Speculum* 71.4 (1996): 907–24.

Jung, Marc-René. "L'empereur Conrad, chanteur de poésie lyrique: Fiction et vérité dans *Le roman de la rose* de Jean Renart." *Romania* 101 (1980): 35–50.

Kay, Sarah. *Subjectivity in Troubadour Poetry.* Cambridge: Cambridge University Press, 1990.

Keller, Adelbert. *Romvart: Beiträge zur Kunde mittelalterlicher Dichtung aus italiänischen Bibliotheken.* Mannheim: Bassermann, 1844.

Kelly, Douglas. *The Art of Medieval French Romance.* Madison: University of Wisconsin Press, 1992.

———. *Medieval Imagination: Rhetoric and the Poetry of Courtly Love.* Madison: University of Wisconsin Press, 1978.

Koenig, V. Frederic. "*Guillaume de Dole* and *Guillaume de Nevers.*" *Modern Philology* 45 (1948): 145–51.

Krueger, Roberta L. "Double Jeopardy: The Appropriation of Woman in Four Old French Romances of the 'Cycle de la Gageure'." In *Seeking the Woman in Late Medieval and Renaissance Writings: Essays in Feminist Contextual Criticism,* edited by Sheila Fisher and Janet E. Halley. Knoxville: University of Tennessee Press, 1989. Reprinted in Krueger, *Women Readers and the Ideology of Gender in Old French Verse Romance,* 128–55. Cambridge: Cambridge University Press, 1993.

Lachet, Claude. "Présence de Liénor dans le *Roman de la rose* de Jean Renart." In *Et c'est la fin pour quoy sommes ensemble: Hommage à Jean Dufournet, Professeur à la Sorbonne Nouvelle: Littérature, histoire et langue du moyen âge,* edited by Jean-Claude Aubailly, Emmanuèle Baumgartner, Francis Dubost, Liliane Dulac, and Marcel Faure, 2:813–25. Paris: Champion, 1993.

Lacy, Norris. "'Amer par oïr dire': *Guillaume de Dole* and the Drama of Language." *French Review* 54.6 (1981): 779–87.

———. "The Composition of *L'escoufle.*" *Res Publica Litterarum* 1 (1978): 151–58.

Ladd, Anne P. "Lyric Insertions in Thirteenth-Century French Narrative." Ph.D. diss., Yale University, 1973.

Langlois, Charles-Victor. *La vie en France au moyen âge de la fin du XIIe au milieu du XIVe siècle d'après des romans mondains du temps.* 1:36–106. Paris: Hachette, 1924.

Langlois, Ernest. "Notices des manuscrits français et provençaux de Rome, antérieurs au XVIe siècle." *Notices et Extraits* 33.2 (1889): 233.

Lecoy, Félix, ed. *Jean Renart: "Le roman de la rose ou de Guillaume de Dole."* Paris: Champion (CFMA), 1979.

———, ed. *Jean Renart: "Le lai de l'ombre."* Paris: Champion (CFMA), 1983.

———. "Sur la date du *Guillaume de Dole.*" *Romania* 82.3 (1961): 379–402.

———. "Sur quelques passages difficiles du *Guillaume de Dole.*" *Romania* 82.2 (1961): 244–60.

Le Gentil, Pierre. "A propos du *Guillaume de Dole.*" In *Mélanges de linguistique romane et de philologie médiévale offerts à Maurice Delbouille,* edited by Jean Renson, 2:381–97. Gembloux: Duculot, 1964.

Legros, Huguette. "Quand les jugements de Dieu deviennent artifices littéraires ou de la profanité impunie d'une poétique." In *La Justice au moyen âge: Sanction ou impunité?,* 197–212. *Senefiance* 16. Aix-en-Provence: CUERMA, 1986.

Lejeune, Rita. "La coupe dans la légende de Tristan dans *L'escoufle* de Jean Renart." In *The Medieval Alexander Legend and Romance Epic: Essays in Honour of David J. A. Ross,* edited by Peter Noble, Lucie Polak, and Claire Isoz, 119–24. Millwood, N.Y.: Kraus, 1982.

———. "L'esprit 'clérical' et les curiosités intellectuelles de Jean Renart dans le *Roman de Guillaume de Dole.*" *Travaux de linguistique et de littérature* 11 (1973): 589–601.

———. "Jean Renart et le roman réaliste au XIIIe siècle." In *Grundriss der romanischen Literaturen des Mittelalters,* vol. 4, no. 1, 400–53. Heidelberg: Carl Winter Universitätsverlag, 1978.

———, ed. *Jean Renart: "Le roman de la rose ou de Guillaume de Dole."* Paris: Droz, 1936.

———. "Le *Roman de Guillaume de Dole* et la principauté de Liège." *Cahiers de civilisation médiévale* 17 (1974): 1–24.

Lejeune-Dehousse, Rita. *L'oeuvre de Jean Renart: Contribution à l'étude du genre romanesque au moyen âge.* Bibliothèque de la Faculté de philosophie et lettres de l'Université de Liège 51. Liège: Faculté de philosophie et lettres; Paris: Droz, 1935.

Lévy, Claude. "Un nouveau texte de Jean Renart?" *Romania* 99.3 (1978): 405–6.

Limentani, Alberto. "Effetti di specularità nella narrativa medievale." *Romanistische Zeitschrift für Literaturgeschichte* 4 (1980): 307–21.

———. "Jean Renart dal romanzo anti-idillico all'anti-romanzo." In *Mittelalterstudien Erich Köhler zum Gedenken,* edited by H. Krauss and D. Rieger. Heidelberg: Carl Winter Universitätsverlag, 1984.

Limentani, Alberto, and Laura Pegolo. "Marote ou de l'amour bourgeois." In *Epopée animale, fable, fabliau: Actes du IVe Colloque de la Société Internationale Renardienne, Evreux, 7–11 Septembre 1981,* edited by Gabriel Bianciotto and Michel Salvat, 323–31. Paris: PUF, 1984.

Lindvall, Lars. *Jean Renart et "Galeran de Bretagne": Etude sur un problème d'attribution de textes. Structures syntaxiques et structures stylistiques dans quelques romans d'aventures français.* Data linguistica 15. Stockholm: Almqvist and Wiksell International, 1982.

Littré, E. "*Guillaume de Dole.*" In *Histoire littéraire de la France,* 22:826–28. Paris: Welter, 1895.

Loewe, F. *Die Sprache des "Roman de la rose ou de Guillaume de Dole."* Göttingen, 1903.

Love, Nathan Leroy. "The Polite Speech of Direct Discourse in Jean Renart's *Guillaume de Dole." Studi Francesi* 97 (1989): 71–77.

Lyons, Faith. *Les éléments descriptifs dans le roman d'aventure au XIIIe siècle (en particulier "Amadas et Ydoine," "Gliglois," "Galeran," "L'escoufle," "Guillaume de Dole," "Jehan et Blonde," "Le castelain de Couci").* Geneva: Droz, 1965.

Mattioli, Carmela. "Sulla datazione del *Guillaume de Dole." Cultura Neolatina* 25 (1965): 91–112.

Micha, Alexandre, trans. *Jean Renart. "L'escoufle": Roman d'aventures.* Paris: Champion, 1992.

Miller, Susan Lee Snouffer. "The Narrative Craft of Jean Renart." Ph.D. diss., Catholic University of America, 1980.

Mussafia, Adolf. *Zur Kritik und Interpretation romanischer Texte, "Guillaume de Dole."* Sitzungsberichte der Kaiserlichen Akademie der Wissenschaften in Wien, Philosophisch-historische Classe 136. Vienna, 1897.

Paden, William D. "Old Occitan as a Lyric Language: The Insertions from Occitan in Three Thirteenth-Century French Romances." *Speculum* 68 (1993): 36–53.

Page, Christopher. "Music and Chivalric Fiction in France, 1150–1300." *Proceedings of the Royal Musical Association* 111 (1984–85): 1–27.

———. *The Owl and the Nightingale: Musical Life and Ideas in France, 1100–1300.* Berkeley: University of California Press, 1989.

———. *Voices and Instruments in the Middle Ages: Instrumental Practice and Songs in France, 1100–1300.* Berkeley: University of California Press, 1986.

Paris, Gaston. "Bele Aaliz." *Mélanges de littérature française du moyen âge* (1910–12): 616–24.

———. "Le cycle de la gageure." *Romania* 32 (1903): 481–551.

Paris, Paulin. *Histoire littéraire de la France,* 23:557, 618. Paris: Welter, 1895.

Payen, Jean-Charles. "Encore *Guillaume de Dole* 'sanz moi', v. 647." *Romania* 84.3 (1963): 376–80.

———. "Structure et sens de *Guillaume de Dole.*" In *Der altfranzösische höfische Roman,* edited by Erich Köhler, 170–88. Darmstadt: Wissenschaftliche Buchgesellschaft, 1978.

Poirion, Daniel. "Fonction de l'imaginaire dans l'*Escoufle.*" In *Mélanges de langue et littérature françaises du moyen âge et de la Renaissance offerts à Monsieur Charles Foulon,* 1:287–93. Rennes: Institut de Français, Université de Haute-Bretagne, 1980.

Psaki, Regina, ed. and trans. *Jean Renart: "The Romance of the Rose or of Guillaume de Dole" (Roman de la rose ou de Guillaume de Dole).* New York and London: Garland, 1995.

Régnier-Bohler, Danielle. "Geste, parole et clôture: Les représentations du gynécée dans la littérature médiévale du XIIIe au XVe siècle." In *Mélanges de langue et de littérature médiévales offerts à Alice Planche,* edited by Maurice Accarie and Ambroise Queffelec, 2:293–404. Annales de la Faculté des lettres et sciences humaines de Nice 48 (1984). Paris: Belles Lettres, 1984.

———. "Imagining the Self." In *A History of Private Life,* vol. 2, *Revelations of the Medieval World,* edited by Georges Duby, translated by Arthur Goldhammer, 311–94. Cambridge: Belknap Press of Harvard University Press, 1988.

Renart, Jean. *Le lai de l'ombre.* See Lecoy, Félix, ed.

———. *Le roman de la rose ou de Guillaume de Dole.* See Lecoy, Félix, ed.

———. *L'escoufle.* See Sweetser, Franklin, ed.

Rey-Flaud, Henri. *La névrose courtoise.* Paris: Navarin, 1983.

Sasu, Voichita. "Romanul medieval—In cautarea aventurii." *Revista de Istorie si Teorie Literara* 35.3–4 (1987): 200–204.

Servois, G., ed. *Le roman de la rose ou de Guillaume de Dole.* Paris: Firmin Didot, 1893.

Solterer, Helen. "At the Bottom of Mirage, A Woman's Body: *Le roman de la rose* of Jean Renart." In *Feminist Approaches to the Body in Medieval Literature,* edited by Linda Lomperis and Sarah Stanbury, 213–33. Philadelphia: University of Pennsylvania Press, 1993.

Struyf, Marie-Claude. "De la sylve au jardin: La fête printanière dans *Guillaume de Dole.*" In *Vergers et jardins dans l'univers médiéval,* 361–71. *Senefiance* 28. Aix-en-Provence: CUERMA, 1990.

———. "Les orphelins de père dans l'oeuvre romanesque de Jean Renart." In *Les relations de parenté dans le monde médiéval,* 275–85. *Senefiance* 26. Aix-en-Provence: CUERMA, 1989.

———."Le personnage de Jouglet dans le *Guillaume de Dole:* Une figure de l'écrivain." In *Figures de l'écrivain au moyen âge,* edited by Danielle Buschinger, 381–88. Actes du Colloque du Centre d'Etudes Médiévales de l'Université de Picardie, Amiens, March 18–20, 1988. Göppingen: Kümmerle, 1991.

———. "Symbolique des villes et demeures dans les romans de Jean Renart." *Cahiers de civilisation médiévale* 30.3 (1987): 245–61.

Stults, Cathy Lynn. "Mendacity in Three 13th-Century Old French Romances: *Le roman de la rose ou de Guillaume de Dole, La Chastelain de Vergi,* and *Le roman du castelain de Couci et de la dame de Fayel.*" Ph.D. diss., Ohio University, 1986.

Sweetser, Franklin, ed. *Jean Renart: "L'escoufle": Roman d'aventure.* Geneva: Droz (TLF), 1974.

Terry, Patricia. "Hearing and Seeing in the Works of Jean Renart: What Is Believing?" *Romance Languages Annual* 4 (1993): 156–58.

Terry, Patricia, and Nancy Vine Durling, trans. *The Romance of the Rose or Guillaume de Dole.* Philadelphia: University of Pennsylvania Press, 1993.

Todd, Henry Alfred. "Guillaume de Dole: An Unpublished Old French Romance." *PMLA* 2 (1886): 107–57.

Vigneras, Louis-André. "Sur la date de 'Guillaume de Dole'." *Romanic Review* 28.2 (1937): 109–21.

Walter, Philippe. "Tout commence par des chansons . . . (Intertextualités lotharingiennes)." In *Styles et valeurs: Pour une histoire de l'art littéraire au moyen âge,* edited by Daniel Poirion, 187–209. Paris: SEDES, 1990.

Warren, F. M. "The Works of Jean Renart, Poet, and Their Relation to *Galeran de Bretagne. I and II.*" *Modern Language Notes* 23 (1908): 69–73, 97–100.

Woledge, Brian. "Bons vavasseurs et mauvais sénéchaux." In *Mélanges offerts à Rita Lejeune, Professeur à l'Université de Liège,* 2:1263–77. Gembloux: Duculot, 1969.

Zink, Michel. *Belle: Essai sur les chansons de toile.* Paris: Champion, 1978.

———. *Roman rose et rose rouge: "Le roman de la rose ou de Guilluame de Dole" de Jean Renart.* Paris: Nizet, 1979.

Zumthor, Paul. *Essai de poétique médiévale.* Paris: Seuil, 1972.

Contributors

John W. Baldwin is Charles Homer Haskins Professor of History at Johns Hopkins University and author of *The Medieval Theories of the Just Price: Romanists, Canonists, and Theologians in the Twelfth and Thirteenth Centuries; Masters, Princes, and Merchants: The Social Views of Peter the Chanter and His Circle; The Government of Philip Augustus: Foundations of French Royal Power in the Middle Ages;* and *The Language of Sex: Five Voices from Northern France around 1200.*

Maureen Barry McCann Boulton is professor of French at the University of Notre Dame. She has edited *Les Enfances de Jesu Crist* and *The Old French "Evangile de l'enfance"* and is the author of *The Song in the Story: Lyric Insertions in French Narrative Fiction, 1200–1400.*

Nancy Vine Durling has taught French and comparative literature at the University of California, Santa Cruz, and at Florida Atlantic University, Boca Raton. She has translated (with Patricia Terry) *The Romance of the Rose or Guillaume de Dole.*

Nancy A. Jones has taught French and comparative literature at Hobart and William Smith Colleges, Baruch College of the City University of New York, and Harvard University. She is the coeditor of *Embodied Voices: Representing Female Vocality in Western Culture.*

Regina Psaki is associate professor of romance languages at the University of Oregon, Eugene. She has edited and translated *Le roman de silence* and has recently completed a new edition and translation of *Le roman de la rose ou de Guillaume de Dole.*

PATRICIA TERRY is retired from the University of California, San Diego, where she taught French and comparative literature. Her many translations include *The Song of Roland, Renart the Fox, Poems of the Elder Edda, The Honeysuckle and the Hazel Tree,* and (with Nancy Vine Durling) *The Romance of the Rose or Guillaume de Dole.*

HENDRIK VAN DER WERF is professor of musicology emeritus at Eastman School of Music at the University of Rochester. He is editor of *The Extant Troubadour Melodies* and author of *The Chansons of the Troubadours and Trouvères: A Study of the Melodies and their Relation to the Poems; The Emergence of Gregorian Chant: A Comparative Study of Ambrosian, Roman and Gregorian Chant;* and *The Oldest Extant Part Music and the Origin of Western Polyphony.*

MICHEL ZINK is a professor of French medieval literature at the Collège de France, Paris. His many publications include *La prédication en langue romane avant 1300; La pastourelle: Poésie et folklore au moyen âge; Roman rose et rose rouge: "Le roman de la rose ou de Guillaume de Dole" de Jean Renart; Belle: Essai sur les chansons de toile;* and *La subjectivité littéraire autour du siècle de Saint Louis.*

Index

Song types and first lines of songs are treated as proper names. Names of singers and of historical characters appearing in *Guillaume de Dole* are listed alphabetically; other characters are listed under the work in which they appear. (The names of the characters Lïenor, Conrad, and Guillaume de Dole occur too frequently for inclusion.)

Aachen, 47, 58, 67
"Aaliz main se leva," 189, 197
Accarie, Maurice, 106, 114
Acre, 53
Active Life, 20, 21
Adolf of Altena, archbishop, 58
Aelis. *See Escoufle*
Aigret de Grame, 201
Alain de Roucy (Alains de Roussi), 56
Albéric, archdeacon of Paris, 63
Albert de Cuyck, 55
Albert II, 57
Albigensians, 64, 77–78n.50
Aleyde de Béthune, 60–61, 63, 78–79n.51, 79n.52
Alix de Dreux, 60
Alix de Namur, 49
Alost, 56
"Amours a non ciz maus qui me tormente," 96, 206
Andreas Capellanus: *De amore*, 72n.9
Anglès, Higinio, 221
Ansold (Eudes), lord of Ronquerolles, 56
Argentan, 58
Arques, 53
Arthur (Plantagenet), 68
Arthur, King, 52, 165
Artois, 56
Aucassin et Nicolette, 15, 180
Aumale, countess of, 61
Austria, duchess of (duchesse d'Osteriche), 177, 192

Baldwin, John W., 6, 143, 165
Ballade, 170, 173
Balleul, 56
Bar(-le-Duc), count of (li quens de Bar), 57
Bartsch, Karl, 168, 170, 173, 182
Baudouin, 50
Baudouin VI, count of Hainaut. *See* Baudouin IX
Baudouin IX, count of Flanders, 47, 49, 51, 52, 53, 54, 55, 57, 60, 61, 62, 63, 64, 70
Baumgartner, Emmanuèle, 112, 130
Bavaria, duke of (duc de Baiviere), 56
Beatrix of Swabia, 68
Beauvais, 50, 51

Bec, Pierre, 94, 169
Bédier, Joseph, 10n.14
Bele Aeliz, 89, 172, 173, 188–89
Bele Aiglentine, 94–95, 116–17, 129–30
"Bele Aiglentine en roial chamberine," 198
Bele Doete (de Troies), 96, 205
"Bele m'est la voiz altane," 206, 221
"Belle Doette as fenestres se siet," 182
Bennett, Judith, 30–31
Benoît de Sainte-Maure. *See Roman de Troie*
Berengaria, 68, 69
Bergren, Anne, 17
Bernard, Saint: pass of, 53
Bernart de Ventadorn, 97, 115, 118, 222
Béroul, 48
Berte as grans piés, 15, 30
Bertran de Born, 58
Béthune family, 61–62, 65, 80n.53, 80n.54. *See also* Aleyde de Béthune; Jean de Béthune
"Bien me cuidai toute ma vie," 217
Blanche de Castile, 50
Bligger of Steinach (Steinahe Blikêr), 35
Boidin, 55
Bond, Gerald A., 210
Boulogne, counts of, 48, 54
Boulton, Maureen Barry McCann, 7, 14
Bouvines, 48, 55, 57, 60, 61, 63, 64, 68, 75n.32
Brindisi, 53
Brittany, 51; matter of, 15
Bruno of Sayn (provost of Bonn), 58
Burgundy, 57

Cambrai, 61–64
Canso, 96, 97, 98
Cantigas de Santa Maria, 175, 221
Cantilena rotunda, 169
Cantus, 182
Cantus gestualis, 180
Capetians, 48–70
Carole, 7, 89, 97, 98. *See also Rondet de carole.*
Carruthers, Mary, 38–39
Carstens, Henry, 210
Caux, 53
"Cele d'Oisseri," 203
Cerquiglini, Jacqueline, 105
"C'est la gieus, en mi les prez," 209
"C'est la gieus, la gieus, q'en dit en ces prez," 209
"C'est la jus desoz l'olive," 192
"C'est la jus en la praele," 197
"C'est tot la gieus, el glaioloi," 191
"C'est tot la gieus, enmi les prez," 192
Chaalons (minstrel [?] of), 206
Champagne, 33, 34, 39, 49, 52, 56; count of (li quens de Champaigne), 75n.32
Chanson: à refrains, 170; *avec des refrains*, 170–71; *courtoise*, 88; *d'amour*, 85, 91, 96, 97; *de femme*, 97; *de geste*, 85, 107, 168, 178, 180–81, 182; *de toile*, 23–25, 27, 38, 39, 85, 93, 94–95, 96, 97, 98, 106, 129, 168; *d'histoire* (*historique*), 85, 129–30, 137
Chansonnette (chançonete), 87, 164, 165, 175, 190
Chansonniers, 37, 166–67, 175, 183, 210
"Chans, quan non es qui l'entenda," 120–21n.9
Chantefable, 180
Chartres, Vidame de, 88, 204, 220
Chartres Cathedral, 20
Chastelain de Coucy, 212
Châtillon-Nanteuil: family of. *See* Nanteuil-la-Fosse: family of
Chrétien de Troyes, 9n.5, 22, 48; *Chevalier au lion*, 3; *Chevalier de la charrete*, 3, 71n. 7, 72n. 9, 139n.11; *Cligès*, 65, 67 (Alis, 65; Cligès, 65; Fénice, 65, 69); *Conte du graal*, 71n.7; *Erec et Enide*, 28, 33, 71n.7, 98, 139n.11
Christina of Markyate, 22
Christina of Sweden, Queen, 4
Chronique de Gislebert, 49, 50, 52, 55
Church of the Holy Sepulcher, 54
Cîteaux, 62
Clermont, count of, 59

Clermont-en-Hesbaye, 59
Cologne, 30, 54, 55; archbishop of, 47, 58, 64, 67
Comedy, New, 15
Conrad, archbishop of Mainz, 58
Conrad III, Emperor, 68, 69, 86
Conrad of Scharfenburg, 56
Constance of Castile, 68
Constance of Sicily, 48
Constantinople, 49
Contemplative Life, 20, 21
"Contrel tens que voi frimer," 198, 216
Couchi, damoisiele de, 110
Crusade, Fifth, 51
Crusade, Fourth, 49, 51

Dagsburg, count of (conte d'Aubours [d'Auborc]), 56, 57, 177, 192
Dam, 61
Danmartin (uns chevaliers de), 97, 115–16, 207
Dares, 152–53n.22
Daude de Pradas, 221
"De Renaut de Mousson," 201
"Des que Fromonz au Veneor tença," 195
Dietrich, count of Cleves (li quens de Cleve), 57
Dietrich of Hengebach, 58
Dinant, 54
Dinant (neveu au segnor de), 201
Dole, 54, 93, 143
Doon le Veneor, 93
Doss-Quinby, Eglal, 169, 171, 173
Dragonetti, Roger, 14, 40, 46, 144
Duby, Georges, 17
Dufournet, Jean, 5, 36, 40, 107, 146
Durling, Nancy Vine, 144, 147

Eleanor of Aquitaine, 50
Elizabeth, countess of Saint-Pol, 60
Enguerrand, lord of Couci (cil de Couci), 56
"E non Deu, sire, se ne l'ai," 190
"En un vergier les une fontenelle," 182
Enide. *See* Chrétien de Troyes
Erec. *See* Chrétien de Troyes
Escoufle: Aelis in, 14, 29–32, 49, 53, 66, 69; date of, 51, 64–65; dedicatee of (count of Hainaut), 49, 51, 54; embroidery in, 2, 6, 14–40; geographical setting of, 6, 29–33, 52–54; Guillaume in, 30, 31, 32, 49, 53, 66–67, 69–70; imperial succession in, 6, 45–70; prologue to, 51–52; Richard, count of Montivilliers in, 53, 67, 69; Ysabeau in, 31, 32
Eslit, 49, 51
Eudes de Sully, bishop of Paris, 63

Fauchet, Claude, 3–4
Ferrante, Joan, 130
"Fille et la mere se sieent a l'orfrois," 24, 193
Flanders, 36, 39; counts of, 48
Florence de Rome, 15, 30
Fourrier, Anthime, 107
France: matter of, 15
Franche Comté, 54
Francien, 52
Frank, Grace, 93
Fratas, 173
Frederick I (Barbarossa), 57–58, 67, 68
Frederick II, 46–48, 65–66, 68, 69
Frederick, duke of Swabia. *See* Frederick I (Barbarossa)
Froissart, Jean: *Espinette amoureuse,* 107; *Meliador,* 106
Fromont, 93, 196
Frye, Northrop, 15

Gace Brulé (monsegnor Gasçon; mon segnor Gasson), 88, 90, 117, 163, 193, 203, 211, 216
Galeran de Bretagne, 1, 15, 16, 17, 30, 31
Galerans de Lamborc, 200
Garan (Galran de Lanborc), 57
Gaucher II de Châtillon, 60
Gaucher III de Châtillon (Gauchiers de Chastillon), 56, 60, 64
Gaucher II de Nanteuil, 60–61, 77–78n.50, 78–79n.51, 79n.52
Gautier de Joigny (Gautier de Joëgni), 56
Gauvain, 65

Gennrich, Friedrich, 168–69, 171, 188
Geoffroi IV, count of Perche, 62
Gerbert de Metz, 93, 135, 166, 195, 196
Gerbert de Montreuil. *See Roman de la violette*
Gislebert of Mons. *See Chronique de Gislebert*
Gontier de Soignies (Gautier de Sagnies), 88, 96, 115, 208
Gottfried von Strassburg: *Tristan,* 35–36
Grand chant courtois, 7, 88, 90, 92, 94, 130, 166, 168
Gregorian chant, 181
Grocheio, Johannes de, 169, 180, 181, 182
Gueldre (li quens de Guerre), 56
Guillaume de Champagne, 50
Guillaume de Dole: Cupelin in, 146–47, 174, 177, 202; date of, 5, 15, 51, 64–65, 165; dye imagery in, 6, 13–14, 36–37, 40; early critical references to, 3–5; editions of, 4–5; ekphrasis in, 136; embroidery in, 5, 6, 13–40, 94, 98, 135–37, 150; geographical setting of, 6, 52–55, 86; gynaeceum in, 17; heraldry in, 59, 76–77n.47; historical characters in, 5, 6, 7, 45–70; imperial succession in, 6, 45–70; Jouglet (Jouglés; Juglet) in, 86, 127, 133, 143, 144, 146, 162, 163, 174, 177–78, 179, 193, 196, 197, 198, 201, 204, 205; letters in, 163; literary references in, 2, 86, 98–100, 123–24, 135–38, 142, 148–49; Milon de Nanteuil (dedicatee) in, 33–34, 39, 40, 49, 50–51, 52–53, 60–64, 68, 70, 162; mother in, 24, 29, 38, 106, 117, 134, 144, 163, 193; ms. Vatican reg. 1725, 2, 3–4, 8, 9n.5, 87, 107–8, 119, 126, 160–61, 183; names (significance of) in, 128, 143–44, 146; nephew of, 96; Nicole in, 24, 116, 128–29, 163, 177, 178, 193, 195, 196; portraits in, 148, 150; prologue to, 6, 13–14, 29, 32, 33–34, 36, 40, 85, 87, 88, 89, 106–9, 112, 134, 146, 149, 157, 160, 162, 164; proverbs in, 146–47, 148; reception of (thirteenth century), 2; seneschal, 23, 25–27, 29, 39, 58, 92, 94, 95, 96, 124, 134, 137, 151; singing and reading of, 87–88, 160, 162, 179–80; songs in, 2, 4, 6, 7, 8, 13, 85–100, 105–19, 122–38, 147, 148–49, 157–222; superlatives in, 147–48; terms referring to compositional activities in, 162–63; translation(s) of, 5, 6, 7, 142–51; understatement, 148; and Welf thesis, 5, 6, 45–46
Guillaume de Lorris: *Roman de la rose,* 4, 148 (Oiseuse, 148)
Guillaume des Barres (li Barrois), 56
Guillaume, lord of Mauléon (uns autres de Maulïon), 56
Guy de Paray (-le-Monial?), 62, 63
Guy II de Châtillon, 60

Hainaut: count of, 33; county of, 52, 57
Hartmann of Aue (Hartman der Ouwaere), 35–36
Heinrich III, 47, 48, 57, 68
Helen of Troy, 28, 98, 135–36, 150–51
Helvide de Nanteuil, 60
Henri III, King, 3
Henri, duke of Louvain and Brabant, 47, 55, 57, 60, 68
Henry the Lion, duke of Saxony, 47–48, 54, 58
Henry V, Emperor, 62, 67
Henry VI, Emperor, 46–48, 53, 59, 68
Heudes de Rades de Crouci, 144
Holy Land, 54, 69
Hoppin, Richard, 175
Hues, 174
Hugues de Pierrepont, 51, 55, 60, 62, 74n.24
Huot, Sylvia, 37, 112, 121n.12
Huy, 54

Igny, 51, 60, 78–79n.51
Infancy Gospels, 18, 21
Ingeborg, Queen, 63
Innocent II, 67
Innocent III, 22, 47, 50, 58, 62, 65, 66

Italy, 47, 53

"Ja de chanter en ma vie," 204, 219
James, Book of, 18
"Ja ne lairai pour mon mari ne die," 111
"Ja ne mi marïerai," 114
Jaufré Rudel, 92, 116, 170, 213
Jean de Béthune (bishop of Cambrai), 61, 62, 63, 64
"Je di que c'est granz folie," 203, 217
Jerusalem, 54
John, count of Mortain, 54
John, King, 47–48, 61, 64, 68
Johnson, Barbara, 142
Jones, Nancy A., 6
Jung, Marc-René, 85, 97, 105, 112, 130, 150

Kaiserwerth, 54
Kay, Sarah, 112, 121n.12, 139n.4
Keller, Adelbert, 4
Kowaleski, Maryanne, 30–31
Krueger, Roberta, 125, 130, 131, 139n.8, 139n.9

"La bele Doe siet au vent," 24, 194
Lacy, Norris, 123
"La gieus desoz la raime," 201
Lai de l'ombre, 48, 119, 124, 127, 135; date, 51; dedicatee, 49, 51
"La jus, desoz la raime," 190
La Marche, count of. *See* Otto of Brunswick
"Lanquan li jorn son lonc, en may," 92
Lateran Council (1215), 48, 64
Lecoy, Félix, 5, 87, 107, 166, 168, 170, 188, 190, 210
Lejeune(-Dehousse), Rita, 5, 6, 45, 46, 55, 142, 143, 144, 146
Lendit, 52
Liège, 45, 54, 55, 59, 62, 163; bishop of, 47, 57; bishop of (nephew [niés l'envesque dou Liege]), 97, 115–16, 207
Limburg, duke of, 57
Limentani, Alberto, 123
"Li noviaus tens et mais [et violete]," 193, 212
"Loial amor qui en fin cuer s'est mise," 196, 214
Loire, 48
Lombardy, 53
Longueau, 60
Looz, 54; count of (le conte de Los), 57
Lorraine, 53, 57
Lorrains, 93
Lorris, 52
"Lors que florist la bruiere," 115, 208
"Lors que li jor sont lonc en mai," 116, 170, 195, 213
Los (un vallez le conte de), 201
Lothar, duke of Saxony, 67
Lotharingia, 51, 55
Louis VI, 62
Louis VII, 67, 68, 69
Louis, count of Looz, 57
Louix IX, King, 50
Louvain, duke of (duc de Louvain), 57
Lowlands (Avalterre), 48, 57
Ludwig, duke of Bavaria, 56
Luxemburg, count of (li quens de Lucelebourc), 89, 177, 191

Maastricht, 54, 55, 86, 89, 94
Machaut, Guillaume de, 105–6
"Main se leva bele Aeliz," 172, 188, 191
"Main se leva la bien fete Aeliz," 173, 189, 192
"Main se levoit Aaliz," 189, 192
Maine, 56
Mainz, 46, 47, 54, 55, 57, 58, 86; archbishop of, 67; *fête de mai,* 95
Manekine, 15
Marguerite, bele, 203
Marie de Brabant, 59, 68
Marie de Champagne, 49–50, 72n.9
Marie de France, 48; *Bisclavret,* 139n.11; *Chevrefeuille,* 184n.7; *Fables,* 71n.7; *Fresne,* 16; *Lanval,* 98–99; Prologue to the *Lais,* 34, 71n.7
Marseilles, 53
Martin, Rebecca, 34
Mary, Virgin, 18–21

Mathilda of England, 47, 48, 58
Mathilda of Saxony, 62
Mathilde de Blois, 62
Matthew Paris, 59
"Mauberjon s'est main levee," 200
Mayence, duke of (sister), 113
Maximin, St., 21
Menard, Pierre, 142
Meuse, 54, 55
Michel de Harnes (Michiel de Harnes), 56
Miller, Susan, 116
Milon de Nanteuil (Miles de Nantuel). *See Guillaume de Dole*
Mons[-en-]Hainaut, 49, 54
Montivillers, 53
Montpellier, 29, 31, 32, 49, 53
Mortain, 64
"Mout est fouls, que que nus die," 202
"Mout me demeure," 197, 215

Namur, 54
Nanteuil-la-Fosse: family of, 60–65, 68. *See also* Gaucher, Helvide, Milon, Sophia
Nichols, Stephen, 148
Niort, châtelaine of (Alïenor, castelainne de Nïor), 110
Nivelle, 54
Normandy, 48, 52, 53, 61, 69
Normendie: une dame de, 110–11; uns bachelers de, 94, 116, 198

Occitania, 166
"Or aroie amouretes," 117
"Or vienent Pasques les beles en avril," 115, 207
Otto of Brunswick, 45, 47–48, 54–66, 68, 69; heraldry, 59, 76–77n.47
Ourscamps, 50

Page, Christopher, 94–95, 175–76
Paris, 30–31, 48, 50
Paris, Paulin, 4
Parker, Rozsika, 18, 21
Pastourelle, 85, 93, 95, 96, 168
Paul, Saint (saint Pol), 132–33
Pentecost, 66
Perceval, 174, 197
Perche, 56
Péronne, 64
Pétau, Paul, 4, 9n.11
Peter, Saint, church of (Mainz), 58, 64
Philip Augustus, 45, 47, 48, 50, 56, 57, 60–64, 67
Philip of Swabia, 46, 47, 56, 57, 61, 62, 63, 65–66, 68
Philippe de Dreux, bishop of Beauvais, 50
Philomena, 16, 17, 22–23; Progne, 23; Tereus, 23
Pierre des Vaux de Cernay, 64
Pillet, Alfred, 210
Poitou, 56; count of. *See* Otto of Brunswick
Polixena. *See* Roman de Troie
Pont de l'Arche, 53
"Por quel forfet ne por quel ochoison," 203, 218
Progne. *See Philomena*
Proverbs, 18
Psaki, Regina, 5
Pseudo-Matthew Gospel, 18
Pseudo-refrains, 170–71, 173

"Quant de la foelle espoissent li vergier," 202
"Quant flors et glais et verdure s'esloigne," 117, 193, 211
"Quant ge li donai le blanc peliçon," 147, 203
"Quant la sesons del douz tens s'asseüre," 204, 220
"Quant revient la sesons," 205
"Quant voi l'aloete moder," 97, 115, 118, 208, 222
"Que demandez vos," 97, 206

Raoul de Houdenc: *Meraugis de Portlesquez*, 3
Raymond de Miraval, 120–21n.9
Raymond VI, count of Toulouse, 54
Razos, 174
Refrain, 85, 88, 110, 130, 170–72; *cité*, 171, 172; *répété*, 171
Régnier-Bohler, Danielle, 17–18

Reims, 49, 50, 51, 52, 53, 61, 62, 63, 64
Renart, Jean: anagrams, 10n.14, 48, 71n.6, 151; attribution to (*Auberée* [*fabliau*], 8n.2; *De Renart de Piaudoue*, 8; *Escoufle*, 1, 4; *Galeran de Bretagne*, 1, 8n.2, 101n.5; *Lai de l'ombre*, 1, 4, 48; *Plait de Dammartin contre Vairon son roncin*, 8n.2; *Roman de la rose ou de Guillaume de Dole*, 1, 4); identity of, 1
Renaud de Boulogne, count (li quens Renaus de Boloigne), 54, 56, 64
"Renaus et s'amie chevauche par un pré," 201
Renaut de Baujieu, 88, 91
Renaut de Sabloeil, 88, 204
Rethel-Pierreponts, 62
Reverdie, 115
Rey-Flaud, Henri, 144
Rhineland, 36, 54, 55, 57
Rhine Palatinate, 47
Richard, count of Montivilliers. *See Escoufle*
Richard, King (the Lionheart), 47, 53–54, 61, 62, 63, 68, 69
Robert of Courson, 50
Roederer, Charlotte, 175
Roman d'Alexandre, 149
Roman de la rose, 175. *See also* Guillaume de Lorris
Roman de la violette, 3, 7, 15, 52, 110–19
Roman de Renart, 1, 48, 151
Roman de Silence, 139n.11
Roman de Troie, 98, 135–36, 149–51; Achilles, Hector, Paris, 98, 135; Memnon, Priam, 98, 135, 150; Polixena, 148. *See also* Helen of Troy
Roman du comte d'Anjou, 15, 30
Rome, 62, 63, 66, 69; matter of, 15
Roncevaux (Rainceval), 174, 197
Rondeau, 97, 98, 110, 113, 114, 168–70, 172, 173
Rondet. See Rondeau
Rondet de carole, 85, 88, 89, 90, 96, 101n.4, 169. *See also Carole*
Rotrou IV, count of Le Perche, 62
Rouen, 30–31, 32, 53, 54, 67, 69
Round Table, 52

Sagremors, li quens de, 191
Saint-Germain-des-Près, 67
Saint-Gilles, 49, 53; count of, 53, 54
Saint-Pol, conte de (sister), 110
Saint-Trond, 53, 54, 55, 56, 57, 60, 64, 116
Salians, 67–68
Sancho of Navarre, King, 68
Santiago de Compostela, 49
Saracens, 53, 54
Savoy, count of, 113, 177
Saxony, duke of (chevalier de Saissoigne / et . . . duc), 57, 69
"Se mes amis m'a guerpie," 89, 190
Seneschal. *See Guillaume de Dole*
Sens, 52
Servois, Gustave, 4
Sicily, 46, 47
Sicily, king of, 66
Siegfried of Eppstein, 58
"Siet soi bele Aye as piez sa male maistre," 24, 194
Son poitevin, 97, 118
Sophia, lady of Nanteuil, 60, 77–78n.50
"Sor la rive de mer," 201
Spanke, Hans, 210
Speyer, provost of (prevost d'Espire), 56, 192
Staufens, 45–70
Steiner, George, 142
Suger, 67

"Tant cuidoie savoir," 97
"Te Deum laudamus," 207
"Tendez tuit voz mains a la flor d'esté," 207
Tereus. *See Philomena*
Terry, Patricia, 7
Testament, New, 181
Testament, Old, 15, 181
Thibaut du Perche, 50, 62
Thibaut I, 57
Thibaut IV, count of Blois, 62
Thomas of England (Tumas), 48, 164
Tobler-Lommatzsch, 107
"Tot la gieus, sor rive mer," 205

Touart (uns chanterres de vers), 209
Toul, 53
Toulouse, 53
Tournai, 52
Tournoi de dames, 85
Tré (li fils le conte de), 200, 201
Tristan et Iseut: Iseut (Yseut; Ysolt) in, 65, 69, 98–99, 139n.11, 149, 164, 184n.5; King Marc in, 65, 89, 99, 149; Tristan in, 65, 67, 98–99, 149, 164, 184n.5, 184n.7
Tristan. See also Béroul, Gottfried von Strassburg, Thomas
Tristan (prose), 8, 164–65, 184n.7; date of, 165; ms. Paris, B.N. f. fr. 776, 165; ms. Vienna, B.N. 2542, 165; songs in, 164–65
Trojan war, 23, 28–29, 135–37, 149–51

"Un petit devant le jour," 187n.44

van der Werf, Hendrik, 8, 211
Vidame de Chartres. *See* Chartres, Vidame de
Vidas, 174
Vieille truande, 107
Virelai, 107, 170, 173

Wallincourt, 56
Walram III, 57
Walther von der Vogelweide, 59
Wautre, 55
Welfs, 45–70
Wenceslas de Luxemburg, 106
Worms, bishop of, 58

York, count of. *See* Otto of Brunswick
Yudkin, Jeremy, 175

Zink, Michel, 5, 7, 8, 24, 27, 46, 94, 123, 124, 144, 147
Zumthor, Paul, 89, 96

Carleton College Library